Approaches to Teaching
the Works of David Foster Wallace

Approaches to Teaching the Works of David Foster Wallace

Edited by

Stephen J. Burn

and

Mary K. Holland

The Modern Language Association of America
New York   2019

MLA and the MODERN LANGUAGE ASSOCIATION are trademarks owned by
the Modern Language Association of America. For information about obtaining
permission to reprint material from MLA book publications, send your request
by mail (see address below) or e-mail (permissions@mla.org).

Library of Congress Cataloging-in-Publication Data

Names: Burn, Stephen, editor. | Holland, Mary, 1970– editor.
Title: Approaches to teaching the works of David Foster Wallace /
edited by Stephen J. Burn and Mary K. Holland.
Description: New York : The Modern Language Association of America, 2019. |
Series: Approaches to teaching world literature, ISSN 1059-1133 ; 156 |
Includes bibliographical references.
Identifiers: LCCN 2019017074 (print) | LCCN 2019017447 (ebook) |
ISBN 9781603293921 (EPUB) | ISBN 9781603293938 (Kindle) |
ISBN 9781603294645 (hardcover : alk. paper) |
ISBN 9781603293914 (pbk. : alk. paper)
Subjects: LCSH: Wallace, David Foster—Study and teaching.
Classification: LCC PS3573.A425635 (ebook) |
LCC PS3573.A425635 Z5225 2019 (print) | DDC 813/.54—dc23
LC record available at https://lccn.loc.gov/2019017074

Approaches to Teaching World Literature 156
ISSN 1059-1133

Cover illustration of the paperback and electronic editions:
Marilyn Louise MacCrakin, *Summer Storm on the Cornfields*
(2 July 2015, Sacramento, California).

Published by The Modern Language Association of America
85 Broad Street, suite 500, New York, New York 10004-2434
www.mla.org

This volume is dedicated to Charles B. Harris (1940–2017)—
pioneering scholar of innovative fiction and Wallace studies,
generous colleague and friend.

CONTENTS

Part One

MATERIALS

Introduction

While David Foster Wallace began publishing in the mid-1980s, it was really the next decade that would see his work generate sustained scholarly readings and the publication of associated pedagogical materials. The justly famous 1993 *Review of Contemporary Fiction* issue devoted to Wallace, William T. Vollmann, and Susan Daitch anchored early criticism of Wallace's fiction to developing debates about the end of postmodernism. Within a few years, his short fiction began to appear in volumes that placed his work in a similar context, including such teacher-friendly anthologies as *Postmodern American Fiction*, edited by Paula Geyh and others (1998), which reprinted "Lyndon"; *Innovations*, edited by Robert L. McLaughlin (1998), which began with "Little Expressionless Animals"; and *After Yesterday's Crash: The Avant-Pop Anthology*, edited by Larry McCaffery (1995), which included "Tri-Stan: I Sold Sissee Nar to Ecko." A solid body of critical work developed across Wallace's lifetime, with early, influential essays by Tom LeClair (1996) and N. Katherine Hayles (1999) establishing *Infinite Jest* in particular as a subject of serious scholarly attention in academic journals. At the same time, his mainstream cultural relevance was bolstered by the publication of such seminal review essays as A. O. Scott's February 2010 *New York Review of Books* essay, "The Panic of Influence." The sheer volume of both academic and popular writing about Wallace, however, grew exponentially in the dark shadow cast by his suicide in 2008, as younger writers—and specialists from other disciplines—pressed his work into broader territories.

This volume appears in the context of that post-2008 expansion of interest in Wallace's work. The survey associated with this volume invited instructors to comment on which of Wallace's works they teach and in what contexts, which secondary supplements they assign to students or employ for their own research, and which thematic and formal issues they emphasize. More than one hundred educators replied, and the information provided in this section is informed by their helpful responses.

Novels and Short Fiction

Over twenty years David Foster Wallace published five books of fiction: the story collections *Girl with Curious Hair* (1989), *Brief Interviews with Hideous Men* (1999), and *Oblivion* (2004), and the novels *The Broom of the System* (1987) and *Infinite Jest* (1996). His final work-in-progress, *The Pale King*, was assembled by his longtime editor, Michael Pietsch, and published posthumously in 2011. These books can be thought of in three pairs (each combining a novel-length work with a collection of short stories) that represent his early, mid, and late career phases:

Broom and *Girl* were both largely drafted during Wallace's student years; *Infinite Jest* and *Brief Interviews* represent his highly successful middle period; and *Oblivion*, parts of which were originally intended to be part of *The Pale King*, forms a natural partner to Wallace's posthumous volume. Taken together, these works are diverse in thematic content and technical accomplishment, and their pedagogical challenges range from those raised by unsettling material (e.g., *Oblivion*'s "Incarnations of Burned Children") to those presented by sheer length (e.g., the thousand-plus pages of *Infinite Jest*).

Despite the scale of *Infinite Jest*, the majority of survey respondents concentrated on this work, following the critical orthodoxy that has established Wallace's long novel as his signature achievement. Beyond *Infinite Jest*, teachers variously draw on every stage of Wallace's career, from his earliest published story, "The Planet Trillaphon as It Stands in Relation to the Bad Thing" (1984), through to *The Pale King*. Amid these diverse selections, *Oblivion*'s "Good Old Neon" is the most frequently chosen individual story, presumably for its condensation of the mature Wallace's essential themes. Despite its relative length, "Westward the Course of Empire Takes Its Way" is the next most frequently taught story, no doubt for its close relation to Wallace's seminal essay "E Unibus Pluram." In order, the next most frequently taught stories are "The Depressed Person," "Incarnations of Burned Children," "My Appearance," "Octet," "Little Expressionless Animals," "Lyndon," and "The Soul Is Not a Smithy."

Nonfiction and Reviews

Wallace published two book-length nonfiction works (*Signifying Rappers* [1997] and *Everything and More*, a history of mathematical infinity [2003]) and two collections of nonfiction essays (*A Supposedly Fun Thing I'll Never Do Again* [1997] and *"Consider the Lobster" and Other Essays* [2005]) during his lifetime; a third collection (*Both Flesh and Not* [2012]) and a speech (*This Is Water* [2009]) were published posthumously. It is a testament to the power and richness of this nonfiction, and to the myriad ways it complements Wallace's fiction, that survey respondents report assigning all or part of every one of these nonfiction works to their classes. *Both Flesh and Not*, while most recently published, contains some of Wallace's earliest nonfiction work, including his first published essay, "Fictional Futures and the Conspicuously Young," in which he lays out elements of his arguments about his place in literary history and his critique of contemporary visual culture that he would later develop in the better-known "E Unibus Pluram" and interview by Larry McCaffery. Many teachers assign one or more of these texts to introduce Wallace's work in relation to his postmodern ancestors and to the ironic culture his work often challenges. Alongside "E Unibus Pluram," most often assigned are "Consider the Lobster" (often in composition, philosophy, or animal studies), "A Supposedly Fun Thing I'll Never Do Again" (in writing classes or alongside *Infinite Jest*), and *This Is Water* (alongside pretty much everything by Wallace).

While instructors use the diverse abundance of the rest of Wallace's nonfiction to suit their own various purposes, the essays do suggest some obvious themes. "Greatly Exaggerated" argues for Wallace's own contrarian view in postmodernism's "death of the author" debate (Barthes), which sets him apart from that literary ancestry, while "David Lynch Keeps His Head," "Some Remarks on Kafka's Funniness," "Joseph Frank's Dostoevsky," and "Borges on the Couch" can be used to situate Wallace's work in a context and history wider than America and literature. Other essays, however, build intimate visions of Wallace's America, particularly "Getting Away from Already Being Pretty Much Away from It All" and the post-9/11 "The View from Mrs. Thompson's"; the extensive "Up, Simba" (published separately as *McCain's Promise*) gives us Wallace's view of American politics and might be excerpted alongside *The Pale King*. Two essays from *"Consider the Lobster"* confront issues of gender, power, and feminism head-on—"Big Red Son," Wallace's exposé of the pornography industry, and "Certainly the End of *Something* or Other," ostensibly a review of Updike—and so could be taught fruitfully alongside *Brief Interviews with Hideous Men* in particular. The early work "The Empty Plenum," a critical essay on David Markson's *Wittgenstein's Mistress*, also raises complex questions about gender and fiction writing while more overtly presenting some of Wallace's ideas about the usefulness of metafiction. Finally, several composition instructors report using Wallace's masterful "Authority and American Usage," from *"Consider the Lobster"* (or the shorter version published as "Tense Present" in *Harper's*), to bring Wallace's characteristic humor and cleverness to their teaching of English usage.

Readings for Students

Survey respondents report teaching Wallace's work in a wide range of contexts; consequently, their assigned topical readings range widely as well. These readings concern postmodern theory, media, and culture; debates within postmodernism, such as the "death of the author," and surrounding the end of postmodernism; metafiction and image fiction; literary journalism; rhetoric and writing strategies; philosophy, especially of consciousness and language; and Wallace's forerunners and contemporaries, particularly John Barth and Jonathan Franzen. Instructors reach for a wide range of criticism to accompany their teaching of Wallace, most often assigning portions of Marshall Boswell's *Understanding David Foster Wallace* and Stephen J. Burn's reader's guide to *Infinite Jest*; when teaching *Infinite Jest*, some also rely on excerpts from Greg Carlisle's *Elegant Complexity* as well as on two earlier essays on the novel, N. Katherine Hayles's "The Illusion of

Autonomy and the Fact of Recursivity" and Mary K. Holland's "Braving the Narcissistic Loop of *Infinite Jest*" (which also appears in *Succeeding Postmodernism*). Many educators introduce Wallace's work as a whole using the 1993 McCaffery interview, which they tend to pair with the "E Unibus Pluram" essay from the same issue of the *Review of Contemporary Fiction*, in order to explore Wallace's ideas about contemporary culture, fiction, and the uses of irony in both. Others assign interviews from Burn's *Conversations with David Foster Wallace*, or the interview by Charlie Rose in 1997 ("David Foster Wallace Interview"), excerpts of which they play in class. On Wallace's innovations in irony, teachers assign articles by Paul Giles ("Sentimental Posthumanism"), Lee Konstantinou ("No Bull"), and Adam Kelly ("David Foster Wallace and the New Sincerity"). Many accompany these critical sources with excerpts from biographical ones, most often D. T. Max's *Every Love Story Is a Ghost Story* (or, for brevity's sake, Max's article "The Unfinished" from *The New Yorker*), but also David Lipsky's *Although of Course You End Up Becoming Yourself*. One respondent wisely paired such excerpts with "The Intentional Fallacy" (Wimsatt and Beardsley).

When placing Wallace's work in the context of postmodern theory, teachers assign excerpts from Fredric Jameson's *Postmodernism; or, the Cultural Logic of Late Capitalism*, Jean Baudrillard's *Simulations*, and Marshall McLuhan's *Understanding Media*, as well as Jacques Derrida's "Structure, Sign, and Play in the Discourse of the Human Sciences"; when connecting Wallace's work to that of early postmodernists including Barth, they use Barth's "The Literature of Exhaustion." In situating Wallace in relation to post-postmodernism, they use Robert McLaughlin's essay "Post-Postmodern Discontent," Burn's chapter "A Map of the Territory," and excerpts from Holland's *Succeeding Postmodernism*. Instructors frequently teach Wallace in relation to the fiction and nonfiction of his contemporaries, most often pairing his *Brief Interviews* with Zadie Smith's chapter "*Brief Interviews with Hideous Men*: The Difficult Gifts of David Foster Wallace" (sometimes juxtaposed with James Wood's essay on "hysterical realism") and pairing Wallace's work more generally with essays by Jonathan Franzen, including "Farther Away," "Why Bother?," and "Mr. Difficult." Emphasizing Wallace's philosophical roots, they use excerpts from Wittgenstein's *Tractatus* and *Philosophical Investigations*, as well as essays by René Descartes, Aristotle, Paul Ricoeur, and Stanley Cavell.

The Instructor's Library

Interviews and Biographical Materials

The frequency with which teachers select Wallace works that deal (albeit in displaced fashion) with personal suffering, such as "Good Old Neon" and "The

Depressed Person," anecdotally indicates how the proximity of Wallace's suicide informs classroom discussion of his work. Many respondents draw on Max's detailed biography of Wallace's suffering as a way of exploring "how biography becomes a curious kind of paratext" (Christopher Schaberg), while others simply see it as inescapable or as something that the students find particularly compelling. Some teachers match individual stories to particular moments in *Every Love Story* where Max recounts the context or writing of that work. Lipsky's book-length interview with Wallace, *Although of Course You End Up Becoming Yourself*, is used less frequently in class, though it is often assigned as secondary reading. Other biographically inflected sources deserve mention. Wallace and Bryan A. Garner's *Quack This Way* offers a transcript of a long interview about usage from 2006. Charles B. Harris's *Proofread or Die!* was published after our survey, but its collection of writings by Wallace's former students offers teachers intriguing juxtapositions (e.g., Suzanne Scanlon's "Final Exam" might be set next to the various "interviews" from *Brief Interviews with Hideous Men*).

Just as many respondents disdain the full biography, considering it "too journalistic for sustained attention" (Joseph Tabbi), and instead emphasize a text-based approach. Even in such cases, Wallace's reflections in interviews on his own position remain important. Interviews archived online, such as Wallace's appearance on *Charlie Rose* or his discussions with Michael Silverblatt, are popular resources, and there are two print anthologies of Wallace's interviews. Stephen J. Burn's *Conversations with David Foster Wallace* collects twenty-two interviews from across Wallace's career. *David Foster Wallace: The Last Interview* contains six interviews, three of which are also in Burn's volume. By far the most important interview—as attested by the survey and by two decades of Wallace scholarship—is Larry McCaffery's *Review of Contemporary Fiction* interview (the version collected in *Conversations with David Foster Wallace* restores about two thousand words that were cut from the version first published [xv]).

Archival Materials

The Harry Ransom Center at the University of Texas, Austin, holds extensive archival materials that relate to every major Wallace work except *Signifying Rappers*. These materials include handwritten notes and drafts, interview and research notes, typescript drafts, proofs, and promotional materials, as well as personal documents including some of Wallace's teaching syllabi; correspondence with his editors and with other authors, most notably Don DeLillo; and more than three hundred books, many heavily annotated, from Wallace's library. Most of these materials are accessible only to those who travel to the archive, though some of them are available on the Ransom Center's Web site (and are also collected at thehowlingfantods.com). One respondent reported students' delight at seeing Wallace's intimate and intellectual notes in the marginalia of his own writing and of others' books. Early and late drafts allow study of Wallace's writing process, which is also often under discussion in Wallace's correspondence with Don DeLillo. Exchanges with other authors can illuminate Wallace's revisions, such as the changes he made to "Mister Squishy" after responding to a question from Dave Eggers on a draft. Wallace's marginalia in other writers' books can be used to consider influence and to trace his sense of literary history: for example, using his very heavily annotated copy of Barth's *Lost in the Funhouse*. For fun and by way of introduction, Wallace's syllabi—characteristically funny, casual, and demanding at the same time—can be used to discuss his ideas about reading, writing, and learning, both as a teacher and as a writer.

Critical Studies

Book-Length Studies

The recent boom in Wallace studies means the body of criticism available to teachers and scholars is rapidly changing. As of this writing, eight monographs on Wallace's work exist, two of them exclusively on *Infinite Jest*. Burn's *David Foster Wallace's* Infinite Jest: *A Reader's Guide* (2003, 2012) offers a concise but detailed and wide-ranging examination of the novel's structure, allusions, and themes; chapters on Wallace's legacy and poetics; and an appendix containing a chronology of the novel's events. Carlisle's *Elegant Complexity* (2007) presents the novel as divided into twenty-eight thematically unified chapters and provides a host of useful tools for orienting oneself in the novel's chaos, including a thematic outline, character lists, its own chronologies, a setting map, and an indexed list of references. Carlisle's *Nature's Nightmare* (2013) gives the same focused attention to *Oblivion*, relating its analyses of each story in the collection to Wallace's career and to his last two novels.

Other monographs expand their frameworks across Wallace's oeuvre. Boswell's *Understanding David Foster Wallace* (2003) remains the sole book to provide a comprehensive introduction to and treatment of each of Wallace's major works through *Brief Interviews with Hideous Men*, balancing theoretical and literary frameworks, close reading, and reader friendliness. Recent monographs have a narrower focus: Clare Hayes-Brady's *The Unspeakable Failures of David Foster Wallace* (2016) examines Wallace's resistance to closure and the commodification of language; Adam Miller's *The Gospel According to David Foster Wallace* (2016) uses short scenes from *Infinite Jest* and *The Pale King* to explore religion, boredom, and distraction in the twenty-first century; and David Hering's *David Foster Wallace: Fiction and Form* (2016) uses archival material to relate Wallace's evolving compositional structures to his works' themes. Most recently, Lucas Thompson's *Global Wallace* (2016) challenges the orthodox view of Wallace as a narrowly American writer and places his work in dialogue with world literary studies; Jeffrey Severs, in *David Foster Wallace's Balancing Books* (2017), examines Wallace's interest in financial crises, and in the social implications of neoliberal policies in the twentieth and twenty-first centuries, as expressed over his entire oeuvre.

Essay Collections and Special Issues

As Wallace's critical profile has risen, his work has been the subject of several special issues of academic journals and essay collections. This trend began with the *Review of Contemporary Fiction*'s 1993 special issue on younger writers but has rapidly gained pace in the last six years. Many collections originate in conferences devoted to Wallace: David Hering's *Consider David Foster Wallace* gathered papers from a conference in Liverpool; Boswell's special double issue of *Studies in the Novel* (later republished in book form as *David Foster Wallace and "The Long Thing"*) partly collects papers from a 2011 conference devoted to *The Pale King*, as did Luc Herman and Toon Staes's 2014 special issue of *English Studies: Unfinished: Critical Approaches to David Foster Wallace's* The Pale King. Zeroing in on Wallace's novels or on *The Pale King*, specifically, these later collections follow a trend toward increasingly specialized focus on a particular book or aspect of Wallace's work that is reflected in Roberto Lucchetti and Roberto Natalini's special issue of *Lettera Matematica* (2016) on Wallace and mathematics, Steven M. Cahn and Maureen Eckert's *Freedom and the Self: Essays on the Philosophy of David Foster Wallace* (2015), and Robert Bolger and Scott Korb's *Gesturing Toward Reality* (2014). Boswell and Burn's *Companion to David Foster Wallace Studies* (2013), by contrast, attempts to take in the full range of Wallace's literary output by including essays on each of Wallace's volumes of fiction alongside essays that address large themes in Wallace's work. Samuel Cohen and Lee Konstantinou's *The Legacy of David Foster Wallace* (2012) helpfully mixes biographically oriented profiles with critical commentaries.

Web Sites and Other Electronic Resources

The popularity of Wallace's work in general (and of *Infinite Jest* in particular) with readers predisposed toward decoding, connecting, and obsessing has produced an impressive presence of Wallace-related materials on the Internet, some of which instructors will find helpful in orienting themselves or their students to Wallace's work and worlds or in drawing connections between that work and students' contemporary experience. One might start with Nick Manaitis's *The Howling Fantods*, a Web site that gathers "David Foster Wallace news and resources since March 97." The Web site lists and links to biographical and bibliographical materials, interviews, Wallace's appearances in popular culture, and even uncollected fiction held at the Ransom Center, while also providing notes on Wallace conferences, a (rather incomplete) list of critical sources, and readers' notes on *Infinite Jest*. It also links to the Wallace-l Listserv, run by Matt Bucher, where Wallace fans debate minutiae of Wallace's life and works. The Wallace Research Group at the University of Glasgow hosts a regularly updated online bibliography devoted to academic criticism of Wallace.

For all things *Jest*, try the *Infinite Jest* Wiki (infinitejest.wallacewiki.com), which offers character diagrams; an alphabetic index of names, places, and events from the novel; readers' annotations of the novel by page; overviews of characters, plot, events, and settings; and links to *Jest*-inspired works of art. Internet searches will also turn up a slew of setting and event maps, including maps of Eschaton, of *Jest*'s Boston, and of its reconfigured North America; *Infinite Atlas* offers an interactive map that identifies important locations, events, and characters from the novel on a contemporary map of the Boston area and beyond. Sam Potts's *Infinite Jest Diagram* expresses the relationships among all the major (and most minor) characters. Such sites, along with many other *Jest*-inspired products and documents, can be fun as well as genuinely helpful as students navigate the novel for the first time. The archived Web site of the first Infinite Summer—a communal reading of *Jest*, organized by Matthew Baldwin, in which readers around the world used a blog to discuss their reading experiences (infinitesummer.org)—also offers helpful introductory materials for first-time *Jest* readers, such as "How to Read *Infinite Jest*" (Bucher), while linking to yet more online reader resources. It can also be used as a template for organizing one's own communal reading experience of the novel, in or outside class.

Many respondents report bringing Wallace's own voice into the classroom while teaching his writing, most often by playing clips of his interviews with Charlie Rose and with Michael Silverblatt and by playing the audio (video is not available) of his 2005 commencement speech at Kenyon College, later published as *This Is Water*. This speech never fails to move students while clarifying some of the core ideas that motivate Wallace's fiction. Teachers also use clips of Wallace reading his fiction (including "Incarnations of Burned Children" and excerpts from *The Pale King* [www.youtube.com/watch?v=UoU3l8trOnY]) and nonfiction (including "Consider the Lobster" [www.youtube.com/watch?v=_fZOl7C_vDI] and "Big Red Son" [www.youtube.com/watch?v=pJv_dxh6meE]).

Finally, as the "contemporary" world of Wallace's writing recedes, savvy instructors have begun to supplement that writing with relevant cultural context, for example, playing commercials Wallace mentions in "E Unibus Pluram," along with clips of shows—including *Saturday Night Live* and *The David Letterman Show*—he uses in his arguments or in his fiction. Students may also enjoy seeing a truly contemporary pop culture imagining of a key scene from *Infinite Jest*—the Decemberists' video for "The Calamity Song," which stages the disastrous Eschaton battle; or Wallace's appearance as a cruiser wearing a tuxedo T-shirt on an episode of *The Simpsons* titled "A Totally Fun Thing Bart Will Never Do Again" (complete with a ship named *Nadir*). While this *Simpsons* reference is only available as captured images, all other clips mentioned here are currently available on *YouTube*.

Part Two

APPROACHES

Introduction

Stephen J. Burn and Mary K. Holland

Reading David Foster Wallace's mammoth *Infinite Jest* (or trying to) has become almost a rite of passage for all kinds of word-hungry, culturally savvy, or intellectually curious young readers, many of whom end up in our classrooms. A darling of erudite pop culture, Wallace is now a widely recognized symbol of hip intelligence, his three-pound masterpiece, lugged around or casually propped on a bookshelf, more effective than ironic nerd glasses at signaling serious cool. At the other end of the literary spectrum, Wallace's 2005 commencement speech at Kenyon College, published posthumously as *This Is Water*, has been equally effective in creating Wallace fans; the audio recording on *YouTube* of Wallace delivering the speech has become so popular—with over a quarter million views as of this writing—that it's hard to find a classroom of students who have not encountered it, even if they have yet to read a word of Wallace's considerable output. Others may arrive in class well versed in the mythos of the man—his decades-long struggles with depression and addiction; his tragic death by suicide; his famous shyness; that bandana—and ready to consume or detest his literary work on the basis of bloggers' rants about his work or of Jason Segel's performance of the mythos in the 2015 film *The End of the Tour.* So any teacher engaging students with Wallace's work must not only confront its infamous difficulty—its multiple narrators and points of view, its fragmentation and lack of closure, its footnotes, its fascination with jargon, and its many flavors of irony—but also speak to and around the cultural expectations students bring to it and to its author.

Fortunately, many enjoyable inroads into Wallace's literary work exist between these popular extremes of hyperdifficult novel and easy-listening speech—for example, the essays, such as "A Supposedly Fun Thing I'll Never Do Again," in which Wallace depicts himself in that most American place—a cruise ship—wearing a tuxedo T-shirt at dinner and mildly harassing his feckless table mates; or "The View from Mrs. Thompson's," in which he processes the horror of 9/11 and the changing landscape of the American heart in front of a TV at his neighbor's house in an ocean of Illinois corn. Select short stories offer other inviting avenues into Wallace's characteristic blend of bite, heart, and humor, as in "Good Old Neon," whose narrator discovers a way out of that most human agony, fear of inauthenticity; or "Forever Overhead," which eschews linguistic tricks to tell the story of growing up by learning to see the world anew and to care about other people. Story-length excerpts from the posthumous *The Pale King* provide another way into the work, as in the moving monologue of Chris Fogle, a once disaffected, drugged-out youth who finds his life's purpose (in a college lecture, no less). Texts such as these introduce new readers to the qualities in Wallace's work that have already elicited passionate responses from some of their classmates. Wallace wrote about growing up; understanding the self; struggling to connect with others, especially within the pressures of romantic relationships; family, particularly how children learn from and are hurt by their parents; politics; labor, and finding personal meaning in work; and media, entertainment, and their effects on individuals and relationships—that is, the things that most urgently occupy students' hearts and minds—with at least as much humor and compassion as intellectual difficulty and literary pyrotechnics, and it is this mix of qualities that has catapulted him into a kind of nerdy stardom and made many of his works a natural fit for college classrooms. Another challenge for teachers, then, is engaging students with the aspects of the work that easily spark them, while pushing them to recognize the many academic and technical ways in which Wallace's funny, big-hearted works also make vital, complex interventions into a long history of literary, intellectual, social, theoretical, and philosophical ideas. This is exactly the kind of challenge—to expand the intellect while nurturing the human—that motivated Wallace as a writer and as a teacher.

A famously demanding and fastidious teacher, Wallace peppered his syllabi with sections headed "WARNING" and "CAVEAT EMPTOR" that specified his expectations, from reading every text twice before class to paying close attention to written grammar and mechanics. He went so far as to list the number of times he had assigned every letter grade so far in his teaching career (he reported the average final grade he gave as "B-/C+" ["English 102"]). Yet alongside these apparent attempts to scare off the unreformed Chris Fogle type he included passionate entreaties for students to respect and engage with every question and comment generated by their reading assignments, to be brave enough to disagree with him, and to take responsibility for the ideas they brought into the course and carried out of it. This simultaneously off-putting and seductive pedagogical engagement also describes Wallace's writing, whose earnest appeals pull the reader in even as its often daunting complexity frustrates and overwhelms. Every teacher of Wallace must be prepared to meet and manage, even to encourage, these contradictory aspects of his writing in the classroom.

Despite his work's notorious challenges, Wallace's rise to prominence in scholarly criticism over the last few years has made clear his centrality to American letters. In 1993 *The Review of Contemporary Fiction* cast Wallace as one of the "younger writers" whose impact on American literature was largely felt in the margins, but since the publication of *Infinite Jest*, and certainly since Wallace's death, interest in every facet of his work, from fiction to nonfiction, short stories to unfinished novel, pop culture treatises to undergraduate philosophy thesis, has exploded. The prominent language games and ironic cultural satire of his earliest fiction, combined with the now-famous 1993 interview in which he launched a stern critique of irony in American culture and art, set the stage for an initial critical response that consistently placed his work relative to language theory and postmodernism. More recently, however, and in part because of the availability of Wallace's research and writing materials at the Harry Ransom Center at the University of Texas, Austin, attention has shifted to the many ways in which his fiction intimately relates to the rich literary traditions, both

European and American, that he himself read, loved, and taught. Recent critical trends have also incorporated Wallace's work, so that we see readings of his fiction in terms of cognitive science and theory of mind, ecocriticism, and virtual environments. With the publication of *The Pale King* in 2011, critics began to examine Wallace's inquiries about American politics and neoliberal economics, models of community and questions of civic responsibility, and individual freedom (often filtered through references to works that bracket his career: his undergraduate philosophy thesis and his later commencement speech). Such a combination of abiding American themes and engagement with contemporary critical and theoretical debates ensures his fiction a place not just in critical scholarship but also in a wide variety of classrooms.

Meanwhile, Wallace's relation to earlier writers, which nearly always informs the stylistic choices he made in each work, remains hotly contested. His early, lengthy hybrid of barely veiled attack and homage to John Barth in the novella "Westward the Course of Empire Takes Its Way" places Wallace's fiction squarely in dialogue with the boundary-breaking metafiction of early postmodernism, which was his most immediate literary inheritance. Any consideration of his own innovative uses of popular postmodern devices like self-reflexivity and formal experimentation must acknowledge the significant impact on his writing of American postmodernists including Barth, Donald Barthelme, Vladimir Nabokov, and Robert Coover, but also Jorge Luis Borges and Julio Cortázar. Yet, as Wallace's work developed, and as archival materials were made available, his larger genealogy—one not exclusively tethered to his postmodern roots—became visible. Scholars have begun to trace in his work the influences of pre-postmodern American writers including Nathaniel Hawthorne, Herman Melville, and Flannery O'Connor, as well as non-American writers including Georges Perec, Manuel Puig, Franz Kafka, and Fyodor Dostoevsky.

His exact influence on writers in his wake is, of course, still becoming clear. But it is already indisputable that fiction of the early twenty-first century owes a great debt to Wallace's late-twentieth-century and millennial innovations. If writers working in the wake of *Infinite Jest* have rarely imitated its massive labyrinthine architecture, Wallace's influence is perhaps most evident in the tonal shift of twenty-first-century writing, from the madcap *jouissance* in language play of early Thomas Pynchon and the disaffected irony of late-twentieth-century Don DeLillo to the unabashed earnestness of Jonathan Safran Foer and Dave Eggers and the convoluted earnestness-through-irony of George Saunders. Wallace's agenda for fiction, and his own work's attempts to enact that agenda, stand as precedent-setting models for such a change. His methods for creating that tonal shift to sincerity—so radically different from those of traditional realism, which he and earlier postmodernists had thoroughly criticized—also continue to appear and to evolve in contemporary fiction. We can connect his variety of formal innovations for communicating sincerity or significance—footnotes and endnotes, nonchronological sequencing, self-aware self-reflexivity, and shifting and multiplying point of view primary among them—to the equally productive anti-realist devices that increasingly populate recent fiction by writers such as Steve Tomasula, Jennifer Egan, and Mark Danielewski.

Wallace's fascination with such devices as a way of answering the seemingly signification-challenged language games of early postmodernism provides one of many indicators that his work was a product of the reign of theory that largely defined our ways of reading and writing literature in the 1980s and early 1990s. He was a devoted student of Ludwig Wittgenstein's work, well versed in language theory and in writers' responses to it, and his writing often tries to settle debates about the status of writers, readers, and texts that remain so contentious in theory. Rather than making the text supreme, Wallace, like many writers today, used fictional devices to invoke their authors, the presence in *Infinite Jest* of the ghost of James Incandenza, auteur, perhaps serving as a joke about Roland Barthes's theorized "death of the author." He manifested the author not to wrest authority from the deconstructed text, however, but to make the text a matter of conversation and relationship that are opened up to writer and reader. In this way his works hand textual authority back to the reader, creating a text-reader-writer nexus that demands from the reader the kind of active textual engagement Wallace saw as antidote to passive entertainment. This self-reflection, which requires more of the reader than of the text, differentiates Wallace's methods from the metafictive devices of his literary predecessors and from the indeterminate identity politics of reader-response theory.

While Wallace's longer works can be neatly classified as examples of what Judith Ryan has called "the novel after theory," his writing is also revealing when read in the context of the renewed interest in literature's institutional foundations—especially the role of creative writing programs—presaged by Mark McGurl's *The Program Era*. McGurl notes that Wallace "was said to have been harshly criticized by his teachers in the M.F.A. program at Arizona for his experimental impulses," and, as critics such as Kasia Boddy have shown, the form and content of much of Wallace's earlier work is often dictated by a hidden template provided by a range of writers (Bret Easton Ellis, John Barth) or literary styles (minimalism) that were in vogue in mid-to-late-eighties program culture.

Beyond his engagement with other styles, and with the divide created by the rise of language theory, Wallace's work spans a rich diversity of topics. Equally adept at philosophy and literature while a student at Amherst, Wallace eventually turned his critical mind not just to inventing forms of newly communicative fiction but also to producing a significant body of essays that mounted social critique on topics ranging from the particularly American narcissism of cruising to the particularly male willingness to construct an ego out of colonized others that he observed in the American porn industry. His essays, like his fiction, incorporate popular culture not, 1980s-style, as window dressing to a depressing verisimilitude but as fodder for his trademark self-conscious critique. What his fiction largely struggles to do, his essays more often successfully achieve: not simply diagnosing the ills of contemporary American society but positing, in the same relentlessly recursive logic of intellectual skepticism, new ways of thinking about these ills with the aim of moving readers out of them. Always he balances his mercilessly keen observations with empathy for those who are likely to suffer—whether it's the lobster whose painful death does not diminish the gustatory pleasure of the gourmand or his maligned table mates on the cruise ship *Nadir*, to whom he apologizes retrospectively, in a footnote. This ethic of care, and of paying attention—to individuals, to ways of connecting with them, and to his own limitations in doing so—is often the quality that draws new readers into Wallace's complex world.

The topical concerns of Wallace's writing, then, offer a kaleidoscopic take on a range of current theoretical and philosophical issues that make both his fiction and his nonfiction naturally fit with courses that seek to interrogate abstract concepts. But there are also more purely literary reasons to teach his work. While Robert Alter bemoaned the spread of "tone-deafness" in the "academic study of literature" in 2010, noting the disappearance of a sense of style in an era of "high-speed short-cut language" (10), Wallace's remarkable sentences offer teachers an opportunity to explore the characteristics and purpose of literary style, while his deft use of linguistic shortcuts ("w/r/t," "IYI," and so on) also demonstrates the value of the truncated language that Alter's conservative reservations overlook. As a novelist who listed Philip Larkin, Louise Glück, and W. H. Auden among his favorite writers, Wallace populated his fiction with an impressive array of carefully crafted, often aesthetically stunning, poetic passages, almost any of which can be set as a close-reading exercise to highlight strategic deviations from ordinary usage. The opening passage of *The Pale King* is particularly rich in such examples, where even such small fragments as "Quartz and chert and schist and chondrite iron scabs in granite" (3) can illustrate language's sonic qualities—rhythm, alliteration, assonance—even as the paratactic structure that characterizes the passage as a whole implies a leveling of hierarchies, the value hidden in the quotidian. Elsewhere Wallace's slangy excursions from proper diction—including deviations into the "high-speed short-cut language" Alter dislikes—allow him not simply to generate humor or to convey character, but also, as Dale Peck observed, "to discuss with varying degrees of fluency all sorts of subjects . . . without resorting to academese" (15). Students might be invited to reflect on what happens in a passage such as Pemulis's breezy discourse on math, late in *Infinite Jest*, which can be offered as an exemplum of Wallace's ability to convey complex concepts and allusions through the elastic idiom of a character's speech.

Yet, if the intellectual richness and literary rewards of Wallace's prose can make his work endlessly inviting to professors, his work can be challenging in the classroom. The very same sentences whose sonic qualities and expansive architecture delight advanced students can strike novice readers as deliberately alienating (Wallace confessed to occasionally expressing "hostility" with "sentences that are syntactically not incorrect but still a real bitch to read" [Burn, *Conversations* 25]). Beyond syntax, Wallace's approach to language itself often seems counterintuitive since, as Marshall Boswell first observed, "much of Wallace's inimitable prose is designed to obfuscate what it is actually determined to reveal" (*Understanding* 140). Some of the topics that Wallace's work returns to again and again—namely depression, suicide, addiction, and male oppression of women—can also be off-putting or treacherously provocative for individual readers and in classroom settings. Indeed, issues of gender and power are in the forefront in much of Wallace's work, from his critique in "The Empty Plenum" of David Markson's feminism to his own attempt at writing "a parody (a feminist parody) of feminism," as he described *Brief Interviews with Hideous Men* (Max, *Every Love Story* 247), to his exploration of masculine beauty in "Federer Both Flesh and Not," and are largely crafted from a male or masculinist point of view. Thus it is not unusual to find interest in or empathy with his work divided down gender lines, or for class discussions about, say, layers of irony in *Brief Interviews*' "B.I. #20" to enter charged territory about real-life male appropriations of women's bodies and voices.

Fraught questions of race have also become increasingly prominent in recent Wallace criticism and should inform classroom discussion. While Wallace wrote self-consciously in *Signifying Rappers* about the position of "mainstream whites" looking in "from outside the cultural window" at black culture (23)—an image that cements cultural difference—he was nevertheless willing to enter stylized black voices in his fiction, notably in the controversial Wardine sections of *Infinite Jest*. Tara Morrissey and Lucas Thompson were the first critics to explore representations of race in Wallace studies, finding both concealed debts to Jamaica Kincaid in *Infinite Jest* and "undeniably problematic outcomes" in *Signifying Rappers*' exploration of race. Since then, Samuel Cohen has argued that Wallace "wrote out of an anxiety surrounding race that despite his best intentions may have expressed itself in his work" (233), while Edward Jackson and Joel Nicholson-Roberts have located "a reactionary attempt to shore up the experiences of whiteness and masculinity at the expense of the novel's black and female characters" in readings of *Infinite Jest* that emphasize the so-called new sincerity.

The sheer size and interconnected design of much of Wallace's output does not lend itself to the sequestered units that most comfortably compose a semester: he has no *Crying of Lot 49*, no *White Noise*. This collection, with essays targeting a wide variety of thematic, stylistic, and literary aspects of Wallace's work, is designed to help teachers face these and other challenges. The contents have been grouped to help teachers locate the essays that may most effectively suit their needs. The first section, "Teaching Key Works and Genres," addresses the practical considerations that arise from teaching particular Wallace works. Marshall Boswell offers methods of tackling the terrifying, immensely rewarding feat of teaching *Infinite Jest* in its entirety; his divisions of readings, consideration of the book's "Sierpinski gasket" structure, and suggested secondary sources promise to ease the way for any instructor teaching the book for the first time or looking for new ways to teach it. Of course, teaching *The Pale King*—unfinished, posthumous, existing as much in the archive as in the bound book—

presents its own enormous challenges, which Stephen J. Burn navigates in his essay, not dodging the book's unfinished status but using it to ask students important questions about authorial intent, editorial input, and Wallace's compositional strategies, along with the novel's myriad thematic and formal aspects that continue the conversations about ideas and literature that Wallace's work has sparked with now generations of readers. Turning to the short fiction, Philip Coleman offers a variety of approaches to teaching several of Wallace's short stories—through connective themes, technical challenges, and the history of the form—to suit instructors who assign them as respite from the exhaustion of the big novels. Then Matthew Luter's "Teaching Wallace's Pop Criticism" suggests ways that students might see Wallace both as a consumer of popular culture and as an exemplary instance of a writer who is able to evaluate his material in nuanced fashion, in stark contrast to the flat option to "like" provided by ever-present social media.

Luter's essay also lays groundwork for teaching Wallace's nonfiction in general, which is not the subject of a separate essay in this volume but instead is treated by several essays in a variety of contexts: Mark Bresnan offers ideas for using five different Wallace essays in the composition classroom; Jeffery Severs considers essays from all three of Wallace's essay collections in terms of Wallace's ideas about authorship and in relation to teaching his novels; Robert McLaughlin pairs Wallace essays with similar, contemporaneous ones by authors including Jonathan Franzen and DeLillo; Lucas Thompson uses half a dozen of Wallace's essays and reviews, some little-known, as intertexts between Wallace's fiction and world literature; and Andrew Warren examines four of Wallace's essays in his analysis of Wallace's writerly styles and techniques. Nearly two dozen, or about two-thirds, of Wallace's published essays are enlisted here, in a wide range of teacherly contexts, reflecting the place they occupy in Wallace's oeuvre itself—neither central nor marginal, but interwoven by theme and technique throughout his literary output.

The second section, "Classroom Contexts," offers advice for teaching a variety of Wallace's works in diverse classroom settings. Mike Miley describes a daring context for teaching Wallace—high school—but demonstrates how young students are particularly suited to the project of debunking master narratives that Wallace's work outlines. Miley offers methods for leading them through the embrace, then the explosion, of the postmodern master narrative that will leave them well prepared to encounter theory and critical thinking in college. Mark Bresnan's essay offers a useful way of teaching Wallace in the composition classroom: using Wallace's "recursive" essays to demonstrate to students the extended and multiplicitous, rather than for/against, reasoning necessary to any strong argument. Meanwhile, most teachers who love Wallace find ways to fit his work into their survey courses; Ralph Clare describes a multitude of text pairings and assignments that situate Wallace in relation to several classic American themes, including individualism, innocence and experience, and America's relation to a newly globalized world. At least as daunting, and as rewarding, as tackling the big novels is teaching Wallace's entire oeuvre—where to start? what to leave out? what contexts to use and in what order?—and Jeffrey Severs's essay addresses all these questions, proposing an innovative method of teaching Wallace's work in clusters that bring out thematic and structural connections, rather than chronologically, making plain the recursive nature of Wallace's entire writing career. Finally, Kathleen Fitzpatrick enlarges her pedagogical context beyond the walls of the classroom by moving from the desk and page to the Internet, exploring ways of teaching Wallace's work using distributed pedagogy and distributing technology while recognizing the many ways in which his fiction builds into itself such distribution of text, writer, and reader.

The third section, "Wallace and Literary History: Influences and Intertexts," addresses the clear demand for intertextual commentary made by Wallace's work. Mary K. Holland describes a framework for connecting Wallace's work back to premodernist traditions and examining Wallace as the realist writer he considered himself to be, putting his fiction in conversation with both the early postmodern antirealists he claimed to oppose and his contemporaries who adopt and adapt what he called anti-Realist realist methods, as a way of asking students to consider the complicated histories of realism and metafiction. Patrick O'Donnell's essay then proposes an approach to teaching Wallace's work that acknowledges his particularly American lineage, connecting his characteristically complex and open-ended fiction to the tradition of the systems novel that evolved out of American postmodern authors including Pynchon, DeLillo, and William Gaddis. Robert McLaughlin's essay connects Wallace's own contributions to the intertext of postmodernism with those of his contemporaries, helping students enlarge their understanding of one often oversimplified period while beginning to look ahead to what is coming next. Finally, Lucas Thompson widens the lens through which we can view Wallace's work, with an essay that presents methods for investigating Wallace's global investments, his appropriations of the methods of writers such as Kafka and Dostoevsky, and his "pragmatic" approach to these appropriations.

The final section, "Intellectual and Social Contexts," outlines several key underlying grids that can be used to place Wallace's work in a variety of larger networks of writings, philosophies, and themes. Andrew Warren's essay sets Wallace's early fiction in its institutional context of "the program era," exploring different ways that students might be encouraged to see the work in relation to the spectacular ascent of the creative writing program. Allard den Dulk also considers Wallace's academic background, invoking the author's early philosophical training as a way to read the later work in the context of philosophical problems of "language, consciousness, and meaningful existence." Seeing Wallace at a junction between critique and capitulation, Hamilton Carroll offers ways for students to recognize how Wallace's work adapts the language and positions of second-wave feminism while operating from the very heteronormativity and male oppression it seeks to overcome. Matt Mullins's contribution, "Can Empathy Be Taught?," sees Wallace less as a conduit for institutional power and influence, as in Warren's essay, and more as a model that students might follow in learning to conceive and write of others through empathy. All the essays in this section construct frameworks for studying Wallace's work that admit both inheritance and reaction, and create from that rich tension opportunities for philosophical critique.

The breadth of topics, contexts, methods, and classroom situations addressed by these essays mimics the wide range of subjects, styles, voices, and techniques that make up Wallace's complicated, contradictory body of work. Inspired by an inexhaustible fascination with that prodigious oeuvre, the essays thus provide an abundant range of tools for negotiating its complexities with our students.

Teaching *Infinite Jest*

Marshall Boswell

For all its complexity, erudition, and formidable length, *Infinite Jest* is, in the final analysis, a young person's novel, written for readers in their twenties and thirties by a brilliant and ambitious young man in his early thirties. More than a third of the novel takes place in a boarding school and features a troubled seventeen-year-old lexical prodigy and marijuana addict whose character recalls such figures as Hamlet, Goethe's Werther, and J. D. Salinger's Seymour Glass, among others. In one of his earliest promotional interviews for the book, Wallace openly admitted that he sought to capture a particular brand of "sadness" that he identified not only in himself but also in his peers. Describing his own state of mind when he began the book, he admits, "I was white, upper-middle-class, obscenely well-educated, had had way more career success than I could have legitimately hoped for and was sort of adrift. A lot of my friends were the same way"; he therefore hoped his novel would help those lost and adrift twenty- and thirty-year-olds "find a way to put away childish things and confront stuff about spirituality and values" (Interview with Laura Miller).

This latter agenda is precisely what has activated the upper-level undergraduates whom I have guided through the *Infinite Jest* labyrinth. The novel speaks to them on numerous levels. Its vast range of themes—solipsism, depression, addiction, entertainment—matches their experience as twenty-first-century young adults, and in a way that speaks to Wallace's remarkable prophetic powers. Like the precocious tennis prodigies at Enfield Tennis Academy, Wallace's readers stream endless hours of filmic entertainment through their own real-life "teleputers," i.e., laptops and tablets, entertainment that they absorb largely in isolation, in dorm rooms and rental apartments. Most of them have already embraced the cynical, ironic detachment of Generation X as well as the heart-felt emo ethos of their immediate predecessors, exhibiting a unique blend of self-consciousness and willed naiveté that encompasses the sensibility of Jon Stewart and Stephen Colbert as well as that of John Green. *Infinite Jest* is the most artful and successful expression of this so-called post-postmodern vision. Yet the novel also suggests a way to transform the confusion of one's early twenties into a purposeful and ethically grounded adulthood. The work of reading the book is the price to be paid for its many rewards, and, for the students I have taught, those rewards were well worth the effort.

In this essay I provide a template for an upper-level undergraduate literature course featuring *Infinite Jest* as its centerpiece. This class can function as a topics course or, in my personal case, as a senior seminar. Roughly half the semester should focus on Wallace's novel, resulting in a six- to seven-week study broken up into reading assignments of between eighty and 120 pages, with preliminary texts and a scattering of follow-up works rounding out the bulk of the required reading. The course concludes with a twenty-page seminar paper, complete with a graded annotated bibliography and an in-class presentation. Having taught this course three times, I can affirm that it represents the most rewarding classroom experience I have had in twenty-five years of college-level instruction, and the credit goes entirely to Wallace's remarkable novel.

One of the great challenges in teaching the novel is that instructors can address most of its major themes or motifs at any point in the reading experience. As such, there is no tidy, linear way to take up this theme or that motif. Nevertheless, specific motifs gain importance at key points in the novel's linear progression. In outlining the weekly readings, I identify those pressure points, which can be seized upon as productive moments for more intensive class discussions that can in turn illuminate earlier sections. In addition, I provide suggestions for preliminary readings as well as secondary sources to be assigned as the reading proceeds. I also provide a list of themes and motifs that can be distributed to the class before the reading proper begins. The instructor of record can assign one of these motifs or themes to an individual class member, based on the student's particular interest, and these individuals can in turn serve as the informal experts on those themes or motifs.

Preliminary Readings

To set up the novel's, and Wallace's, fascinating and instructive engagement with metafiction and postmodernism more generally, one might well begin the course by assigning, on day 1, John Barth's "Lost in the Funhouse" in conjunction with his companion essay, "The Literature of Exhaustion," reprinted in *The Friday Book*. These two works lucidly contextualize the metafictional turn in relation to literary modernism and provide a vocabulary with which to talk about both dominants. Students should next read Wallace's "E Unibus Pluram" and one or two pieces from his first story collection, *Girl with Curious Hair*, ideally "My Appearance" and, if there is time, "Westward the Course of Empire Takes Its Way," the latter of which will require roughly two additional class sessions.

"E Unibus Pluram" can be read as Wallace's generational response to Barth's earlier essay, while "My Appearance" fictionalizes the problems Wallace raises in the essay. Just as Barth confronts the difficulty of writing innovative fiction in the wake of modernist experimentation, so too does Wallace wrestle with the challenges of moving beyond the irony and self-reflexivity characteristic of Barthian metafiction and reengaging with readers in a way that transcends mere irony. Wallace's essay also points forward to *Infinite Jest* in its focus on contemporary popular culture, which, in Wallace's analysis, has appropriated postmodern self-reflexivity and institutionalized ironic detachment as a dominant mode. "Westward" meanwhile engages directly with Barth's famous story, and with Barth himself, while pointing the way forward to *Infinite Jest*. Students should also be encouraged to read Wallace's widely cited interview with Larry McCaffery, which can be assigned as required reading or simply made available as an optional text. This important selection of preliminary readings should occupy no more than a week, with perhaps one additional class session in week 2 in the event students read "Westward the Course of Empire Takes Its Way."

Infinite Jest: *The Overture*

As many of the novel's first-time readers will attest, the first one hundred pages are, in many respects, the most difficult. For one thing, readers have to acclimate to Wallace's dense prose, which, although it is addictive over time, is undoubtedly forbidding and challenging at first exposure. For another, the novel's seemingly haphazard narrative structure is never more varied and decentered than in its opening movement. Readers meet dozens of characters whose relation to one another, and to the novel's main plot lines, is deliberately obscured. Finally, the novel's use of endnotes takes some getting used to; the back-and-forth movement from the body text to the appendix requires readers to develop a reading strategy that works best for them. Asking students to read the first 109 pages of the novel before the semester begins will allow them to acclimate to the book at their own pace. Stephen Burn's indispensable reader's guide to *Infinite Jest* will not only help them navigate this early section on their own but also shape their reading of the entire novel as the semester proceeds. When the course begins, students will have met most of the major characters, visited several of the novel's main locations, and been introduced to the book's key plot engine, the mortally addictive Entertainment—and will be eager for guidance going forward.

Whether the students read those first one hundred pages before or during the semester, initial class sessions on this section will likely be spent clearing up various difficulties and providing some guidance as to the novel's elusive structure. The first issue to address is the chronology of Hal Incandenza's opening monologue, which is in fact the final scene in the novel. Hal's concluding line, "So yo then man what's *your* story?" (17), launches the novel proper, which means the subsequent narrative leads up to this opening event and should (though may not) provide an explanation for Hal's condition. Challenge students to track Hal's development over the course of the novel with an eye toward solving the mystery of his inability to talk.

The novel's future setting should also be addressed in this opening week. According to numerous historical references sprinkled throughout the text, Wallace set the novel in the first decade of the twenty-first century, as he projected it in his imagination from his mid-1990s perspective, with the bulk of the action taking place in the Year of the Depend Adult Undergarment, which corresponds to our 2009 (see 223). Why set a novel in this way? How should we as twenty-first-century readers respond to this futuristic setting, now that we have effectively overtaken it? What does this proleptic chronology say about Wallace's relationship to traditional realism and postmodern metafiction? And what are the political, socioeconomic implications of Subsidized Time? Does this imagined development have any analogue in our current culture?

Finally, it can be helpful to provide students with a structural map for the novel, which, though not readily apparent in this confusing opening section, is in fact quite simple. The novel is neatly subdivided among three main narrative strands. The first focuses on Hal and the Enfield Tennis Academy. The second centers on Don Gately and the recovering addicts at Ennet House. The third involves the search for the Entertainment and all the attendant political developments surrounding the emergence of O.N.A.N. and the rise of Quebecois separatism. The Entertainment, produced by Hal's father, is the novel's primary symbol for addiction and joins all three strands, both literally and figuratively. At this stage, students might also be introduced to the figure of the Sierpinski gasket, which Wallace identified in an interview with Michael Silverblatt as one of the novel's governing structural devices. A Sierpinski gasket is a fractal with the shape of an equilateral triangle. The triangle can then be subdivided infinitely into a set of smaller and smaller equilateral triangles (fig. 1).

Figure 1. Sierpinski gasket.

Students can explore how the novel's tripartite narrative structure might be grafted onto the Sierpinski model, which also operates according to recursive sets of three.

Infinite Jest: *Six Weeks of Readings*

With those first 109 pages behind them, students still have nearly nine hundred pages to go, not counting the endnotes. To get through the rest of the book in six weeks, they will have to read roughly 150 pages a week. These pages can be divided into three fifty-page assignments for a course meeting three times a week or weekend assignments of roughly one hundred pages followed by a fifty-page mid-week assignment for twice-weekly classes.

This early stage may be a good time to introduce a list of tropes, allusions, and themes that students can begin tracking as they read. Students might also be asked to select a topic that particularly interests them and to pay special attention to each iteration of that motif or theme as the semester proceeds. In this way, the class can pool its collective wisdom as it unpacks the novel's dense and interlocking network of themes. A possible list might read as follows:

> Alcoholics Anonymous and religion
> Film as trope and structural device
> Optics and lenses
> The Entertainment, DMZ, and addiction
> The Great Convexity/Concavity and environmental ethics
> Quebecois separatism and the United States' foreign policy
> Tennis as trope
> Treatment of sexual abuse and incest
> Mythic allusions
> *Infinite Jest* and the poetics of postmodernism
> Mathematics in *Infinite Jest*
> Allusions to and parallels with James Joyce's *Ulysses* as source text
> Allusions to and parallels with Don DeLillo's *Ratner's Star*
> Allusions to and parallels with Fyodor Dostoevsky's *The Brothers Karamazov*
> Allusions to and parallels with Shakespeare's *Hamlet*
> *Infinite Jest* and the postironic novel
> *Infinite Jest* and the encyclopedic novel

By no means exhaustive, this list nonetheless includes topics that will likely be beyond the students' intellectual scope. But providing students with such a list at the beginning of the reading experience, and inviting them to focus on one theme, gives them not only a sense of the key ideas at work in the novel but also some ownership over their reading experience.

Edward Mendelson's essay "Encyclopedic Narrative: From Dante to Pynchon," the source of the term mentioned in the final entry above, is a useful text to distribute at this early stage. In particular, students should focus on the catalog of features that Mendelson lists as specific to encyclopedic narratives. In his conception, all encyclopedic narratives include "an account of a technology or science" and "also offer an account of an art outside the realm of written fiction" (1270). They "attend to the complexities of statecraft . . . , identify the range of roles and actions that the City provides," and include "vast numbers of jobs and professions, all the varieties of work and labor" (1271). Finally, "each encyclopedic narrative is an encyclopedia of literary styles" (1271). Students will be able to identify nearly every item in Mendelson's catalog, a process that will demystify the book and also connect it to a larger tradition that includes *Moby-Dick*, *Ulysses*, and *Gravity's Rainbow*. James O. Incandenza's filmography, which appears as an endnote on pages 985–93, also highlights the novel's encyclopedic nature and its antagonistic relationship with the postmodernist tradition represented in class by the two Barth texts and in Mendelson's essay by *Gravity's Rainbow*.

Weeks 2 and 3

By the second week of class discussions, the novel will have commenced its sustained treatment of Alcoholics Anonymous (AA). Two key episodes prepare the way for this theme: Ken Erdedy's internal monologue as he waits for his marijuana supplier to return his call (17–27) and Joelle van Dyne's suicide attempt at Molly Notkin's party (219–40). These two episodes can spur a fruitful class discussion about Wallace's particular take on addiction and its sources. In the earlier episode, Wallace connects addiction with paralysis, while in the later one he conflates it with the dangers of pleasure. Students will be quick to connect this multifaceted depiction with the Entertainment and its effect on viewers, but they should also be directed to the various ways that Wallace makes these connections in structural and literary terms, as in the moment when the partygoers at Molly's discuss the Entertainment in earshot of Joelle, who is in the bathroom attempting to commit suicide—or "eliminate her own map" in the novel's specialized argot—by having what she terms "Too Much Fun" with her Substance (231).

Conversely, the major Ennet House passages from this section of the novel open up the novel's counternarrative involving AA and the wisdom embedded in the program's hollow clichés. These sections compel a return to "E Unibus Pluram," with its sustained critique of hip irony and "meta-watching" (33). Class discussion might profitably focus on the conflict between Geoffrey Day and Don Gately that spans pages 270–81. Day functions as one of the novel's key postmodern ironists, and his criticism of Alcoholics Anonymous and its reliance on pithy slogans exemplifies the sophisticated alienation that Wallace diagnoses in "E Unibus Pluram." "I used sometimes to think," Day complains. "I used to think in long compound sentences with subordinate clauses and even the odd polysyllable. Now I find I needn't. Now I live by the dictates of macramé samplers ordered from the back-page ad of an old *Reader's Digest* or *Saturday Evening Post*" (271). For Gately, Day belongs in that class of "newcomers with some education" who "identify their whole selves with their head, and the Disease makes its command headquarters in the head" (272). Conversely, Gately insists that "the cliché directives are a lot more deep and hard to actually *do*. To try and live by instead of just say" (273). In discussing this conflict, students should be warned against merely dismissing Day's criticism and embracing Gately's thoughtful earnestness, particularly given the novel's own intellectual sophistication and its metafictional gestures.

At this point in their reading, students might be introduced to two key thinkers whom numerous critics have cited as important in shaping Wallace's counterintuitively positive depiction of AA, namely Søren Kierkegaard and William James. Hal mentions Kierkegaard explicitly in the novel's opening scene (12), while Randy Lenz hides his organic cocaine "in a kind of rectangular bunker razor-bladed out of three hundred or so pages of Bill James's gargantuan Large-Print *Principles of Psychology and the Gifford Lectures on Natural Religions*" (543). In this subtle way, Wallace reveals two of his major source texts and offers a clear warrant for reading the text in the light of these thinkers.

Allard den Dulk has thus far provided the most thorough accounting of Kierkegaard's influence on Wallace (see in particular "Boredom"). As den Dulk and others have persuasively argued, many of the novel's key concepts exhibit a Kierkegaardian debt. Wallace's critique of irony can be keyed to Kierkegaard's *The Concept of Irony*, while his depiction of addiction and despair borrows freely from Kierkegaard's *The Concept of Anxiety*. An ironist in AA, Gately observes, "is a witch in a church," because AA is an "irony-free zone" (369). Students will benefit greatly from some exposure to Kierkegaard's analysis of irony as a way of being and his complex diagnosis of ironic self-avoidance and despair, all of which sit at the heart of Wallace's depiction of AA testimonials as sites of earnest, unironic empathy and naked self-disclosure.

Unfortunately, both of these works are perhaps too dense and elusive in their articulation to be excerpted for class consumption. One way to overcome this problem is to focus on Kierkegaard's aesthetic/ethical dialectic, which can be presented to students in a way that will inform their understanding of the novel. One of the more lucid accounts of the dialectic can be found in Kierkegaard's *Concluding Unscientific Postscript to* Philosophical Fragments, specifically in an appendix titled "A Glance at a Contemporary Effort in Danish Literature," which reviews, under a pseudonym, Kierkegaard's own *Either/Or*, the dense, two-volume work in which the author first spelled out the aesthetic and ethical realms (251–300). Aesthetic existence focuses on the pursuit of pleasure, a pursuit designed to allow the individual to avoid self-reflection and self-ownership. As Kierkegaard explains, the pleasure-seeking aesthete "holds existence at bay by the most subtle of all deceptions, by thinking. He has thought everything possible, and yet he has not existed at all" (253). Such an existence is, at its root, despair. Conversely, the ethicist abandons pleasure-seeking in favor of "openness" and self-responsibility. Day and Gately fall neatly into the aesthetic and ethical categories, respectively, but students will also quickly see how other characters in the book might be slotted into one of these two realms or placed at some mid-point between the two stages.

Kierkegaard's additional insistence on a purely subjective experience of God links his thought to that of William James, whose seminal work, *The Varieties of Religious Experience: A Study in Human Nature*, was first presented as a series of Gifford lectures in 1901 and 1902. A leading figure in American pragmatism, James explores religion as a fundamental human experience and judges it not on its empirical justification but on its usefulness. Although the text is too long to assign in full, its structure as a series of freestanding lectures makes it suitable for excerpting. Lecture 2, "Circumstriction of the Topic," is perhaps the best section to assign, as it lays out the key contours of James's argument and his approach, while lecture 20, "Conclusions," reprises many of these arguments in the larger context of scientific rationality and pragmatic utility. Gately struggles throughout the novel with his own religious doubt and with AA's insistence that he "surrender" to some sort of "Higher Power," which he experiences as a vast "*Nothing*, an edgeless blankness that somehow feels worse than the sort of un-considered atheism he Came In with" (443). He consoles himself with the "fairly standard Boston AA agnostic-soothing riff about the 'God' in the slogan being just shorthand for a totally subjective and up-to-you 'Higher Power' and AA being merely spiritual instead of dogmatically religious, a sort of benign anarchy of subjective spirit" (366). When he asks the "scary old guys How AA Works, . . . they smile their chilly smiles and say Just Fine. It just works, is all; end of story" (350). A foray into James's work will also illuminate Wallace's exploration of choice and free will as spelled out in the lengthy philosophical dialogue between Hugh Steeply and Rémy Marathe interspersed throughout the novel. David Evans's "The Chains of Not Choosing" is a splendid overview of Wallace's engagement with James's rich corpus.

Weeks 4 and 5

By week 4, students will be well past the novel's halfway mark. At this point in their reading, they will be delving deeper into Joelle van Dyne's indispensable role in both the novel and the samizdat Entertainment. Her paralyzing beauty and the mystery surrounding her veil—is she hiding her ravishing face or a hid-eous deformity?—will be the source of great confusion and debate. One way to harness this debate is to introduce students to Wallace's many allusions to the Medusa myth in particular and to mythic archetypes more generally. Wallace points his readers to the Medusa myth through James Incandenza's film *The Me-dusa v. the Odalisque*, which James's son Mario watches and analyzes at some length (396). Mario's brother Orin nicknames Joelle "The Prettiest Girl of All Time" and labels her "decapitating" effect on males "the Acteon Complex," a ref-erence to the story of Acteon and the bathing Diana found in book 3, lines

138–250, of Ovid's *Metamorphosis* (290). Similarly, in her role as the maternal figure of Death in the Entertainment, Joelle effectively turns her viewers into stone, further confirming her Medusa role. In exploring these archetypal allusions, students might read T. S. Eliot's review of James Joyce's *Ulysses* and his famous description of Joyce's "mythic method." They might also return to Barth's *Lost in the Funhouse*, particularly to such late stories as "Echo," "Menelaiad," and "Anonymiad," which embody Barth's own postmodern revision of modernist mythic allusions.

The Medusa subtext also opens up space in which to discuss the novel's depiction of gender more generally. Does Wallace interrogate the patriarchal biases of the Medusa myth or affirm its misogynistic fear of female power? Laura Mulvey's work is indispensable in shaping a discussion of the Entertainment's complex gender coding. In particular, her groundbreaking essay "Visual Pleasure and Narrative Cinema" is essential reading for its analysis of the "male gaze" and the "phallocentric" bias of cinematic depictions of the feminine. Students should read Mulvey's essay in full, for it will provide the class with a shared vocabulary with which to analyze not only the Entertainment but also Wallace's critique of filmic entertainment more generally, as well as his ambiguous conflation of James Incandenza's films with more traditional postmodernist metafiction, particularly as articulated by Joelle (see 740–41).

Helpfully, Mulvey's essay also includes a cogent paraphrase of Jacques Lacan's "The Mirror Stage" (1–7). As I have argued elsewhere, Lacan appears to have been a major guiding source for the Entertainment's basic premise, in which the viewer is placed in the position of an infant in a cradle as Joelle, as a maternal figure of Death, leans in and apologizes over and over for an unspecified crime (see Boswell, *Understanding David Foster Wallace* 128–32, 151–56; *Infinite Jest* 787–95). A reading of Mulvey's essay will make a subsequent reading of Lacan's brief but dense text much more lucid. Lacan's essay will also help students analyze the novel's sustained use of infant imagery, as in the case of Hal's conception of the truly "human" person as "in some basic interior way forever infantile, some sort of not-quite-right-looking infant dragging itself anaclitically around the map, with big wet eyes and froggy-soft skin, huge skull, gooey drool" (695). At the same time, students might consider the various ways that Wallace swerves from Lacan's theoretical model in the light of the extended set piece dramatizing Hal's accidental attendance at an "Inner Infant" focus group (795–808).

Week 6

Gately's extended hospital stay and the numerous plot developments surrounding the Wheelchair Assassins' possible acquisition of the Entertainment will dominate class discussion during this final week. The disparate sections of the concluding two hundred pages clue readers in to the events that take place immediately after the action ends, and just before the novel's opening scene, and yet the novel carefully sets up these late developments almost from the beginning. For instance, the master copy of the Entertainment turns up unexpectedly through-out the novel. On her way to Molly's party, Joelle apparently walks past what could be the master copy, left unattended in a cardboard display depicting a man in a wheelchair (224); this same copy turns up again at Antitoi Entertain-ment amid a pile of cartridges "Bertand claimed he had picked up literally on the street downtown" (483). The cartridge no doubt appears elsewhere as it makes its way to Enfield Tennis Academy. If students are clued in to such details early enough, they can track the cartridge's progress toward its final destination, a bit of detective work that can help clarify many of the murky details surround-ing the novel's conclusion. Students might be prompted to speculate about which of the novel's main or minor characters put the cartridge into circulation in the first place. Orin Incandenza would appear to be the most logical choice (see 723), but he is far from the only suspect. Such a discussion will compel students to consider various characters' motives and their connections to one another, and hence disclose the plot's many interlocking pieces.

Although Gately's heroic defense of Randy Lenz occurs at around the novel's halfway point (610–11), his resulting hospital stay does not begin until two hun-dred pages later. Nevertheless, Gately remains in that hospital bed for the nov-el's final 172 pages, and so the concluding week presents a rich opportunity to explore Gately's role as the novel's complex, ambiguous hero. Hal's seventh-grade essay on *Hawaii Five-O*'s Steve McGarrett and *Hill Street Blues*'s Frank Furillo provides a good starting place for this discussion, as Hal contrasts McGarrett, the "classically modern hero of action," with Furillo, the "'*post*'-modern hero . . . of *re*action" (140, 141). Hal goes on to ask, "But what comes next? What North American hero can hope to succeed placid Frank? We await, I predict, a hero of *non*-action, the catatonic hero, the one beyond calm, divorced from all stimu-lus, carried here and there across sets by burly extras whose blood sings with retrograde amines" (142). Does Gately fulfill this role, in his catatonic, hospital-ized state, or is this reading undermined by the act of heroism that placed him there? And how might Hal slot into this dynamic, particularly in the light of his possible exposure to the Entertainment?

In exploring this aspect of Gately's character, students should touch upon the various archetypes Gately recalls. Wallace connects him to the mythical figure of Hercules (507) and endowed with a Prince Valiant haircut (449). Meanwhile, his surname may refer to Matthew 7.13–14 in the Bible, where Jesus instructs, "Enter ye in at the strait gate: for wide is the gate, and broad is the way, that leadeth to destruction, and many there be which go in at it. Because strait is the gate, and narrow is the way, which leadeth into life, and few there be that find it." When he finally steps in to take on the Canadians who are attacking Lenz, Gately experiences a "jolly calm" that suggests his intervention is, in some ways, a surrender of his self-control and sobriety rather than a simple, selfless act of heroism. At the moment of decision, he realizes he has "no choice now not to fight," at which point "things simplify radically, divisions collapse. Gately's just one part of something he can't control" (612). These ambiguities complicate

Gately's role and his motives in ways that double back to Hal's essay and prepare the way for his long, concluding internal monologue, during which Gately is repeatedly depicted as floating in a womb (see 815–16).

Perhaps the most important component of that monologue is the appearance of the wraith, who may be the ghost of James Incandenza, the novel's narrator, or a ghostly visitation by Wallace himself (see 829). The wraith suggests Wallace's engagement with Roland Barthes's "The Death of the Author," which Wallace himself addressed at some length in his review of H. L. Hix's *Morte d'Author*, reprinted in *A Supposedly Fun Thing I'll Never Do Again* under the title "Greatly Exaggerated." In what ways does Wallace, as the novel's author, confirm Barthes's notion of the dead author, and how might the ghostly figure of the novel's key *auteur*, and author of the original "Infinite Jest," complicate or refute Barthes's essay? A discussion such as this also inevitably leads to interesting speculations as to the novel's primary narrator. Is it Hal, narrating the novel in retrospect, or is it the dead figure of James Incandenza, taking one more stab at his "Infinite Jest" project? Who is responsible for the "Notes and Errata," and how do we know? Finally, how do we account for the moment, during the Eschaton sequence, when Mike Pemulis steps in to take over the endnotes from Hal (1023)? In framing this debate, instructors might ask students to consider who among the novel's main characters has the strongest motive for narrating the novel as well as the best access to the widest range of settings, characters, and inside information. Discussion might also address the narrator's unique voice, particularly the way it pivots from teenage slang (as in the casual use of "like") to technical precision.

Throughout his literary career, Wallace, the son of educators, also taught literature and creative writing at the college level. The new *David Foster Wallace Reader* even includes samples of his course syllabi. What shines through in these documents is his fierce commitment both to the humanities and to the liberal arts. *Infinite Jest* exemplifies that same dual commitment. Although six to seven weeks is a long time to devote to a single novel, nearly every day discussing *Infinite Jest* in class will open up a new line of inquiry or introduce a new theoretical or philosophical source text. The novel teaches as it entertains, demanding intense intellectual labor to access its many pleasures. In *This Is Water*, Wallace observed, "The single most pervasive cliché in the commencement speech genre . . . is that a liberal arts education is not so much about filling you up with knowledge as it is about, quote, 'teaching you how to think'" (12). *Infinite Jest* is Wallace's most successful attempt to affirm the deep truth of that cliché.

Last Words:
Teaching *The Pale King*

Stephen J. Burn

The length and complexity of many of David Foster Wallace's works raise challenging questions about how exactly they might be taught. The unfinished status of Wallace's final novel, *The Pale King*, arguably raises the contrary question of why it would be taught. The very rawness of *The Pale King*—the fact of its incompleteness—makes it the Wallace text that is hardest to disentangle from more reductive biographical readings. Even having done so, because the published text itself is at best provisional, teachers can easily find themselves in a classroom that includes students reading a paperback edition with scenes that aren't available to their hardback-carrying classmates. These are hardly promising starting points, yet, while such difficulties may be compounded by the book's restless perspectival shifts, catalogue of characters, and lack of resolution, many of these apparent limitations can be recast as the pedagogical opportunities that come from seeing a literary work not as a finished monument—with every feature appearing inevitable—but as a mobile configuration of momentary choices, experimental devices, and chance explorations. Other essays in this volume suggest strategies for teaching individual parts of *The Pale King*, and while some sections can be seamlessly excerpted,[1] this essay explores strategies for teaching the book as a whole. The teaching plan outlined here may seem naturally geared toward advanced undergraduate and graduate courses, but I think *The Pale King* is more accessible than many assume. I first taught the novel along these lines to freshmen at a state school, who were cheerfully free of preconceptions and capable of taking on most of the challenges the book presents.

Preliminaries: Contextualizing the Work in Progress

While Wallace's earlier works can often be effectively paired with key interviews, such combinations are harder to replicate when teaching *The Pale King*, not just because Wallace never spoke directly about his last novel in interviews,[2] but also because he tended to speak less programmatically in later dialogues. Similarly, biographical treatments may be less helpful here. Many develop a narrative based on Wallace's inability to reinvent himself—say, Karen Green's claim that by this point Wallace "didn't want to do the old tricks . . . But he had no idea what the new tricks would be" (qtd. in Max "Unfinished" 50)—which inevitably casts the book as a failure, prematurely setting the terms of a discussion that might better serve students (and critics) if it were left open. It may be more effective, then, to pair the novel with other literary texts, a move that can simultaneously downplay biography-based prejudgments and connect the atomistic novel to overarching (and coherence-lending) themes.

If seminar time is tight, intensive work on the novel can be effectively prefaced by a short discussion of "A Radically Condensed History of Postindustrial Life," a microfiction that Wallace wrote while he was presumably in the early stages of planning *The Pale King*. "Radically" interrogates the nature of narrative itself, using its spareness to ask what makes a story (characters? a social gathering? an exploration of the gap between outward appearance and private motivation?) and attributes its affective black hole to the overarching systems that govern contemporary existence (the postindustrial age), so it concisely frames the initial, exploratory questions that students might be encouraged to ask of the later novel: How do mostly invisible social systems condition human relationships? If "Radically" represents Wallace's fundamental doubt about how short fiction typically works, might *The Pale King* be read as a similar critique of the novel writ large? The latter question, in particular, nudges students unfamiliar with Wallace's work away from seeing the book's incompleteness as a simple failure to erect traditional novelistic machinery (unity of viewpoint, consistent characters, a single plot) and calls attention to Wallace's concern with dismantling traditional forms from the inside out. Especially attentive students will sense a consonance with "Radically" when they spot one of the story's signature phrases, "staring straight ahead," recurring as an index of affectless activity in *The Pale King* (268, 301, 441). When *The Pale King* is being taught as part of a block of Wallace's writing, there are expansive opportunities for juxtaposition: Wallace's more obviously political nonfiction (*McCain's Promise*, "The View from Mrs. Thompson's") angles discussion toward the book's social commentary; pairing the novel's "Author Here" sections with, say, "Westward the Course of Empire Takes Its Way" or the David Wallace character in "Good Old Neon" highlights Wallace's changing approach to self-reflexive strategies; and the series of "Brief Interviews" and "The Depressed Person" can help highlight the manipulative strategies in Meredith Rand's account in section 46.

Outside the Wallace oeuvre, the novel sits comfortably in a thematic framework that interrogates innovative fiction's efforts to map the shaping power of institutional or economic systems. Approaching this theme with an American lens, Henry James's essay "The Question of the Opportunities" can act as a discursive preface providing historical context. Building on this foundation, the class might then investigate works from the twentieth century's later decades. William Gaddis's *J R*, which Wallace included on his syllabus at Illinois State University, is a natural fit in both form and content. Despite its seamless appearance, *J R* (as Steven Moore has shown) is split into discrete scenes, and scene 14 (75–89), documenting a field trip to Wall Street, and scene 41 (251–57), featuring an argument about a suit filed by boy capitalist J R, can be compared to Wallace's novel in terms of their exploration of the way characters internalize the logic of capitalist systems, of how financial jargon functions—and as demonstrations of the art of mixing low comedy with abstract discussion. Richard Powers's *Gain* is another important reference point. Because Powers's novel works according to an alternating rhythm, in which the rise of the Clare Soap and Chemical Company is set against the fall of Laura Bodey, students might contrast this structure with *The Pale King*, asking why Powers sets up a dialectic where financial power is set *against* the vulnerable human, while Wallace explores the human *inside* the financial system.

While discussing Wallace in terms of postmodernism and American fiction places the author in his most familiar critical context, useful reference points may also be found beyond the borders of the United States. Wallace's understudied but important investment in Georges Perec's formal games, for instance, can be probed by having students read Perec's single-sentence novel, *The Art and Craft of Approaching Your Head of Department to Submit a Request for a Raise*. Because this Oulipian novel (which is short enough for students to read in about an hour) is patterned around a bureaucratic flow chart that traps its characters in endless loops, the book can introduce the double binds that are commonplace in *The Pale King*. Students may also notice a cluster of smaller overlaps, such as characters named "X," extravagant vocabularies, and so on.

One virtue of such contrasts is their plasticity, because in each of these instances thematic discussion can become a gateway to talking about technique. Gaddis's cascade of unattributed dialogue, for instance, has obvious counterparts in Wallace's primarily dialogue-driven discussion of masturbation in section 3 (where the technique is used for comic effect) and in section 19's famous civics debate (where it is not). Perec's endless sentence is similarly replicated in *The Pale King* at smaller scale, with section 2 culminating in a sentence that runs to almost three full pages (21–24). Having identified such parallels, classes can then compare Wallace's use of such techniques to that of his postmodern precursors. Does Wallace, for instance, decide not to tag his dialogue in section 2 because his interest in universal experiences means that it doesn't really matter who speaks, whereas Gaddis uses dialogue to reinforce individual identity, as verbal tics cement our sense of a character's specific thought patterns? What makes Claude Sylvanshine especially suited to echo Perec in section 2's concluding run-on sentence? Such discussions can open onto larger questions: While each earlier author was content to maintain one style consistently throughout his book, why does Wallace adopt particular techniques in shorter bursts? What does this tell us about his belief in polyphony or the limitations of a single style, and what consequences does this have for the book as a whole? Similarly, to what extent do these comparisons suggest that Wallace's distinctive voice is paradoxically predicated upon a kind of patchwriting aesthetic?

Pairing Wallace with earlier writers in this way highlights *The Pale King*'s literary ancestry and nudges the class's focus toward questions of literary influence (they should spot, of course, that the novel identifies Gaddis and Perec as "immortally great fiction writers" [73]). The temporal weight of such discussions can easily be reversed, however, by pairing Wallace with younger writers—setting *The Pale King* next to, for instance, the choral we-narration of Ed Park's

Personal Days and Joshua Ferris's *Then We Came to the End*—or, perhaps more directly, with Tom McCarthy's discussion of the bureaucratic uses of boredom in chapter two of *Satin Island.*

Finding a Form

As discussion moves from contextual materials to the novel itself, it makes sense to address *The Pale King's* unfinished status explicitly, either by instructing students to read the "Notes and Asides" before beginning the text proper (an approach that will likely highlight questions of authorial intent in later discussions) or by giving a brief explanation of the book's collaborative birth. It may be helpful to explain to students that Michael Pietsch had actively assisted Wallace in arranging the stories in *Brief Interviews with Hideous Men*, so the sequence of the novel is not necessarily more divorced from Wallace's intent than some of the works he published in his own lifetime; indeed, as James Ramsey Wallen has argued, "the unfinished label" often serves to obscure the fact "that *no one*, has *ever*, finished a work *entirely* by him or herself" (131).[3] This is obviously an opportunity to qualify the misconception that contemporary authors are isolated geniuses, crafting every feature of a given work on their own, and more sophisticated classes may choose to pursue this subject.

After either lecturing on the book's origins or exploring Wallace's earlier attacks on linear structure, I encourage students to read the novel not by seeking a single novelistic arc through continuous episodes but by noting the way disparate sections or passages seem to be linked variations on the same theme. To make such patterns clearer, I begin by splitting the class into groups and asking each to trace and elucidate a particular network of imagery or thematic preoccupation that they will ultimately share with the rest of the class. Students in advanced classes might generate their own area of investigation after some exploratory early reading. In other instances, students can choose from a prescribed list of headings that might range from the particular, such as gathering apparently incidental references to feet, eyes, or divided selves, to the more holistic, such as noting instances of particular plot structures (perhaps Wallace's regular recourse to condensed biographies, or his tendency to organize scenes so they reveal double binds) and tracing the evolution of the book's headline themes (boredom, attention, and so on). At a basic level, this process helps students chart a path through the novel's vertiginous perspectival shifts, while it also makes visible Wallace's strategic substitution of linear narrative succession for imagistic or thematic unity. At advanced levels, such patterns can be the starting point for engagement with Wallace scholarship: students might, for instance, read the early discussion of ground and value in Jeffrey Severs's *Balancing Books* as a way of framing the novel's obsessive references to feet; the book's many mentions of eyes and vision can be read either in dialogue with classic postmodern texts on the image's imperial reign (say, Guy Debord's *The Society of the Spectacle*) or with my essay "Toward a General Theory of Vision in Wallace's Fiction"; boredom and attention naturally lead to Ralph Clare's "The Politics of Boredom."

I typically split the novel into three blocks, devoting two class sessions to each third of the book. The first two classes consider the opening twenty-one sections (pages 3–153); as the novel's pace slows through its middle, the next two meetings discuss six longer sections (154–345); and the final two sessions address the remaining twenty-three episodes (346–548). Because both of the later segments include long, novella-like sections (22 and 46) that offer something closer to sustained plot and character development, the rapid changes in perspective and style that mark the opening section (and particularly the first sixty pages) can be the hardest for students to assimilate. Yet it is exactly this restless early movement that makes *The Pale King* a narrative boot camp for literature students in general as much as it is the last installment for students already immersed in Wallace's oeuvre. To help students cope with any disorientation they may feel, my initial classroom exercises encourage them to concentrate on the part, not the whole: starting with a descriptive goal, I ask the students (normally in groups) to list the techniques Wallace uses in each of the opening twenty-one sections; having mapped the territory, we then begin to think comparatively, asking why particular narrative viewpoints or approaches might serve (or reveal) a specific episode's purpose, while they would undermine the function of a different episode. Wallace's omniscient narration in section 5 (detailing Leonard Stecyk's childhood) and his use of limited third-person narration in section 6 (where Lane A. Dean and Sheri Fisher contemplate an abortion) can serve as a useful initial example. The latter section is predicated on the mind's absolute self-enclosure, whereas the kind of breezy summary of what everyone else secretly thinks that section five's omniscience permits ("Everyone hates the boy" [32]) would leech any dramatic tension out of Lane and Sheri's dilemma. Section 5's broad comedy, by contrast, necessitates a narrative mode that precludes sympathy and so could not work to the same ends with sustained immersion in Leonard's mind. Students will no doubt note the use of documents to narrate in sections 4 and 11; depending on what students have previously read, this technique might be compared to novels that partly rely on epistolary narration—say, *Frankenstein*—or postmodern texts that interrupt routine narration with unexplained documents—such as chapters 31 and 37 of Don DeLillo's *White Noise*. They will also sense the kinship between the kinetic list that opens section 8 and the description that begins the novel, will examine Wallace's various uses of dialogue, and will discuss why the "off-camera prompt"'s (128) of section 18 mark it as a satellite that has drifted free from section 14's videotape files. The connections and contrasts students identify will help them better understand the scope and limitations of different narrative techniques and, crucially, help them recast the book's refusal to settle on a single style or viewpoint as functional and not as a simple symptom of its incomplete status.

Teasing out the book's connective architecture and hidden logic strikes me as the most important aim in early classes on *The Pale King*, but, where class time permits and students are sufficiently advanced, the opening chain of episodes offers many opportunities for more detailed investigation. The visual plenitude of section 1 is an obvious and rewarding first port of call: at a basic level, students can be encouraged to trace the contours of Wallace's poetics—his emphasis on language's sonic qualities, his tendency to repurpose properly poetic forms for prose (this tendency might be made more vivid by introducing the students to other list poems, by Walt Whitman or others), and so on. At a more advanced level, students might be asked what Wallace may have meant by describing this scene as a "Reply to Theory" in his notes. Moving forward, the appearance of "David Wallace" and his disdain for "cute, self-referential paradoxes" (67) invites discussion of Wallace's career-long engagement with this postmodernist legacy. David Cusk's flop sweat in section 13 distills the way conscious thought in Wallace's fiction often creates imprisoning spirals (section 46 provides a clear opportunity to return to this topic). Finally, section 19's civics discussion in a stalled elevator (encourage students to reflect on the importance of location in many of the early scenes; even as Wallace blurs timelines, spatial coordinates remain vital) is the obvious entry point for approaching the book's economic argument, and Boswell's essay "Trickle-Down Citizenship" is required reading in this context.

In the Heart of the Heart of the Service

Students will likely have fewer problems in the second week because the book's pace decisively slows through these six episodes (sections 22–27) to more closely approximate the kind of sustained narrative development readers have been trained to see as the natural goal of prose fiction (an impression that's surely strengthened when the reappearance of characters such as section 4's Frederick Blumquist gives the misleading impression of diverse strands coming together). They will also detect the plot's gradual evolution: while the opening episodes counterbalanced scenes from the Internal Revenue Service with pivotal moments that shaped different workers or led them into the service, Chris Fogle's long section offers the last substantial conversion narrative as the book's narrative gravity subtly shifts to center, now and for most of the rest of the book, on life at the REC (Regional Examination Center).

As an overarching rubric for these episodes, students might be introduced to the concept of *exformation*, outlined in an excerpt from one of the book's source texts—Tor Nørretranders's *The User Illusion*—and its discussion of communication theory (92–96), or by Wallace's gloss on the concept in "Some Remarks on Kafka's Funniness." Nørretranders defines exformation in terms of the difficult task of transferring what is in the sender's head into the recipient's head: while the specific words used in communication are a message's information, exformation is the vital communicative material that is omitted yet nevertheless evoked by that raw information. As such, exformation indexes a message's relative depth, and it works symbiotically with information: "information without exformation is vacuous chatter; exformation without information is not exformation but merely discarded information" (95). Nørretranders concisely explicates the term by listing words (information) that immediately evoke contexts and spark associational chains (exformation): "'Yesterday.' 'Christmas.' 'Tax return'" (94). Wallace illustrates it with reference to jokes. Students might find narrative parallels in the stark poetics that underwrites short stories by Ernest Hemingway or Raymond Carver.

Students will spot many isolated scenes in this part of the book where information without exformation is presented as redundant chatter (e.g., Fogle's description of the Christian girl's story as "just data" [214]) or where the process of discarding information to create exformation is addressed discursively (e.g., "The whole point . . . is to get rid of the information you don't want" [340]). The real goal here, however, is not to connect the dots between source material and individual scene, but to help students see the way this concept ties together several disparate episodes in this part of the book, by showing how Wallace tests the limits of Nørretranders's explanation. Rather than employing exformation (as, say, Carver and Hemingway do), these episodes ask in different contexts: How much information in any given communicative sequence is too much? What can be discarded? What might evoke exformation? What do we miss when we discard too much? Chris Fogle's long narration, in the first instance, raises such questions at the level of the life story, where exformation is explored through the notion of the recollected epiphanic moment amid irrelevance (the particularly personal nature of some exformation, for instance, is suggested by Fogle's tendency to invest the Jesuit's words with more weight than they merit). Section 24 raises the stakes of this exploration to engage the question of writing, both through the episode's form, where footnotes containing vital data make it unclear what is central and what is discarded overspill, and through its content, which assembles detailed minutiae that's every bit as irrelevant as Fogle's digressions. Finally, section 25 addresses the same questions at the level of consciousness: how does failure to discard information cause us to miss potentially richer bits of information? This episode might be juxtaposed with the *New York Review of Books* review of *The Pale King*, which confidently describes the chapter as empty of exformation, containing just "around 1,300 words . . . in which a host of named people simply turn pages" (Raban).

Beyond following such connective arcs, there are—again—many individual moments instructors might examine through the book's central portion: Fogle's encounter with the Jesuit, for instance, merits comparison with encounters with Jesuit teachers in Joyce's *Portrait of the Artist as a Young Man* and DeLillo's *Underworld*; the scene where Fogle's father returns to encounter the aftermath of the wastoid party can be set next to Wallace's famous description of the writer's situation after postmodernism at the end of his interview with Larry McCaffery (it's "like the way you feel when you're in high school and your parents go on a trip, and you throw a party" [Burn, *Conversations* 52]); and the moment in section 27 when David Wallace's story is relayed through a third-person lens also rewards examination.

Things Fall Apart?

In my experience, at least, the final third of *The Pale King* is the least satisfactory section to teach, in part because there are awkward shifts in characterization (as in the way Sylvanshine is seemingly reduced to a stock comic figure in section 49) and unsponsored developments (such as the appearance of Clothier and Aylortay in section 48), but also because the sense of an unfolding, if incomplete, narrative plan becomes harder to sustain even as there remain many rewarding episodes to consider. Connections certainly continue to emerge, but they often work on a smaller scale: that the last scene involving Sylvanshine denies him his usual position as the narrating consciousness in section 49 parallels section 27's switch to a third-person view of David Wallace; section 29's catalogue of shit stories ties into earlier apparently incidental references to bodily waste (including the punning abbreviation of taxpayers to TP); the nearly simultaneous setting of section 32 and section 33 should prompt discussion of what Wallace is trying to do with the many-sidedness of the individual moment. Seminar discussion is likely to gravitate toward this third's longest section: the Happy Hour conversation between Rand and Shane Drinion at Meibeyer's (section 46). Students might be encouraged to consider the significance of the fact that this section both shares and inverts preoccupations of the book's other long segment, Fogle's conversion narrative. Both offer extended reflections on attention, for instance, but Drinion's narrow purview is obviously meant to counterpoint Fogle's early dissipation. References to machine consciousness also come to a head in this section, while the fact that the bar is suffused in "fake flames" casting a "red light" (473n) can be used to tie together strands of katabatic imagery (not to mention the presence of ghosts) that insistently develop earlier in the novel.

   To counter these increasingly centrifugal energies without betraying the book's authentically diffuse format, I typically devote less time in the final week to minute examination of individual scenes and more time to asking questions that draw together the students' experiences of the book. These questions range from those posed by the text itself (e.g., who are the two "unborable" men [438]?) to more overarching queries; this is an opportunity for the students to share (and attempt to explain) the patterns of imagery and thematic variations they've noted, but also to ask how Sylvanshine's position as a fact psychic might be a model for the many interruptions within individual sections, as much as for the random-seeming shifts between episodes. Similarly, the book's multivalent engagement with memory (its dependence on fragments [162], its relation to the senses [283], and so on) can also be explored at this point.

Yet, having approached the book by way of novelistic history—invoking *J R* or Perec—I see part of the value of teaching *The Pale King* in its ability to unsettle its generic label. In the final session, I encourage students to consider the subtitle "an unfinished novel" by asking how the novel's failure to fit the traditional template both helps us see what we mean when we describe something as *novelistic*, and how Wallace evades that label. Why, in this light, does Wallace identify the book's narrative particles as sections and not chapters? Why did Wallace nearly always describe himself in interviews as a fiction writer, and virtually never as a novelist? Pursuing this line, how does labeling the book a novel inform the way reviewers and critics have responded to it? How might the relative independence of *The Pale King*'s individual parts be compared to the structure of contemporary story cycles by writers ranging from Louise Erdrich to George Saunders and Jennifer Egan? Students will respond to the richness and humor of many sections of the book, but teaching *The Pale King* is also an opportunity to probe larger questions about how genres condition our expectations and critical judgments.

NOTES

[1] Allard den Dulk, Ralph Clare, and Jeffrey Severs, for instance, each explore how section 22 might be taught as a discrete segment.

[2] This problem can be somewhat circumvented by setting the text next to *Oblivion*-era interviews. Because some parts of *Oblivion* were originally conceived as *Pale King* chapters, Wallace's discussion with Steve Paulson on boredom and "The Soul Is Not a Smithy" (Burn, *Conversations* 128–30), or his talk with Michael Goldfarb about the workplace (137–40), can be placed alongside the novel as representations of its general concerns. As I suggest later, the McCaffery interview provides a notable exception.

[3] Wallen's essay may be a provocative text for advanced classes, particularly in terms of his concluding claim that "a crucial element of postmodernism" might be located in the "compromise between unfinalizability and finitude" that emerges out of the "Golden Age of Unfinishable Novels" (140), a period that runs from Flaubert's death to Musil's demise.

Teaching Wallace's Short Fiction

Philip Coleman

Because David Foster Wallace published three collections of short fiction, containing a total of forty-one pieces,[1] it can be difficult for instructors to know what to select when teaching his work for the first time. In this essay I describe a number of strategies that have been successful for me in different teaching contexts, from courses focused solely on Wallace's work to more general surveys of American literature and the American short story. Whether the pedagogical focus is on close reading or on a consideration of the ways in which texts engage with the contexts of their composition, or a combination of both, the published corpus of Wallace's short fiction provides a wide range of possibilities for discussion and analysis in the undergraduate classroom and beyond. Indeed, the movement of this essay from a consideration of Wallace's first published piece of short fiction to his later work maps the author's evolving concerns with the relation between texts and their contexts. The evolution of Wallace's career as a writer of short fiction was marked by a preoccupation with style, but his stylistic and formal experiments were also bound up with a broader sense of engagement with other texts and their social and cultural contexts. In short, by studying Wallace's short fiction one is given an immediate insight into an important contemporary author's thinking about literary texts and their multifarious intertextual points of reference, from stories by other authors to television game shows.[2] The dialectic between these different kinds of textual experience and production is central to Wallace's art, but it is possible to explore it with particular effectiveness in the classroom by focusing on his short fiction.

Starting from "Planet Trillaphon"

Wallace's first published short story, "The Planet Trillaphon as It Stands in Relation to the Bad Thing," provides a useful starting point for sustained classroom considerations of Wallace's writing styles, influences, and interests. The story demonstrates the presence of key themes Wallace established at the beginning of his career, such as the idea of academic achievement; the imagination of alternative realities; the experience of mental illness, substance abuse, and alienation; and the role of the family and the importance of relationships. These themes can be traced across Wallace's work—in *Infinite Jest*, for example, where they are given extensive treatment—but they are also taken up in important later short stories such as "The Depressed Person" and "Good Old Neon." "Trillaphon" also represents the earliest iteration of what Kevin Dettmar calls Wallace's occasionally "faux-yokel Midwestern" voice (Wallace, *David Foster Wallace Reader* 20), which can be compared to the voice in some of Wallace's essays, such as "Getting Away from Already Pretty Much Being Away from It All." Drawing parallels like this from across Wallace's work helps students think about how different texts speak to one another, and it also prepares the way for larger considerations of context and intertextuality as students become more deeply acquainted with the author's methods and interests.

In a course focusing chiefly on Wallace's work, this movement between genres—from short story to novel to essay—can help students appreciate the different ways in which Wallace used literary form and language throughout his career. It is an approach that also teaches students about genre itself—how to differentiate between various kinds of literary fiction (such as the short story and the novel) and nonfiction—and it encourages them to see how Wallace's treatment of key themes, such as depression, changed over time. While some of Wallace's early portrayals of mental illness are darkly comic, for example, especially in "Trillaphon" and in his novel *The Broom of the System*, students can debate the extent to which his later representations might be seen as more challenging both in their formal complexity and in their ethical and social implications. A good classroom exercise is to get students to compare descriptions of depression, for example, drawn from texts written by Wallace at different points in his career—from "Trillaphon," say, and "The Depressed Person." Wallace's sense of the complexity of the subject of depression as a topic worth revisiting several times throughout his career is emphasized by the comparison, but the task also allows students to appreciate the difficulty of literary representation in itself as they observe a serious author returning to a specific theme as part of an ongoing attempt to understand its significance not just in relation to his own experience but more generally in his cultural and historical moment.

Before broader contexts and intertexts can be considered, however, the literature teacher must start with the text, and "Trillaphon" is a good place from which to begin a discussion of Wallace's approach to the minutiae of literary language and style. Considering the opening sentences of the story, for example, students might be asked to comment on the narrative function of the words *what, really, say,* and *obviously.* How would this passage sound and how would the narrative voice be heard without those single-word interjections? The relation between sentence length and punctuation—which is a particular point of interest for Wallace—can also be analyzed in careful detail so that students can appreciate the connection between style and the creation of a fictional voice and persona:

> I've been on antidepressants for, what, about a year now, and I suppose I feel as if I'm pretty qualified to tell what they're like. They're fine, really, but they're fine in the same way that, say, living on another planet that was warm and comfortable and had food and fresh water would be fine: it would be fine, but it wouldn't be good old Earth, obviously.   (5)

Close attention to even such short passages as this can show students the strategic importance of punctuation and syntax and lead to more detailed considerations of Wallace's style. The fact that this passage attempts to represent a speaking voice is also important here, because it is related to Wallace's desire to connect with his readers through literary form. The colloquial, conversational narrative style creates an illusion of amenability that is worth exploring so that students can appreciate early on the strategic ways in which Wallace sought to direct his readers' response to his work.

This close reading exercise can be conducted with passages drawn from many of Wallace's shorter works, from very short fictions such as "A Radically Condensed History of Postindustrial Life" to the opening paragraph of "Mister Squishy." Other shorter pieces by Wallace, such as "Everything Is Green" and "Incarnations of Burned Children," are also useful starting points for courses focused solely on the author's oeuvre. Whichever text one begins with, however, this process of close textual analysis helps students appreciate the ways in which voice operates as a function of style, not just in Wallace's writing but in all productions of language, including their own. By attending to Wallace's particular approach to language and form—and especially his handling of syntax—students are prepared for the often more complex constructions that occur in his longer works, and they are given tools that will serve them well elsewhere in their literary (and nonliterary) studies. An analysis of the different kinds of sentence structure used in "Radically Condensed History" is helpful here, for example, as one moves from the relatively straightforward opening sentence ("When they were introduced, he made a witticism, hoping to be liked") to the final one, which seems closer to poetry than to prose in its unexpected use of repetition ("One never knew, after all, now did one now did one now did one"). The repeated phrase "now did one" introduces a sense of open-endedness and mystery, and the emphasis on knowing/not-knowing ("One never knew") goes to the heart of Wallace's project because it suggests that the kind of knowledge we obtain from the stories we tell each other about ourselves may, ultimately, be unreliable. What is the narrator suggesting can "never" be known here? Is it the minds of others, the truth of other people's stories, or both? These questions, prompted by one of Wallace's shortest short fictions, apply across the range of his writing and are relevant, too, to many other writers. Indeed, the question of what kind of knowledge is to be gained from the stories we tell ourselves, which may be this story's central theme, is flagged in the title of the piece as something that concerns the entire "history of postindustrial life." This phrase, in turn, suggests an expansive textual and cultural horizon, far beyond the five sentences of the story, within which Wallace's work asks to be read.

Wallace's Short Fiction in Survey Courses on American Literature or the Short Story

Wallace's three collections of short fiction differ strikingly in their uses of the short story form. Of the three volumes, *Brief Interviews with Hideous Men* is arguably the most unified in thematic terms given its focus on questions of sexuality, gender, and violence. Whether they are taught in their entirety or not, however, Wallace's separate short story collections speak to late-twentieth-century cultural and social experience in the United States—the "postindustrial" context named in the opening story of *Brief Interviews*—in significant ways. "The Suffering Channel," from *Oblivion*, is particularly apposite in its focus on the culture of the United States in the period leading up to and around the terrorist attacks on the nation in September 2001, but several other stories, including "Little Expressionless Animals" and "My Appearance" from *Girl with Curious Hair* and "Mister Squishy" from *Oblivion*, open up discussions about the relation between self and world in the contemporary era, especially how we understand connections between private life and the public sphere—between the personal life of the individual who speaks or narrates and his or her place within a larger global and historical ("postindustrial") frame of reference.

In a more focused course on the short story's development in anglophone literary culture from the beginning of the nineteenth century to the present, Wallace's short fiction affords striking formal and stylistic contrasts with earlier texts. His writing provides several illuminating points of contact and continuity with some of the most important early contributors to the development of shorter forms of narrative, including the novella, and it can be usefully read alongside authors ranging from Edgar Allan Poe and Nathaniel Hawthorne to George Saunders and Lydia Davis. For example, the frequently violent self-obsessions and delusions of protagonists in tales by Poe such as "The Tell-Tale Heart" and "The Fall of the House of Usher" may be compared with figures drawn by Wallace in texts ranging from "Girl with Curious Hair" to certain sections of *Brief Interviews with Hideous Men* (most notably "B.I. #20") and "Mister Squishy." This pairing of writers from very different social and cultural contexts encourages comparative perspectives that allow for an expansive sense of literary history to emerge over the course of a semester studying American short fiction. By reading Wallace in relation to early-nineteenth-century American authors and teasing out various formal and thematic continuities and discontinuities between them, students are given an opportunity to think about questions of literary history and tradition in the United States. They may wonder, for example, why selfhood is such a central and recurring theme in the literature of the nation, and especially with regard to the self under extreme forms of emotional and psychological pressure, as one finds throughout the tales and stories of Poe and Hawthorne. If the short story can be seen as a form that has particular importance in American literary history, and if one accepts that there is a close relation between the development of the short story and the creation of American cultural identity during the nineteenth century, students can be asked to consider the ways that Wallace's short stories contribute to and complicate this critical argument. Do his stories reinforce or refute the rhetoric of American exceptionalism? How do they construct or, indeed, dismantle and reconstruct earlier versions of the American self? These questions are relevant to several of Wallace's short stories, and exploring them in comparative literary contexts can illuminate the strategic intertextual expansiveness of Wallace's writing.

Because of this expansiveness, Wallace's stories can also be read within the traditions of modernism and postmodernism in survey courses on American literature and the short story. Sections of *Brief Interviews with Hideous Men*, including those after which the volume is named and the three "Yet Another Example of the Porousness of Certain Borders" pieces, can be contrasted with a text like Sherwood Anderson's *Winesburg, Ohio* as radically different contributions to the development of the short story cycle in twentieth-century American literature. Anderson's experiments with the short story cycle, in particular, can be contrasted with Wallace's experiments with narrative interconnectedness and seriality in *Brief Interviews* and elsewhere. Students might be encouraged to consider the role of narrative continuity and discontinuity in the two cycles, exploring different approaches to the development of character, setting, and plot. Working individually or in groups, students can also learn a great deal about the movement from literary modernism to postmodernism in this exercise as they compare Anderson's and Wallace's handling of narrative perspective and form from different ends of the twentieth century. When teaching the "Brief Interviews," I have found it useful to ask students to draw up maps and chronologies that provide a sense of where each of the narrators is based—using the information given at the start of each piece (such as "08-96" and "St. Davids PA" in "B.I. #14" [*Brief Interviews* 14]). This allows us to create a visual constellation of the various narrators—to tell us where each voice is coming from, as Eudora Welty might put it[3]—and allows the text's Americanness to be perceived in geospatial terms that are fractured, discontinuous, and ruptured. When compared with the ostensible demographic cohesiveness of *Winesburg, Ohio*, Wallace's text presents students with a radically altered version of American space, how it is inhabited, and the different ways that writers have sought to represent it.

A survey course on American literature (or the American short story) beginning with Poe, including Anderson, and ending with Wallace could include any number of writers and encompass a broad range of themes and contexts. In my experience of teaching Wallace in this general context, often over the course of a full academic year, texts by Welty ("Where Is the Voice Coming From?"), Nathaniel Hawthorne ("Rappacini's Daughter"), Herman Melville ("Bartleby, the Scrivener"), Henry James ("In the Cage"), F. Scott Fitzgerald ("Winter Dreams"), Ernest Hemingway ("Hills Like White Elephants"), Flannery O'Connor ("A Good Man Is Hard to Find"), Richard Wright ("Big Boy Leaves Home"), Donald Barthelme ("The School"), Raymond Carver ("What We Talk About When We Talk About Love"), Lydia Davis ("The House Plans"), and George Saunders ("Tenth of December"), provide illuminating points of comparative contact. These and other texts can be used to explore possible intertextual allusion or reference in Wallace's work, but they can also be used to provide comparative backgrounds against which the originality of Wallace's own achievement, in terms of his formal and stylistic methods, can be appreciated. Although the field is continually expanding, Wallace continues to make a very strong claim to pedagogic significance in courses on the short story and on the more general American literature survey. Often, indeed, this is based as much on student demand as it is on the author's own high critical standing.

From Context to Paratext and Back Again

Many of Wallace's short fictions are fascinating in the way they engage with the personal development of the human subject. In stories such as "Little Expressionless Animals" and "Forever Overhead" in particular, his examination of sexuality and the relation between personal and social constructions of sexual identity is poignant and profound. Wallace's short stories often speak to the tension between private and public experience, and in "The Suffering Channel," for example, questions regarding the relation between the creation of art and the public sphere are examined, especially with regard to moments of particular personal and social crisis. Because of the oblique way in which Wallace approaches 9/11, "The Suffering Channel" challenges students to consider the idea of the responsibility of the artist to respond to public events. At the same time, it invites them to consider the very idea of art itself as a way of responding to the world, which is a major theme for authors ranging from Poe, Hawthorne, and Melville to O'Connor, Saunders, Franz Kafka, and Jorge Luis Borges. In "The Suffering Channel," Wallace brings the events of 9/11 and the first Gulf War together through journalist Skip Atwater's preparation of an article on the veteran Brint Moltke's ability to create art, literally, out of his own feces. As in other stories, there is something darkly comic about this—a point given further resonance through a quotation of one of Jonathan Swift's scatological poems, "The Lady's Dressing Room," at one point in the narrative (265)—but Wallace is making a serious point here about the proximity between private experience and public awareness.

He is also exploring a theme that was of interest to him from the beginning of his career, as it was to Thomas Pynchon before him, concerning the ways we deal with waste in the twentieth century and how it threatens to consume us. Atwater's "sanitized" account of Moltke's unique method of artistic production addresses society's handling of difficult and so-called taboo topics—the phrases in square brackets here are Atwater's insertions:

> It was on a field exercise in basic [training in the US Army, in which Moltke later saw action in Kuwait as part of a maintenance crew in Operation Desert Storm], and the fellows on shitter [latrine, hygienic] detail—[latrine] detail is they soak the [military unit's solid wastes] in gas and burn it with a [flamethrower]—and up the [material] goes and in the fire one of the fellows saw something peculiar there in amongst the [waste material] and calls the sergeant over and they kick up a [fuss] because at first they're thinking somebody tossed something in the [latrine] for a joke, which is

against regs, and the sergeant said when he found out who it was he was going to crawl up inside the [responsible party's] skull and look out his eye-holes, and they made the [latrine] detail [douse] the fire and get it [the artwork] out and come to find it weren't a[n illicit or unpatriotic object], and they didn't know whose [solid waste] it was, but I was pretty sure it was mine [because subj. then reports having had prior experiences of roughly same kind, which renders entire anecdote more or less pointless, but could foreseeably be edited out or massaged].   (256)

In "The Suffering Channel," Wallace seems, on one level, to avoid 9/11—the story concerns events leading up to the day before the terrorist attack on the United States—but in a more complex way he is dealing directly with the meaning of art during a time of war and public crisis for everyone from the creators of the art to those who package it, analyze it, or consume it.

The theme of public engagement with art and the related idea of authorial responsibility can be traced in different ways throughout Wallace's short fiction, not least because his stories frequently feature identifiable places, figures, and events. In several stories collected in his earlier volume *Girl with Curious Hair*, for example, including "Little Expressionless Animals," "Lyndon," and "My Appearance," Wallace refers to figures, events, and cultural phenomena that students may already know something about, such as the television shows *Jeopardy* and *Late Night with David Letterman* or the thirty-sixth president of the United States, Lyndon B. Johnson. Although Wallace cautions readers in a note at the start of this collection that these stories are "100 percent fiction" (*Girl* vi), it is useful to ask students to identify the real-world referents in these and other texts and to explore the ways that Wallace's work employs and manipulates them in the context of late-twentieth-century popular and political culture. In these and other texts, Wallace complicates our sense of what *context* means. Indeed, while students may usefully research the historical figures and events evoked in many of Wallace's stories so that their sense of his contextual references can be clarified and developed, they should also be reminded of the ways that Wallace reimagines and defamiliarizes the world in his writing. While a character such as Brint Moltke is completely imagined, for example, to what extent, if at all, can the character called Lyndon be known or related to the historical figure with whom he shares a name? How are we to reconcile Wallace's sense of "fiction" with official versions of reality as documented in newspapers or historical studies? These are important questions that recur throughout Wallace's writing and ultimately relate also to the author's own self-representations, especially in the later story "Good Old Neon" and *The Pale King*, texts that feature characters who share the same name as the author.

In a more detailed examination of Wallace's manipulations of syntax and form, students could be asked to consider how to read the strange linear diagrams that appear throughout the text in "Little Expressionless Animals" or the questions and statements marked by the letter Q in the "Brief Interviews." They might also be invited to consider the function of Wallace's dedications, such as "For K. Gödel" under the title of "Here and There" (*Girl* 149), or his epigraphs, like those that precede "Westward the Course of Empire Takes Its Way" (attributed to Anthony Burgess and John Barth). These insertions expand the intertextual frame of reference of Wallace's work and encourage students to see his writing in relation to a wide range of American and international contexts. However, they also allow instructors to introduce technical issues such as the idea of the paratext—items ranging from preliminary notes to cover art—which are extremely important in Wallace's work.[4]

The questions and topics suggested here provide useful points of entry into the relation between Wallace's formal and stylistic methods and his thematic concerns. A consideration of Wallace's strategic use of narrative gaps and absences in the "Brief Interviews," for example, might refer back to the importance of minimalist techniques in the stories of Hemingway, Barthelme, Carver, Davis, and others, while the self-reflexive moments of narration in stories such as "Octet" can be read in response to earlier experiments in metafiction such as those by John Barth in his collection *Lost in the Funhouse*. Barth is a key figure in any discussion of Wallace's short fiction, especially because of the central role he plays in the novella that ends *Girl with Curious Hair*, "Westward the Course of Empire Takes Its Way," which makes clear reference to the title story of Barth's collection and to works by Cynthia Ozick. In the preliminary pages to *Girl with Curious Hair*, Wallace states that "[p]arts of 'Westward the Course of Empire Takes Its Way' are written in the margins of John Barth's 'Lost in the Funhouse' and Cynthia Ozick's 'Usurpation (Other People's Stories)'" (vi). My students have often asked why they should read the texts mentioned here in addition to what is already a long and complex piece of writing. Teaching "Westward" is a challenge, not least for this reason. Even a consideration of its title, however, with regard to the mural that shares its name by Emanuel Leutze in the United States Capitol Building, can be revealing, in terms of both the radical intertextual expansiveness of Wallace's shorter texts and his concern with cultural ideas of progress and myths of idealism throughout the history of the United States. As a text about writing itself, on one level, "Westward the Course of Empire Takes Its Way" advances Wallace's interest in the self-reflexive forms of narration common in high postmodern literature from Barth to Italo Calvino, but beyond its technical complexity it is also a work that speaks to the author's desire to create stories that reveal the fragility of the human subject. Its closing paragraphs, indeed, could be used to preface any discussion of Wallace's work where an instructor wishes to assure students in advance that the difficulty of reading him is often rewarded with very particular kinds of ethical and aesthetic understanding. In this regard, "Westward," by its very complexity, can help instructors illustrate the movement toward "sincerity" that some critics, such as Adam Kelly, have seen as a central motivation and aim in his work as a whole.

"The Mind of Those Stories"

The first story in *Brief Interviews with Hideous Men* ("A Radically Condensed History of Postindustrial Life") flags both the formal and the contextual coordinates of Wallace's work in clear terms. The idea of a "radically condensed" text speaks immediately to the short story form, which is predicated on ideas of textual compression, brevity, and economy of scale, while the notion of "postindustrial life" signals Wallace's concern with personal and cultural experience in the postmodern (if not the post-postmodern) era. Comprising two short paragraphs, "Radically Condensed History" takes a very big idea ("postindustrial life") and compresses it into a very short narrative about two people being introduced for the first time. For all of its concision, however, the story is deeply ambiguous, and its closing sentence affirms the kind of epistemological uncertainty that underlies so much of Wallace's writing—a kind of not-knowing that pervades all aspects of our personal and public lives. Reading Wallace, in short, it is appropriate at times to say that one does not know what a story means or what is going on, exactly, between its first and last words. That this particular short story should be positioned on a page numbered zero is in itself the basis for a very interesting classroom discussion about the methods and intentions of Wallace's work. What does it mean to begin on page zero? Is Wallace suggesting that the best place to begin is with nothing? To put it another way, students can benefit from being encouraged to leave what they think they already know about Wallace (perhaps concerning his popularity, his biography, or the perceived complexity of his writing) to one side as they approach his work for the first time.

For all that Wallace's short fiction appears to deal so comprehensively with so many subjects of personal and public import, it is essential for students to appreciate that the author's work retains an abiding sense of doubt and confusion in response to the realities of the contemporary world, as suggested in the final sentence and pagination of "Radically Condensed History." In many of his short stories, as outlined above in relation to "Westward the Course of Empire Takes Its Way," Wallace drew on other texts to create the fabric of his own stories. "Little Expressionless Animals" "makes use" (as he puts it) of John Ashbery's poem "Self-Portrait in a Convex Mirror" (*Girl* vi) in a way that invites readers to consider the boundaries of textual experience—where Ashbery's poem ends and Wallace's story begins, where author becomes reader, and vice versa. In an essay on Borges first published in 2004, Wallace argues that "the mind of those stories [by Borges] is nearly always a mind that lives in and through books" ("Borges on the Couch" 293). He continues:

> Whether for seminal artistic reasons or neurotic personal ones or both, Borges collapses reader and writer in a new kind of aesthetic agent, one who makes stories out of stories, one for whom reading is essentially—consciously—a creative act. This is not, however, because Borges is a metafictionist or cleverly disguised critic. It is because he knows that there's

finally no difference—that murderer and victim, detective and fugitive, performer and audience are the same.   (294)

In thinking about the relationship between reader and writer in this way, Wallace also affirms the expansive intertextual method of his own writing process. This is one of the reasons why his short fiction can be read so fruitfully alongside the texts by other authors discussed above. By engaging with his work, students and scholars gain not only critical knowledge about his own experiments with literary form and style but also insights into the development of the short story as one of the major modes of expression across the contours of American literary culture.

NOTES

[1] Some of Wallace's stories, especially in *Brief Interviews with Hideous Men*, are gathered under the same title and are clearly interconnected. It can be interesting for students to examine these groups of stories together in class by considering the chronological and geographical distribution of the "Brief Interviews," for example, or the mysterious numbering of the "Yet Another Example . . ." sections. These texts include the four sections entitled "Brief Interviews with Hideous Men" (17–34, 82–124, 213–34, 287–318); "Yet Another Example of the Porousness of Certain Borders (XI)" (35–36), "Yet Another Example of the Porousness of Certain Borders (VI)" (211–12), and "Yet Another Example of the Porousness of Certain Borders (XXIV)" (319–21); two pieces entitled "The Devil Is a Busy Man" (70–71, 190–93); and "Adult World (I)" and "Adult World (II)" (161–82, 183–89). Page numbers refer to the Back Bay edition.

[2] The term *intertextuality* is understood here to include "literary" and "non-literary" texts, as Graham Allen suggests in his study *Intertextuality* (1).

[3] Welty's widely anthologized short story "Where Is the Voice Coming From?" might also be read in relation to the theme of private and public experience discussed in this essay.

[4] The idea of the paratext is developed in particular by Gérard Genette in his study *Paratexts: Thresholds of Interpretation*. It is possible to teach Wallace's short fiction without drawing too heavily, if at all, on literary or critical theory. However, a course beginning with Poe, for example, could include a discussion of his essay "The Philosophy of Composition," which outlines Poe's ideas about compression and "unity of effect" in literary works. As Charles E. May (xv) and others have argued, contemporary short story theory originates with Poe.

Teaching Wallace's Pop Criticism

Matthew Luter

Many of our students read music, film, and television reviews of one sort or another, but not all of them think of pop cultural criticism as conversational, complex, or comprising a journalistic tradition. This has become especially true as
social media has turned every consumer into an amateur critic, leading to countless think pieces in the last decade regarding the role of criticism in an age that
often seems to have replaced thoughtful cultural discussion with the decision
whether or not to click a "like" button. Popular online review aggregators like
Rotten Tomatoes reduce all film reviews to either a positive judgment or a negative one; *Metacritic*'s hundred-point scale allows for a larger spectrum of responses but still jettisons much argumentative subtlety by turning every review
into a numerical evaluation. To students who interact with pop criticism primarily in order to decide whether or not to purchase something (another binary,
yes/no decision, a good/bad assessment), criticism that seeks to analyze pop ar-
tifacts with complexity and even ambivalence can be unfamiliar territory—even
for those who read and produce criticism in literature courses. Equally unfamiliar to many is the idea of pop criticism as a distinct American literary tradition
with a canon of influential writers.

I find it useful to introduce students to landmark pieces of pop criticism in
order to explain that Wallace's critical nonfiction—particularly in a book like *Signifying Rappers* or essays like "Host" and "The (As It Were) Seminal Importance of *Terminator 2*"—stands firmly within an American literary tradition, not
unlike the ways in which Wallace is an heir of Thomas Pynchon, William Gaddis, Don DeLillo, and others as a fiction writer. I also find it useful to introduce
students to criticism that seeks to do far more than review. For some students,
the idea that a pop critic might do more than dictate whether or not one ought
to consume a product is genuinely new. For instance, after encountering portions of *Signifying Rappers* on the syllabus of a composition course centered on
writing about pop music—a course that introduced students to ways that pop
music discourses raise questions of gender, race, law, politics, sexuality, history,
and aesthetic philosophy—a few students commented on how pleasantly surprised they were at the breadth of topics covered within what they had sus-
pected might be a course devoted to studying record reviews. These students,
voracious music listeners already, benefited from introduction to a fuller range
of critical contexts for the culture they consumed. In writing critically about
culture (literary or not) on their own, such students may need help moving from
thinking evaluatively (am I entertained by this work?) to thinking analytically
(what is this writer trying to say, and how does he or she pull it off?).

A class devoted to writing on pop culture offers a wonderful opportunity to
introduce students to Wallace's critical writing on cultural topics with which they
are likely already familiar: action movies, hip-hop, and television. The complex-

ity and deep ambivalence with which Wallace approaches pop texts can encourage students to write with intellectual care and to examine their subjective reactions. That said, Wallace's pop criticism frequently insists on the value of its subjectivity and can function as a useful model for critical writing that moves past mere reaction while never denying that a biased human being is doing the writing. For those who use Wallace's nonfiction in the classroom to demonstrate what analytical criticism can accomplish, Wallace's writing about pop culture can be held up as a model of critical complexity.

Toward two ends—illuminating Wallace's intellectual context as an inheritor of the American pop-critical tradition, and illustrating how those critics most influential on Wallace have shaped his nonfiction—I suggest some pairings of Wallace's essays with major essays by important American pop critics. I also suggest key questions for classroom discussion and a few writing assignments that encourage students to think of themselves not as readers, listeners, viewers, or reviewers but as apprentice cultural critics borrowing fruitfully from Wallace's critical toolbox as they write themselves into a vibrant tradition. I then briefly suggest ways in which thinking about Wallace as a pop critic can shed new light on some of his most pop-centric fiction.

The two American pop critics whose influence on him Wallace has most directly discussed and displayed are the longtime *New Yorker* film critic Pauline Kael and the rock critic Lester Bangs, who wrote for many music publications. Wallace wears his appreciation of both on his sleeve. Asked which nonfiction writers inspired him, Wallace immediately named Joan Didion and Kael, adding, "I think prosewise, Pauline Kael is unequaled" (Burn, *Conversations* 88). He also refers to Kael many times in the conversation that became David Lipsky's *Although of Course You End Up Becoming Yourself.* For her part, Kael admired Wallace's work, praising *Girl with Curious Hair* (Espen 142). Wallace expressed his devotion to Lester Bangs by dedicating *Signifying Rappers* to the late critic. In his preface to a reprint of *Signifying Rappers*, Wallace's coauthor and then-roommate Mark Costello recalls how "the central chunk" of their shared reading passions in the late 1980s was "a group of skitter-smart cultural critics," including "the king of the apartment, Lester Bangs" (vi). Many have noted Bangsian touches throughout Wallace's fiction: for instance, D. T. Max's biography casts a description of Ennet House in *Infinite Jest* as "a passage that sounds as if Lester Bangs had written it" (141).

Kael and Bangs share two qualities that Wallace's pop criticism displays repeatedly: a willingness to defend modes of expression that are frequently critically derided, and an emphasis on the subjective, emotional experience of pop texts, as opposed to an evaluative detachment that holds them at arm's length. Arguably, Kael's most representative single piece of writing is "Trash, Art, and the Movies," whose core claims Wallace has echoed, and which remains highly accessible to movie-minded students today, even as few will recognize etle to which Kael refers. Those passages from *Although of Course* in whiclace discusses relatively mainstream films like *Scrooged, Glory,* and

Runner—all easy to excerpt and quite accessible even if students haven't seen the films in question—borrow their critical lens directly from Kael, who argues that good cinematic entertainment is not necessarily art and that a silly, "trashy" film can be enjoyed on its own terms (Kael 223). One should not perform pseudoacademic interpretive acrobatics, she argues, in order to turn an enjoyably silly movie into a piece of high art for respectability's sake. "[M]ovies are so rarely great art," Kael asserts, "that if we cannot appreciate great *trash*, we have very little reason to be interested in them" (222). Viewers can still "get little things even in mediocre and terrible movies," since "we are so used to reaching out to the few good bits in a movie that we don't need formal perfection to be dazzled" (213, 216). Many students react positively to the idea that films (or any other pop cultural texts) don't have to be consistently perfect or all that original in order to succeed; others will find Kael a bit capricious and inscrutable in selecting "the few good bits in a movie." Either way, she raises an excellent question for students of Wallace: What might be the value of "trash" in a pop cultural context that Wallace agrees is so often full of it?

Wallace echoes Kael's point of view frequently in his writing about film, especially when he focuses on the resonance of specific moments onscreen instead of analyzing what a filmmaker is trying to say. Consider how he contrasts David Lynch and Quentin Tarantino visually, or how skillfully he close-reads the utterance, "You're like me" in Lynch's *Blue Velvet* ("David Lynch" 166, 207). Additionally, much of the conversation about entertainment with Lipsky in *Although of Course* focuses on relatively mainstream fare, especially as Wallace admits that he sometimes finds highly formulaic and disposable television "tremendously compelling" and "*profoundly* soothing" (199). Having students look for and write about what Wallace calls the "little flashes" of significance in their own experience of film (or television or music or literature, for that matter) can help beginning critics learn the vital analytical skill of close reading, or it can help more advanced students begin thinking of themselves as inheritors of Kael's culturally omnivorous tradition (Lipsky 202). Students might also read *The Film Club* for David Gilmour's description of the filmgoers' game of "spot-the-great-moment" (61). This parlor game of sorts could easily become a Kaelian (or Wallacean) analytical writing assignment as students articulate what specific components of a text most help it achieve its intended effects.

If Wallace primarily borrows aesthetic preferences from Kael, he borrows stylistic energy from the intentionally excessive, borderline hysterical Lester Bangs. Bangs makes an ideal pairing with *Signifying Rappers*; in my course on writing about pop music I taught chapter 1B of *Signifying Rappers* with Bangs's sardonic essay "How to Be a Rock Critic" and Greg Tate's "It's Like This Y'all," a notable essay from a *Village Voice* feature on hip-hop's emergence into the mainstream that also has its touches of Bangsian overheated energy (both this piece and the aforementioned Bangs essay are reprinted in Theo Cateforis's *Rock History Reader*). Whereas Wallace positions hip-hop as something genuinely new, Tate places it in a long tradition of African American expression; this can lead to comparative discussions regarding what Wallace might notice and miss about hip-hop as a white listener and consumer.

The title essay in *Psychotic Reactions and Carburetor Dung*, where Bangs's most important work is collected, functions as the most concise distillation of Bangs's style and aesthetic. Its aggressively know-it-all narrative voice may polarize students, though, and its central conceit will need some explaining. Assuming the guise of a stereotypical old-timer, Bangs breathlessly tries to explain the greatness of the music of his youth. "Psychotic Reactions" is a defense of amateurish, disposable garage rock that also seeks to immortalize the near-forgotten San Jose garage rock band the Count Five, whose single "Psychotic Reaction" was a top-five hit in 1965. The central conceit of the essay's second half is Bangs's chronicle of a fabricated five-record discography for the Count Five, who in actuality released only one LP. Like Kael, Bangs valorizes art that might be easily dismissed by more tradition-bound critics: he writes of using the "aggressively mediocre" Count Five to conclude "that grossness was the truest criterion for rock 'n' roll" (10). Obviously, playing the Count Five track for students is helpful. From there, I ask students why critics might seek to rehabilitate forgotten art at all. Do critics have a duty to put their argumentative weight behind art that is underappreciated, or is that an elitist assumption that figures critics automatically know the culture at large better than their audience?

Either of those interpretations of Bangs could inform Wallace's assertions in *Signifying Rappers* that hip-hop circa 1990, disdained by some listeners and critics as outright unmusical, was underdiscussed and misunderstood. Students might also see this approach, which argues that pop forms that are critically unpopular deserve thoughtful reconsideration, in works by Wallace's contemporaries. Examples I have assigned include Chuck Klosterman's memoir *Fargo Rock City*, which also functions as an unlikely aesthetic defense of 1980s heavy metal, and Carl Wilson's acclaimed *Let's Talk about Love: A Journey to the End of Taste*, which starts with its author's disdain for the music of Céline Dion but eventually meditates on aesthetic philosophy from the likes of Kant, Hume, and Bourdieu. Students writing their way into Bangs's tradition through Wallace might then consider which of the texts they consume ought to be considered culturally significant but are not thought artistically important—doing so requires them to move past articulating what they enjoy about a (perhaps guilty) artistic pleasure and to instead imagine what cultural work such a text might perform. This assignment also encourages students to consider multiple interpretive lenses for a single text as they try to conceptualize how a particular film, song, or television show might play to an audience whose demographic is not their own.

When contextualizing Wallace's nonfiction by teaching Kael and Bangs, I also suggest emphasizing the degree to which these earlier critics allow emotional and subjective reactions into their critical work—rhetorical moves adopted by Wallace. As Mark Bresnan discusses in his essay in this volume, many students assume that analytical writing must attempt pure objectivity and impersonality; many have been trained not to use first-person pronouns, while others shy away from building arguments that might leave their ideas open to criticism on grounds of subjectivity. The latter defensive position, of course, runs counter to the idea that criticism is inherently conversational. Instead of attempting to ban subjectivity altogether from students' critical work (which would be next to impossible anyway), I share some intentionally, even aggressively, personal writing that opens discussion regarding how visible we expect a critic's subjectivity to be. Students can discuss when it is (and is not) useful to know details about a critic's background or experiences. How appropriate is consideration of background when critics write of artworks that reflect their experiences (as does Greg Tate in "It's Like This Y'all"), or when the critic approaches work originating in another community (as does Wallace in *Signifying Rappers*)?

To emphasize how potentially useful overt subjectivity and displays of emotion in critical analysis can be, I suggest Kael's reviews of *Shoeshine* (44–45) and *Nashville* (456–62). In the former, Kael describes seeing a classic Italian film "after one of those terrible lovers' quarrels that leave one in a state of incomprehensible despair" (44); in the latter, Kael's famous rave about *Nashville* gets particularly visceral as she calls Robert Altman's film "an orgy for movie-lovers—but an orgy without excess" (456). Like the aforementioned Tate essay on early hip-hop, Kael pairs well with chapter 1B of *Signifying Rappers*, in which Wallace confronts the incongruity of being one of a pair of "highbrow upscale whites" intrigued by this music and admits that he and Costello were less interested in "what we knew than what we felt, listening" (23). As Wallace recognizes his subjectivity and his more emotional than intellectual connection to his subject matter, I ask students to consider what he gains and risks in displaying his own critical biases.

The last piece of instruction I encourage students to take from Wallace's pop-critical nonfiction (and that of his influences and contemporaries) has to do with the value of the ambivalent response. I began this essay by decrying modes of contemporary reviewing that reduce complex artworks by only judging them "recommended" or "not recommended." Wallace's deeply ambivalent essay about television "E Unibus Pluram" is a case study in approaching pop material neither to bury it nor to praise it, but to articulate its value and its limitations with great complexity. Other nonfiction by Wallace builds multifaceted arguments by making clear the (sometimes unexpected) complexity of the texts under discussion: in "Host," Wallace evinces discomfort with the content of John Ziegler's radio show ("*Consider*" 285–88, 343) yet acknowledges Ziegler's mastery of a confoundingly difficult job (293–96), while *Signifying Rappers* cogently argues that hip-hop's emphasis on crime and poverty is this music's most culturally important feature and its biggest potential liability (43–45). I then have students write about a pop text or form that they neither love nor hate (or, as "E Unibus" positions television, a text or form toward which their attitude is complicated). The assignment is not an attempt to remove strong emotion from these students' critical writing, but it does force them to apply their critical acumen in the absence of strong attachment.

The classic writings that I've mentioned serve as models of essays that pass judgment on individual texts and genres while also making larger points about the essential qualities of their respective media. All encourage us to embrace complexity in our experience of popular media, or, as Wallace explained on an undergraduate literature syllabus that included popular fiction by the likes of Stephen King, Thomas Harris, and Jackie Collins, "[t]hese 'popular' texts will end up being harder than more conventionally 'literary' works to unpack and read critically" ("English 102"). I am far from the first reader of Wallace to assert that considering his critical nonfiction in the light of his pop-critical influences can shed additional light on his fiction that engages with popular culture; indeed, one of the earliest significant essays about Wallace is Lance Olsen's "Termite Art, or Wallace's Wittgenstein," which posits Wallace as a clear inheritor in his early fiction of the tradition the film critic Manny Farber names in his classic essay "White Elephant Art vs. Termite Art." To Farber's contrast between plodding Oscar bait (white elephant art) and nimbler, more modest movies (termite art) Olsen adds a characterization of termite art as "concerned with process over progress, question over solution, complex ambiguity over crystalline explanation" (201). Olsen even suggests that Wallace writes definitively termite-art-like individual sentences, quoting a complex periodic sentence from a book review by Wallace before calling it one of the author's typically "maximalist effusions that correspond not to some mathematically pure realm of being but rather to some multidimensional space of becoming intricate as the involved surface of a brain" (207). Olsen, like Farber, values messy complexities over easy conclusions.

Indeed, Wallace's stories about television appear less like easy jeremiads against a potentially destructive medium and more like meditations on the messy complexities of entertainment. "Little Expressionless Animals" and "My Appearance" mock the predictable formulas of the game show and the talk show—programs that Kael would refer to as trash, Bangs as mediocre—while allowing readers to witness moments on those shows that reach toward a transcendent honesty. "Tri-Stan: I Sold Sissee Nar to Ecko" juggles reams of inside-baseball industry jargon while unearthing the mythopoeia at the core of even the silliest television shows. And, while the title cable network in "The Suffering Channel" is ethically questionable to say the least (a fact underscored by the story's quick jabs at reality television), the story takes pains to present its cast of behind-the-scenes media players as professionals with some dignity, not as uncaringly impersonal mercenaries. Wallace resists the temptation to make apocalyptic pronouncements about even this dubious attempt at entertainment.

Some of the films Kael refers to in "Trash, Art, and the Movies" may be unfamiliar to young readers, but her core claim will resonate—as it clearly did with Wallace—with any avid moviegoer who has ever found a single moment revelatory in a film that otherwise doesn't fully succeed. Similarly, Bangs's work will strike a chord with countless readers who have loved a pop cultural artifact as a kind of guilty pleasure (as Wallace, viewer of *Baywatch* and *The Love Boat*, surely did) despite knowing it lacks critical stature. Both will resonate with students who desire (and want to practice) a constructive balance between analytical thought and experiential reflection in critical writing. Wallace's nonfiction work about film, television, and music does precisely what good pop criticism ought to do: it approaches familiar artistic forms with complexity and, often, ambivalence, to produce a response to pop texts that is well informed, reasoned, and undeniably subjective. If we hope to see from our students literary (or film, or television, or cultural, or social) criticism that works with original, multifaceted arguments and embraces complexity instead of shying away from it, Wallace's writing can function well as a model.

Infinite Unrest:
"Octet," High School, and
the Revolving Door of Metanarrative

Mike Miley

Teaching David Foster Wallace to high school students constitutes a trademark Wallace double bind: his work poses probing, vital questions about media, sincerity, and addiction relevant to adolescents entering the adult world—yet those questions are embedded in elusive structures and intimidating terminologies that could easily deter young readers. None of Wallace's themes exhibits this dilemma better than his engagement with and critique of postmodernism, which is so grounded in literary theory and history that attempting to introduce high school students to it would appear to be a nonstarter. I have found, however, that teaching Wallace's short story "Octet" at the end of a carefully sequenced and scaffolded introduction to postmodern literature and theory provokes a passionate and insightful discussion of postmodernism. A course modeled on Wallace's ability to make the theoretical not only relatable but personal encourages students to grapple with what they have learned in the classroom and to apply their learning to the world they inhabit. In relating postmodernism to their world, students engage in critical thinking by interrogating postmodernism's ability to stand outside its own critique. At first, postmodernism appears to be the one truth that survives its own skepticism.

Despite postmodernism's difficulty, students are surprisingly receptive to it. In "E Unibus Pluram: Television and U.S. Fiction," and "Westward the Course of Empire Takes Its Way," Wallace offers insight into why high schoolers are poised to appreciate postmodernism's ironic attack on authority and master narratives: these theories, despite originating in avant-garde fiction and dense theoretical tracts, have been thoroughly absorbed by mainstream culture, particularly television. Today's students have likely been watching since infancy the kind of ironically self-aware programming Wallace laments, and they can recognize it quickly. For them, metafictional techniques are, as Wallace writes in "Westward," "safe to read, as familiar as syndication" (333). In fact, syndication probably provided their first encounter with postmodernism, whether in *The Simpsons'* unrelenting self-awareness or in *South Park's* send-ups of master narratives such as Mormonism and Scientology. If a teacher can connect postmodern theory to pop culture, students will follow because, for all of its challenging verbiage, postmodern theory confirms what rebellious high schoolers already suspect: that the narratives dominating their education, such as American progress, humanism, science, and religious doctrine, are riddled with contradictions and simplifications that fail to capture the world as they experience it. Postmodernism provides them with a name for these suspicions that gives their adolescent rebellion some academic cachet: metanarrative.

I taught Wallace in this context first in a one-semester twelfth-grade honors elective entitled Contemporary Fiction. The class met for forty-five minutes, five days a week, which allowed us to cover more material, and to assess comprehension more frequently, than in a college course. Not everything I outline here will apply to another high school or undergraduate classroom; however, the approach and reading list could be modified, condensed, or expanded into a standalone unit, undergraduate-level semester, or yearlong high school course, depending upon the demands or constraints of the course and institution. The core texts of the course are Zadie Smith's *White Teeth* (which I assign as summer reading), Don DeLillo's *White Noise*, Thomas Pynchon's *The Crying of Lot 49*, Michael Ondaatje's *The Collected Works of Billy the Kid*, Toni Morrison's *Sula*, Ishmael Reed's *Mumbo Jumbo*, and Jeffrey Eugenides's *The Virgin Suicides*. These novels challenge the authority of metanarratives and present students with a multivalent, subjective way of looking at the world around them. This opening up of human experience and literature gets students to consider new perspectives on history, identity, and truth in a safe, encouraging, often humorous way. Wallace's story "Octet" addresses these issues more aggressively and ultimately reveals that metanarrative resembles a series of revolving doors: breaking free of one metanarrative only leads us into the orbit of another.

Before students can understand the persistence of metanarratives, they must first understand what metanarratives are and why they must be questioned. I begin the course with excerpts from important postmodern essays such as Susan Sontag's "Against Interpretation," Jean Baudrillard's "The Precession of Simulacra," Fredric Jameson's "Postmodernism and Consumer Society," John Barth's "The Literature of Exhaustion," and, of course, Roland Barthes's "The Death of the Author." Some of these essays are harder than others for students to grasp and require top-down explanation; however, more often than not, students realize they understand an essay better than they think they do. This discovery boosts their intellectual confidence and allows them to tackle DeLillo and Pynchon with more depth, rigor, and risk because they now possess a foundation for understanding these texts. I find that these theoretical pieces work best when paired with short fiction that illustrates their ideas, so I assign "The Death of the Author" with John Barth's "Autobiography" and Barth's "The Literature of Exhaustion" with his story "Title." These stories work well because they each, respectively, capture Barthes's elevation of the reader as meaning maker and Barth's description of fiction being consumed by its own conventions and techniques. Other pairings I find useful are "The Precession of Simulacra" with George Saunders's theme-park ghost story "Civilwarland in Bad Decline," to illustrate the concept of hyperreality; "Against Interpretation" with Donald Barthelme's deconstructed antistories "The Glass Mountain" and "The Explanation" to showcase the emptiness and hostility behind analysis; and "Postmodernism and Consumer Society" with Saunders's consumer-culture satires "In Persuasion Nation" and "Offloading for Mrs. Schwartz" to amplify Jameson's critiques of advertising and nostalgia. Of course, this introductory unit would not be complete, and students would not be adequately prepared for Wallace's interrogation of postmodernism, without a careful examination of the story that Wallace both imitates and challenges in "Octet": "Lost in the Funhouse." Through the task of explaining how "Lost in the Funhouse" and the other stories illustrate the ideas in the essays, students discover how theory's changing ideas about the relation between the text and the author shapes contemporary literature.

These early classes are among the most exciting because the students are using the essays and stories to challenge metanarratives and destabilize fixed senses of meaning, truth, authorship, and form for the first time. They experience the liberation of repudiating the solve-for-x approach to literary analysis in which they have been trained to reduce texts to singular meanings or themes. Since honors students tend to be eager to please, by the end of these first two weeks I find myself facing a room full of postmodern zealots who come to class each day ready to debunk the next metanarrative.

I admit that there is something of a dirty trick or postmodern game about the course's design, because in making the students so excited about deconstructing all these myths of literature and culture, I am encouraging them to construct a metanarrative of their own in which postmodernism becomes the best explanation for the world as it is. Postmodernism may be an antinarrative, but nevertheless it functions as a school of thought with rules and rationales as codified as the schools my students are discrediting. In this regard, the course itself (in hindsight, at least) takes on the look and feel of a funhouse, one that is built out of the wreckage of dignified traditions and institutions and that must itself be torn apart in order to make students see that we have, to paraphrase Wallace in "Westward," "built a funhouse for lovers out of [stories] that [do] not love" (331).

Although critics commonly regard "Westward" as Wallace's demolition of Barth's postmodern funhouse, the shorter, more coherent (and at once more jarring and more confrontational) "Octet" achieves the same purpose and offers more educational value. "Octet" embodies the takedown of metafiction's take-down of traditional narrative that "Westward" only describes: it is a story that "use[s] metafiction as a bright smiling disguise, a harmless floppy-shoed costume" before unmasking the self-absorbed cynicism at the heart of the genre ("West-ward" 333). We preface "Octet" with the section of "Westward" entitled "Final Interruption," which describes postmodern metafictionalists such as Barth and Barthelme as "gifted old contortionists" whose fiction cannot step outside itself to bring the reader inside; rather than loving the reader, Barth and Barthelme are merely, according to Wallace, pleasuring themselves (332). Dissatisfied with Barth's cleverly self-aware funhouse, Wallace claims in "Westward" that "the way to make a story a Funhouse is to put the story itself in one," to "make the reader a lover, who wants to be inside. Then do him" or her (331). Ironically, Wallace se-duces readers into the funhouse of "Octet" using metafiction's "harmless floppy-shoed costume," then directs them toward fiction of "completely naked helpless pathetic sincerity" ("Octet" 154).[1] This redirection of the reader's position on metafiction constitutes "the involved revelation of betrayal" Wallace outlines in "Westward"—a betrayal that emerges from the design of the story itself. The octet structure, explains the narrator of the story's final section, "Pop Quiz 9," "attenuate[s] the initial appearance of postclever metaformal hooey and end[s] up . . . interrogating the reader's initial inclination to dismiss the pieces as 'shallow formal exercises' . . . forcing the reader to see that such a dismissal would be based precisely on the same sorts of shallow formalistic concerns she was . . . inclined to accuse the octet of" (151–52). In using metafiction both to demolish the devices of Barth's metafictional funhouse and to disarm the reader of his or her familiarity with those devices, Wallace opens the door for a "100% honest . . . obscenely na-ked direct interrogation" of the reader that would reveal the reader and the writer to be truly on the same level, lost in the same funhouse of metanarrative (154).

I use "Octet" at the end of the course precisely because the betrayal Wallace describes above matches the sense of betrayal that the story provokes in students who are newly enamored with postmodernism's commitment to exposing com-monly held truths as illusions. Students' anger in response to "Octet" is matched only by the enthusiasm they brought into those first discussions of postmodern-ism. "Pop Quiz 9" appears to reject everything that the students have spent a semester learning about postmodernism, and it uses postmodern forms and ideas in order to discredit them. Wallace exposes what was so revelatory to students a few weeks earlier as "pseudometabelletristic gamesmanship" and "highly rhe-torical sham-honesty" (150, 147n2). The students are not prepared for such a re-versal. They will want, nay, demand an explanation from their teacher because the concepts they had come to accept as proven have been unmasked as assump-tions. They will feel decentered, uncertain of where to stand, how to proceed, or what to believe. In short, "Octet" will leave them reeling in the throes of a postmodern crisis. In that sense, "Octet" does not debunk postmodernism's at-tack on metanarrative at all. In fact, quite the contrary—it makes the problems regarding metanarrative real rather than theoretical, something that is happening to the students rather than something that was resolved before they started taking the class. In addition to making the course material personal, this experience shows them how postmodern theory grew out of feelings about the world, not academic theoretical spitballing.

Careful structuring enables this class plan to function most effectively. Prior to reading "Octet," students reread "Lost in the Funhouse," followed by the "Final Interruption" section of "Westward," so that they have all of Wallace's points of reference fresh in mind when they read "Octet." Student understanding and interest should guide the first class discussion of "Octet"; some students may want to spend time examining the form of the story, while others will want to discuss how "Pop Quiz 9" precludes the "sham honesty" or "Carsoning" that the story decries (159n17). I like to ask students to list examples of this technique that they have seen on television or in movies—such as when Dave Chappelle and Anthony Jeselnik playfully admonish their audiences about what they do and do not laugh at in their stand-up routines, or when John Oliver deliberately misidentifies countries on a map on his show—and consider how they have reacted to those examples. As a different initial approach, the class could split into groups and each take one of the story's pop quizzes to solve. If students come in with a particularly heated response to Wallace's critique of postmodernism, the class can be dedicated to letting students express their sense of betrayal, with the teacher frequently baiting them by taking Wallace's side.

I spend another class leading students through a textual comparison of "Octet" with "Lost in the Funhouse" to show how Wallace subtly subverts Barth's story using Barth's self-aware techniques, demonstrating that what appear in one light as barrier-busting innovations can also be seen as cynical strategies for avoiding emotional truth. I spend most of the time comparing Barth's direct address to the reader throughout his story with Wallace's in "Pop Quiz 9," from their choices of pronouns *we* and *one* in "Funhouse"; *you* and *she* in "Octet") to their tones (professorial and assured in Barth; confessional and insecure in Wallace) to their insights on the conventions of fiction. I also call attention to the stories' endings, because, while both protagonists become hopelessly lost in mazes of their own design, they draw markedly different conclusions. I ask students to explain how Ambrose's choice to become both architect and "secret operator" of funhouses ("Lost" 97) differs from the fiction writer's decision to resolve the failed octet by approaching the reader "100% hat in hand" ("Octet" 154). Incorporating the "Final Interruption" section of "Westward," especially the passage claiming that the writer and reader must "walk arm in arm . . . through the grinning happy door" (331), helps students understand Wallace's position in "Octet": Wallace's reading of "Lost in the Funhouse" sees Barth's writer hero choosing to sequester himself in the funhouse, forever apart from (and perhaps above) the regular people (readers), whereas Wallace's story ends with writer and reader "quivering in the mud of the trench" together (160).

As this discussion progresses, however, it becomes important to avoid embracing wholesale Wallace's scathing interpretation of Barth (explicit in "Final

Interruption," implicit in "Octet"). That would, after all, be yet another meta-narrative, one that mistakenly prevails in Wallace studies. Getting students to see something self-serving in Wallace's undermining of Barth is important, and I ask students to rebut Wallace's claims that Barth's story is only cold and clever by finding moments of emotional truth and sadness in Barth's story as well as other stories from the course, such as Oedipa's scene with the drunk man on the mattress in *Lot 49*, to show how Wallace's reading may overlook or ignore aspects of these works that do not fit his own metanarrative. While this approach may appear to actively undermine the previous day's discussion by contradicting Wallace's criticisms of Barth and metafiction, it teaches students that the impulse to construct metanarratives is unavoidable, even for Wallace, and that embracing any claim or school of thought without examination or qualification invites a closed-off, ideologically based way of looking at the world, the very thing that postmodernism and, ideally, educators attempt to deconstruct.

In the third class, we examine how "Borges on the Couch," ostensibly a review of Edwin Williamson's *Borges: A Life*, is actually Wallace's rereading of Borges against Barth. Wallace challenges the way "The Literature of Exhaustion" champions Borges as proto-postmodern by demonstrating how Borges's stories render him not a metafictional Daedalus but a fellow reader. The discussion should spend significant time on this passage:

> . . . Borges the writer is, fundamentally, a reader. The dense, obscure allusiveness of his fiction is not a tic, or even really a style . . . Borges collapses reader and writer into a new kind of aesthetic agent . . . one for whom reading is essentially—consciously—a creative act. . . . because he knows that there's finally no difference—that murderer and victim, detective and fugitive, performer and audience are the same.   (293–94)

After discussing this passage, I guide students to see how Wallace's reading of Borges becomes a revision of postmodernism itself. Barth's "Funhouse" is Borges's "Library of Babel" carried out to its metafictional end point. For Barth, "when the characters in a work of fiction become readers or authors of the fiction they're in, we're reminded of the fictitious aspect of our own existence" ("Literature of Exhaustion" 73). Barth sees (and admires) the *regressus in infinitum* at the heart of Borges, and "Lost in the Funhouse" ends with Ambrose (and the author) trapped in the story, cut off from direct interaction with the reader. However, the end of "Octet" shows Wallace reading Borges's library differently: the fiction writer's decision to descend from the "Olympian HQ" at the end of "Pop Quiz 9" to "quiver" with the reader shows that the writer and the reader are not cut off but united in an intimate relationship seeking to make sense of stories together (160). For Wallace, Borges does not retreat into fiction as Barth's character does in "Funhouse" but uses fiction for "yanking people out of themselves and into the world," the writer included ("Little Expressionless Animals" 20). This discussion should show students how, by going back to an earlier postmodern source in Borges, Wallace turns American postmodernism inside out, redirecting the course of the postmodern empire away from what he sees as solipsistic metafictional games that cannot break out of themselves and toward an intimate engagement with another human being in the world, the reader.

Thanks to Wallace's reading of metafiction in "Octet," every topic of the course becomes reanimated and recontextualized; everything is back on the table, nothing is finished. The rejection of metanarratives is itself a metanarrative, the dead author is a living reader, and, arguably, the exhausted is reinvigorated. At this moment, I bring the discussion back to the theoretical essays that began the course (especially "The Death of the Author") because, rather than negating the discoveries of the entire course, "Octet" synthesizes them. Wallace's reading of Borges revises and enhances the class's understanding of Barthes because "Octet" does not set out to kill the author so much as it tries to make the author one of us. I ask students how Wallace's approach differs from that of Barthes, but, more important, I ask them how the two are similar. Does the author have to be "dead" in order for the reader to be born? Is the author in "Octet" an author who refuses to die, or perhaps a fellow reader? Or is this author "a self-consciously inbent schmuck, or like just another manipulative pseudopomo bullshit artist" (159)? Is the distinction between writer and reader itself a metanarrative that must be exploded? Does "Octet" succeed in achieving this? How would dissolving the line between the two, regarding fiction writing as readers talking to each other across the lonely divide, affect the avowed purpose of fiction? These questions go beyond postmodernism and engage students with the purpose of all art.

For the fourth class, I ask students to consider how works studied earlier in the semester can help us answer the above questions. Their reevaluation of the course material gives me a snapshot of what they have learned, and in asking them to articulate it I encourage them to take another step toward retaining it. Despite time constraints, Wallace's story demands we also raise some big-picture questions that we do not always get the time to address: what changes in us when we are incredibly self-aware (and aware of that awareness)? How do we go forward with the business of being human beings, when the age-old problems persist as strongly as ever but all the coping mechanisms have been exposed as clichés, metanarratives, and myths? Has anything we have studied this semester (or ever) helped us engage with these questions at all? Is there any way out of metanarrative, or are we locked in a cycle of constructing new metanarratives out of the detritus of the old ones?

These questions also provide students with a new way to read the pop quizzes in the story, and I ask them to think about how each quiz functions as an analogue for this new, fragile relationship between writer and reader that Wallace calls "the new aesthetic agent" in "Borges on the Couch." How can two people share one coat ("Pop Quiz 1")? How can a person say how he or she feels in all honesty without jeopardizing a relationship ("Pop Quiz 6" and "Pop Quiz 6A")? How can a parent provide for a child through absence ("Pop Quiz 7")? How can we communicate the universal experience of being human through art and formal games ("Pop Quiz 9")? As the fiction writer in the story must learn, both the writer and the reader are freezing cold, and Wallace shows us that the writer and the reader must, as the students might say, update their relationship status in order for either of them to survive.

This approach to Wallace's story ought to help students come to see the meta-fictional devices in "Octet" as being about the necessary risk of being genuine and honest with another person, even if that honesty results in failure. Wallace uses the games in order to get to something real, not to evade it by retreating into style and formal experimentation. His strategy, as the end of the story attests, involves enormous risk on the part of the writer because he or she will have to abandon the "wise or secure or accomplished" position readers frequently accord writers and instead "look fundamentally lost and confused and frightened and unsure . . . more like a reader . . . instead of a *Writer*" (160). "Octet" becomes a story about knowing the dangers but going ahead anyway because articulating "this queer nameless ambient urgent interhuman sameness" is necessary. It is worth asking students whether the feelings that gave rise to postmodernism represent that "queer nameless ambient urgent interhuman sameness" Wallace wishes to communicate in "Octet" by breaking apart the conventions of meta-fiction and "address[ing] (or interrogat[ing]) the reader directly" (157, 147n2). If the class accepts this notion, they can discuss whether postmodern theory or Wallace helps us get closer to articulating this sameness as well as talking openly about the role risk plays in interpersonal relationships.

The teacher who presents postmodernism in high school runs the risk of indoctrinating students to believe that postmodernism is the answer to everything. The goal of imitating and unpacking the elaborate double fake-out maneuver in Wallace's story as I have outlined here is to avoid that indoctrination. Instead, the hope is that students will regard postmodernism as another approach to making sense of the world that has the same challenges, benefits, and pitfalls as any other. In absorbing a new way of thinking and finding it challenged before it has lost its novelty, students will truly think through a position on postmodernism, synthesize a wide variety of information, and arrive at a unique, personal position. Studying Wallace's critique of postmodernism in "Octet" will not just help them understand the postmodern sensibility better; it will show them the necessity of maintaining critical thinking skills, especially when confronted by post-modernism's skeptical, seductive mode of thinking.

This approach certainly requires a lot of the teacher, who must be well versed in postmodern theory, literature, and pop culture, but the rewards of making the course material relevant to the students' immediate surroundings and culture, and making them think critically about it, are huge. Furthermore, the course becomes a bonding experience for students, who leave with a common vocabulary and understanding of postmodernism that they employ long after the course has ended. Finally, this course introduces students to theory in a way that encourages their personal engagement with it, preparing them not only to have meaningful encounters with it at the college level but also to guide their frustrated classmates through it. This last benefit validates the initial impulse to teach Wallace in high school: Wallace exposes young people to complex theory and makes it relevant to real-world dilemmas and everyday problems of human interaction in a way that does not scare students off but actually invites them to dive more deeply into theory and work through it with one another. This makes Wallace a teacher's best friend, because his fiction makes students want to do the work.

NOTE

[1] This essay uses the Back Bay edition of *Brief Interviews with Hideous Men*.

Considering Composition: Teaching Wallace in the First-Year Writing Classroom

Mark Bresnan

Near the end of "Consider the Lobster," David Foster Wallace confesses his concern that he might be alienating his audience, the readers of *Gourmet* magazine for whom the Maine Lobster Festival is most likely a simple culinary event rather than an occasion for ethical reflection: "I'm curious about whether the reader can identify with any of these reactions and acknowledgments and discomforts. I am also concerned not to come off as shrill or preachy when what I really am is confused" (253). Confusion, discomfort, and contradiction are familiar tropes in Wallace's nonfiction, and passages like this one often spark resistance when I teach his essays in my first-year writing class. My students sense that Wallace flagrantly ignores the central demand of most of the thesis-driven writing assignments they undertake in both high school and college: a clear statement of argument or idea that is articulated in one sentence near the beginning of the essay and reiterated throughout. It is precisely because of the gap between Wallace's style and my students' assumptions that "good" writing must be animated by a clearly articulated thesis that I regularly teach Wallace's nonfiction in my composition courses. My goal is not to produce a legion of Wallace imitators but instead to defamiliarize the academic research essay, pushing students to think about how evidence is gathered and analyzed and to consider both the potential and the limits of argument itself. Once the conventions of the academic essay are exposed and analyzed, students can employ them with more precise intention in a variety of writing occasions, both in and out of the classroom. Reading, discussing, and responding to Wallace's nonfiction shows students that effective writing can be both flexible and rigorous. His essays highlight the habits of mind that are essential to academic growth.

While the writing skills and practices of first-year college students range widely, most of my incoming students share common experience with a secondary educational system that situates writing in contexts that aggressively restrict the level of curiosity and flexibility essential to Wallace's essays. The timed writing assessments that have been incorporated into standardized tests over the last two decades encourage American high school students to quickly generate ideas and spend more time organizing and drafting arguments than examining evidence and considering questions. For instance, the third of three questions on the 2015 Advanced Placement English Language and Composition free-response section asks students to "develop [a] position on the value or function of polite speech in a culture or community with which you are familiar." Students are encouraged to use forty minutes to respond to this prompt and are given no evidence to work with. (The other two questions do include brief pieces of evidence but are also meant to be completed in forty minutes.)

The merits of this sort of writing assessment are the topic for another essay. It is clear, though, that first-year writing instructors must help students reenvision writing and research as an iterative process that unfolds, changes, and develops over time. While clear arguments are essential to academic writing, framing a thesis statement too quickly actually prevents students from attaining the level of complexity that college-level writing requires. Over the past several decades, composition scholars have established a consensus that effective writing must be undertaken as a recursive process; key texts in the field include *Hearing Ourselves Think* (Penrose and Sitko) and *Making Thinking Visible* (Flower et al.). As Ann Penrose and Barbara Sitko write in the introduction to *Hearing Ourselves Think*:

> In short, [our research] has shown us that the way students think about writing affects the way they write and determines the ease and confidence with which they engage in reading and writing tasks. We can help students become better writers not by simply telling them what or how to write but by helping them understand how writing works. . . . A writer does not choose a strategy, an example or a line of argument by formula; she chooses in response to the needs and expectations of her audience, the conventions of genre, discipline, and culture, the specific demands established by the teacher and institutional setting, and in accordance with her personal goals, needs, and history. (5–6)

Wallace, perhaps more than any other contemporary essayist, makes visible the ways that writers think. His essays are explicitly recursive—in their contradictions, asides, and footnotes, and, most important for first-year students, in the rigor with which they examine evidence before articulating their ideas. Ironically, it is precisely these elements of Wallace's nonfiction that lead my students to conclude that there is no overlap between his work and their own. They assume that work that features idiosyncratic and lyrical language, first-person perspective, and complicated, contradictory ideas cannot also be rooted in evidence and analysis. In other words, they feel that academic writing must be brief, direct, and explicitly focused on a narrowly defined argument, and Wallace's nonfiction fails those tests.

A key first step in teaching Wallace's nonfiction, then, is to redescribe the essays with academic language that is familiar to students. For instance, "The View from Mrs. Thompson's" could be discussed as a reply to the Advanced Placement prompt about polite speech mentioned above. In that context, Wallace's opening paragraphs clearly establish a focus on politeness and communication that is just as important to the essay that follows as patriotism and the September 11 attacks:

> In true Midwest fashion, people in Bloomington aren't unfriendly but do tend to be reserved. A stranger will smile warmly at you, but there

> normally won't be any of that strangerly chitchat in waiting areas or checkout lines. But now, thanks to the Horror, there's something to talk about that overrides all that inhibition, as if we were somehow all standing right there and just saw the same traffic accident.   (128)

The point I stress in the classroom is not that this sort of digressive, lyrical, and reflective beginning is inherently superior to a thesis-driven opening paragraph—a more conventionally structured essay could also address the issue of polite speech in a fascinating way. Instead, I emphasize the contingent, partial, and provisional nature of the thesis-driven model. Writing that expresses a clear and easily digestible argument or idea is only one of many choices an author can make, a choice that is suitable for many academic and professional contexts but not for all of them. As Penrose and Sitko write, the ability to recognize the contingency of essay structure is a fundamental goal of first-year composition pedagogy: "Instead of looking to us for formulas such as the five-paragraph theme or the authoritative opening quote, we want students to observe a writer choosing an opening move and to ask why that move was chosen—what goals or circumstances led to that choice?" (6). In this spirit, I ask my students to consider why Wallace might have chosen to resist framing an explicit argument in the opening paragraphs of "Mrs. Thompson's." How might his decisions have been influenced by rhetorical issues of audience (the readers of *Rolling Stone*) and occasion (the weeks after September 11)? What does the lack of a clear thesis tell us both about the topics the essay explores and about Wallace himself?

Once students can recognize Wallace's work as academic writing, we can discuss and analyze the decisions he makes in crafting his essays. "Mrs. Thompson's" begins, like so many of Wallace's essays, with observations that may at first seem both banal and needlessly detailed: "A lot of homeowners here have those special angled flag-holders by their front door, the kind whose brace takes four Phillips screws. . . . A good number of vehicles have them wedged in their grille or attached to the antenna" (129). Wallace neither explicates his argument in the opening paragraphs nor frames any explicit questions; the opening paragraph begins with the heading "SYNECDOCHE" (128), which accurately describes the associative logic that governs the opening paragraphs of many of Wallace's essays.

My students find this associative organizational strategy counterintuitive, especially given the controversial topics Wallace explores in *"Consider the Lobster" and Other Essays*. Pornography, politics, language, patriotism, and vegetarianism are all topics that students can imagine (and have probably seen) being addressed in the pro/con template of persuasive writing and debate. The collection's titular essay, for instance, transcends the controversial nature of its topic to offer something richer and more complex than the arguments about eating meat with which students are often already familiar, and working with that essay can help students understand ways to transcend the argumentative modes they relied on in high school. "Consider the Lobster"'s motivating question ("Is it all right to boil a sentient creature alive just for our gustatory pleasure?") does not appear until the thirteenth paragraph, at which point it is immediately expanded, complicated, and deconstructed (243).

As my students become more engaged with Wallace's work, some of them develop objections to this deferral of argument that are much more sophisticated than their initial reflexive resistance to his style. "Big Red Son" is especially notable in this regard, as the essay's opening paragraphs are evasive about vital questions of gender, sexuality, ethics, and exploitation. After a beginning constituted by several paragraphs of specific details and narrative asides, Wallace admits that "[t]he adult industry is vulgar" before immediately moving to complicate that idea: "But of course we should keep in mind that *vulgar* has many dictionary definitions and that only a couple of these have to do w/ lewdness or bad taste. At root, *vulgar* just means popular on a mass scale" (7, 8). As the essay continues, Wallace emphasizes this sense of the industry's vulgar popularity through frequent acknowledgements of and allusions to his own personal consumption of pornography. In class, I ask my students to consider whether or not this is a responsible rhetorical act. What avenues of inquiry and understanding does Wallace open by refusing to make an explicit argument about such a problematic industry? What possibilities does he forestall? Why does Wallace defer judgment in this piece but go boldly on the attack in the collection's next essay, which describes John Updike's *Toward the End of Time* as "a novel so clunky and self-indulgent that it's hard to believe the author let it be published in this kind of shape" (52)?

As these questions suggest, my first-year writing class spends much more time discussing Wallace's craft, structure, and style than it spends exploring his ideas. While this emphasis on style over content certainly represents a sacrifice, it is necessary precisely because, in my experience, incoming students see the thesis-driven model not as a choice but as an ironclad law: all essays begin with a clearly stated thesis followed by three supporting arguments and reiterated in the conclusion. While students will indeed need to construct thesis-driven essays in many of their college courses, they cannot transfer their skills to unfamiliar writing tasks (a long research essay, a case study, a press release) unless they develop an understanding of the genre's internal logic, its potential, and its limits.

This level of metacognitive skill—which allows one not only to complete a writing task but also to reflect upon and justify the decisions made when doing so—is repeatedly emphasized in "Framework for Success in Postsecondary Writing," produced by the Council of Writing Program Administrators, the National Council of Teachers of English, and the National Writing Project in 2011. The document identifies and prioritizes eight "habits of mind" that, in conjunction with experience in reading, writing, and critical analysis, serve as "foundations for writing in college-level, credit-bearing courses" (2). These eight habits include curiosity, openness, engagement, creativity, flexibility, and metacognition—all hallmarks of Wallace's nonfiction. While these may sound like obviously beneficial skills, they don't match my students' notions of what makes successful writers. In our discussions early in the semester, they most frequently emphasize knowledge and mastery—good writers succeed because they know more than bad writers and because they have mastered a fixed set of skills related to (for instance) sentence structure, thesis formulation, and citations. "Framework" emphasizes teaching practices that guide students away from genres and modes that they are familiar with; it asks students to "take risks by exploring questions, topics, and ideas that are new to them"; "practice different ways of gathering, investigating, developing, and presenting information"; and "examine processes they use to think and write in a variety of disciplines and contexts" (4–5).

Focusing on Wallace's use of structure is only one way to highlight his mastery of these skills. His essays also provide helpful models in their use of evidence and in their development and testing of unfamiliar ideas. To help students analyze Wallace's use of evidence, I return to familiar academic language. In class, we construct a works-cited list for "A Supposedly Fun Thing I'll Never Do Again," noting how Wallace contextualizes his personal experience on the cruise with careful analysis of Celebrity Cruise Line's promotional materials, *Fielding's Guide to Worldwide Cruises*, interviews (and attempted interviews) with cruise employees, Captain Nico's navigation lecture, and even a phone call to the author Frank Conroy, who wrote an essay for the Celebrity Cruise brochure. While the essay is unimaginable without Wallace's personal experience, it is also deeply informed by exterior evidence. Wallace's essays occupy a subset of the participant-observer genre in which embodied experience and academic research not only coexist but also inform, deepen, and complicate each other. "A Supposedly Fun Thing I'll Never Do Again" and "Getting Away from Already Being Pretty Much Away from It All" are my two favorite Wallace essays in terms of modeling this relation between experience and evidence. What follows describes in-class work I have done with these essays and writing that my students have produced in response to them.

My contention that Wallace makes thinking visible rests not only on his expression of abstract ideas and reasoning but also on his tendency to vividly dramatize his own research and evidence-gathering. By characterizing himself as a frazzled researcher frantically recording information, Wallace frames the essay genre as a bold and at times overwhelming exploration of the unfamiliar. Wallace depicts himself not as a master of easily knowable information but as an intrinsically limited pursuer of knowledge. As such, scenes of Wallace trying and failing to record everything he sees, hears, and reads become tropes in these two essays. He initially forgets to bring a notebook to the Illinois State Fair, and then he buys one only to have it ruined by rain (85, 91). Even when he finally procures one he is reduced to "basically scribbling impressions" as he "jog[s]" (132). He also finds the gathering of information logistically difficult on the cruise ship, especially when he again forgets his notebook and has to take notes with a highlighter on napkins. As he reviews the napkins at the ship's café, he finds "the job of deciphering the big Rorshachian blobs of my Navigation Lecture notes so taxing" that he exceeds his self-imposed daily coffee limit, "which may help explain why the next few hours of this log get kind of kaleidoscopic and unfocused"

(335–36). Wallace's relentless pursuit of evidence—his quixotic desire to know everything about his subjects—produces both physical and mental exhaustion.

At the same time, "A Supposedly Fun Thing" suggests that evidence without interpretation, reflection, or analysis is worthless, most notably through Wallace's depiction of Captain Video, who he notes is always recording even the most mundane moments on the cruise:

> Pretty much everybody on the Nadir qualifies as camera-crazy, but Captain Video camcords absolutely everything, including meals, empty hallways, endless games of geriatric bridge—even leaping onto Deck 11's raised stage during Pool Party to get the crowd from the musicians' angle. You can tell that this magnetic record of Captain Video's Megacruise experience is going to be this Warholianly dull thing that is exactly as long as the Cruise itself. (307–08)

These scenes dramatize research not as a tedious obligation but as a sincere passion while marking a distinction between the mindless recording of information and a more thoughtful approach. While I don't begin my first-year writing courses by assigning a fully developed research-driven essay, I do want my students to think deeply about the relation between their experiences and their reading and to write essays that are cognizant (implicitly or explicitly) of that relation. After reading and discussing "A Supposedly Fun Thing" and "Getting Away" with emphasis on Wallace's representation of the relation between experience and research, I asked my students to visit a public park and to write an essay analyzing their experience through the lens of at least one of the texts we'd read in class (either of the Wallace essays, Walker Percy's "The Loss of the Creature," or selections from Rebecca Solnit's *Savage Dreams*). My hope was that they would be able to emulate Wallace's openness in their approach to their own experiences and to the ideas they discovered in the reading. My student Christine Ercole's essay was an especially successful example of taking this charge seriously. "Like Wallace," she writes, "I find that I am so consumed with the many things I feel I must do that I am being tugged in several different directions at once. In his words, 'It seems journalistically irresponsible to describe [the attractions] without experiencing at least one of them firsthand'" ("Getting Away" 134). The remainder of her essay explored Wallace's ideas about entertainment, recreation, and overstimulation as reflected in her observations at the park, placing text and experience in a dialogue that deepened her analysis of both.

While the use of personal experience and first-person perspective called for in this assignment might make some thesis-oriented writing professors nervous, I stressed to my students that their essays could not merely record their impressions or channel Wallace. They also needed to express a coherent idea—not necessarily a thesis, as they entered the class understanding that word, but an idea that was produced by the synthesis of experience and text. While some students struggled with this challenge, the ending of Ercole's essay is notable for its expression of and support for a sophisticated idea; it demonstrates the extraordinary potential of an approach to first-year writing that is rooted in both experience and textual evidence. Her conclusion reads, in part:

> I marvel at the fact that even at my most contented, it is as though a weight has settled upon my shoulders, urging me onward to what I presume to be greener and greater pastures. Wallace, surely, would urge us to separate ourselves from the immediacy of the moment; to simply close our eyes, and feel the heat of the sun on our closed lids until, though the constant chatter doesn't cease, it is almost as though we have entered some state of suspended animation. There is a vulnerability inherent in the act of cutting yourself off from the world and all it has to offer; it is foreign and fantastic, to sit in silence, and think of other things.

The nuance and sophistication of this idea leads me to my final point of emphasis in teaching Wallace—the construction, revision, and complication of ideas and arguments that is perhaps the defining feature of his nonfiction. The verb *consider* is essential both to Wallace's writing and to my own teaching. While she did not explicitly invoke Wallace's work in her response to the essay prompt outlined above, another student, Tracy Tauro, exemplified the level of careful consideration that we highlighted in our discussion of "A Supposedly Fun Thing" and "Getting Away." Scrutinizing her own assumptions about nature, she writes that

> Nature does not have to be beautiful or grandiose or stunningly overwhelming. This is something I learned at Bryant Park. My experience there showed me that I need to expand my concept of nature and appreciate its smaller notes. . . . It is important to be open to being wrong or having personal beliefs tested, [and] just because it does not correspond with my ideal of nature . . . does not mean that Bryant Park has nothing to offer.

Tauro's phrase—"It is important to be open to being wrong or having personal beliefs tested"—is a simple but elegant restatement of the habits of mind outlined in "Framework for Success in Postsecondary Writing" and a fundamental element of any mode of critical inquiry. Wallace's nonfiction is so useful in the first-year writing classroom because it complements this openness to being wrong with a vividly described desire to understand the unfamiliar. Reading and responding to Wallace helps my students begin to understand the necessity of this mindset for effective academic writing.

Wallaceward the American Literature Survey Course Takes Its Way

Ralph Clare

Finding a comfortable fit for David Foster Wallace's work in the American literature survey is a challenge that raises a host of questions regarding Wallace and American literature itself. Wallace criticism has tended to situate his oeuvre in relation to postmodernism in general and, more specifically, to postmodern metafiction. This is an important critical task, to be sure. Like many, I have taught Wallace's stories, essays, and novels in an array of courses, including twentieth-century American literature, postmodernist literature, and the single author course, all formats in which I had a luxurious amount of time to get students acquainted with Wallace's complex on-again, off-again relationship with that often exciting, if sometimes terrifying, thing called postmodernism. But what happens when Wallace is not the focal point of a course, or when a course reaches back before the twentieth century, or when students read only one of Wallace's shorter pieces at the tail end of a course packed with numerous writers and poets, some of whose works seemingly have nothing in common with Wallace's? What gets inevitably overlooked in the limited, though nuanced, context of twentieth-century or theme-based courses that feature Wallace is his work's relation to the American literary tradition as a whole, as well as questions about the ways in which we can understand Wallace's place in the ever-evolving American canon. Teaching Wallace in the survey course provides a prime opportunity to address such pressing concerns.

One of the unique features of the literature survey is that it provides a *longue durée* that establishes shared concerns and themes and demonstrates their transformation over time. Placing Wallace in the context of the survey means that we ought to consider him as one of many writers who have significantly questioned and altered how we view literature, ourselves, and America in ways that are relevant beyond the present in which they wrote. Hence, this essay will explore two specific ways in which Wallace might fit into the American canon beyond the obvious post-postmodern periodization of his oeuvre, and it will consider which of Wallace's works are best suited to the aims of the survey.

The American Self

The Chris Fogle chapter, section 22, in *The Pale King* is quite possibly the best candidate of Wallace's fiction to complement the survey course. Though the chapter is an excerpt from a novel, it works well as a stand-alone piece that contains many of Wallace's familiar themes; its novella length makes it a readable size for a survey; and, perhaps most important, it forges connections with texts likely to have been covered earlier in the course, especially in the longer survey.

Postmodernism, when it arrives in the survey, earns at best a few weeks at the end of an exhausting semester. When and if the question of post-postmodernism arises, students are probably already studying for finals and frantically finishing papers, hence the benefit of finding a work by Wallace that enters into dialogue with several of the works the class has read over the semester.

If one can manage it, setting aside two classes to discuss Fogle's narrative of his transformation from a self-described "wastoid" and "nihilist" into a serious and driven IRS agent will serve students best. The first day can be spent exploring the story's themes of freedom, choice, and individualism, as well as the ways in which Wallace turns Fogle's story into an allegory about the ongoing political and cultural challenges facing America in the twenty-first century. The second day offers an opportunity to discuss the story's generic and formal features and its links to earlier American literary genres and to consider how Wallace works within tradition while reworking it.

Some preliminary remarks about Wallace's critique of postmodernism will establish a useful framework for students to think about the story. By this point in the course, we will just have finished roughly two to three weeks on postmodernism, usually having read Pynchon's "Entropy," Barthelme's "The Balloon," and Hunter S. Thompson's *Fear and Loathing in Las Vegas*. Having at least one high postmodern text in this grouping is helpful in that postmodernism's penchant for textual play and disinterest in fleshed-out characters is something that Wallace's work reacts against. Indeed, one could bring in an excerpt from Wallace's McCaffery interview to emphasize this point.

For new college students, many of whom are still acclimating to university life and deciding on their majors, Fogle's first-person narrative relating his struggle to find himself in life is sure to resonate. Students are likely to see Fogle's dilemma primarily as an existential one, raising such fundamental questions as, What is the meaning of life? What is truly worth doing? To what degree do the expectations of my family or society matter in my decisions? To be sure, these questions underlie Fogle's experiences, but the trick is to get students to see that Wallace is up to much more than telling simply another coming-of-age tale.

The existential question of the burden of freedom, in the broadest sense, is a theme most students will have homed in on; a good question to pose students at the beginning of discussion is, in what ways is Fogle free during his college years? Students will surely note that Fogle is exemplary of someone with the freedom to do whatever he wants, which he exercises by essentially doing nothing but partying, taking drugs, dropping out of school, and making cynical fun of the world around him. He sees himself as a rebel, and students will probably have strong opinions regarding the familiar figure of the American rebel or maverick so often depicted as free from society's petty and hypocritical constraints.

Since the discussion of freedom up to this point will have been fairly abstract, it will be necessary to start directing it toward the story's greater concerns regarding American democracy. To this end, a quick poll asking students to write down what freedom means to them will generate some common answers: freedom of (consumer) choice or thought, freedom from intrusive government, freedom to pursue happiness, freedom to do whatever you want so long as it does not harm someone else, etc. After listening to these answers, it is important to point out to students that they are equating freedom with individual freedoms or liberties. The next question should address whether Fogle as an individual is using or abusing his freedoms. Is there a positive and negative way to use freedom?

Undoubtedly some students will point out that Fogle is wasting his life and thus his freedoms too. This is a perfect opportunity to have students parse Fogle's realization that "I drifted . . . because nothing meant anything, no one choice was really better. That I was, in a way, too free, or that this kind of freedom wasn't actually real—I was free to choose 'whatever' because it didn't really matter. . . . I had somehow chosen to have nothing matter" (223). Here, students should consider how Fogle can be "too free" and what "real" freedom entails—active engagement instead of passive acceptance. Handing out an excerpt from Alexis de Tocqueville's *Democracy in America* will also help to spur a more focused discussion about the interrelation of freedom, self-interest, and the greater community. Democracy, Tocqueville writes, "at first, only saps the virtues of public life; but, in the long run, . . . attacks and destroys all others, and is at length absorbed in downright egotism" (98). Tocqueville's warning recalls early American texts that ponder the promise and perils of a young nation, such as J. Hector St. John de Crèvecoeur's letter claiming that Americans' "labour is founded on the basis of nature, *self-interest*; can it want a stronger allurement?" (44) as well as John Winthrop's "A Model of Christian Charity," with its religious argument and corporeal metaphor for the establishment and bonding of community through love. With these texts in mind, students can explore what freedom of choice means politically, and not just existentially, in statements like "[i]f I wanted to matter . . . I would have to be less free, by deciding to choose in some kind of definite way" (*Pale King* 224). In short, Wallace shows how Fogle's dilemma, and our own, is still related to fundamental questions about the relation between the one and the many, and between personal liberties and governmental authority. Students should benefit from Wallace's renewal of these questions that can sometimes seem stuffy or dated but are as relevant and urgent as ever.

Once students have grasped the personal-as-political stakes of Fogle's story, they should be prepared to identify larger questions regarding the sustainability of American democracy. Pointing out that Fogle accidentally attends the lecture that will change his life instead of taking a final exam on *The Federalist Papers* will allow the class to revisit the question posed in *Federalist No. 1* as to "whether societies of men are really capable or not of establishing good government from reflection and choice" (Rossiter 27) and the argument elaborated in *Federalist No. 10* apropos of "the numerous advantages promised by a well-constructed Union, [such as] its tendency to break and control the violence of faction" (71). In the light of *The Federalist Papers*, I recommend asking students what "factions" or sides exist in the story and what the qualities are of each. Following students' suggestions, drawing this schema on the board will yield a division between Fogle's father, a representative of the conservative 1950s, and Fogle (and his mother), representative of the "Me Generation" in bloom after the heady years of the '60s (*Pale King* 165–68). This visual chart illustrates the gaping generational chasm and resulting authority vacuum. Fogle describes a culture in which the father's moral authority no longer holds sway, having been rightfully criticized by a radical '60s politics. Yet, as the story shows, without a replacement for that authority, "pretty much every red-blooded American in [the] late-Vietnam and Watergate era felt desolate and disillusioned and unmotivated and directionless and lost" (213). At this point reminding students about Wallace's position vis-à-vis literary postmodernism and the postmodern era should help them see the ways in which Wallace is criticizing Fogle and his generation's failure to respond to troubled times with anything but irony and cynicism, for "all of the directionless drifting and laziness and being a 'wastoid' which so many of us in that era . . . believed was cool and funny . . . was, in reality, not funny" (223).

Students will recall that the goal of *The Federalist Papers* is not to end but to manage faction by arguing that states should adopt the Constitution and submit to a strong central power for the good of the nascent nation. What, students might consider, represents such a power in the story? Directing students to the passage in which Fogle describes his encounter with the Jesuit professor will make for a provocative discussion, since Fogle's statement that "a real authority was not the same as a friend or someone who cared about you, but could nevertheless be good for you, and that the authority relation was not a 'democratic' or equal one yet could have value for both sides" (227) may at first strike students as counterintuitive. What value might be accorded an authority that is not democratic? Does this mean that one should unquestionably submit to whoever holds power, and does this not lead to tyranny or fascism? After some discussion, pointing out that the *Federalist No. 10* proposes a republican form of government and not a "pure democracy" (76) should help students to see that Fogle's situation as a "free" individual at war with his father's generation is analogous to the antifederalists who resisted relinquishing any power to a strong central government for fear of tyranny. What Fogle eventually realizes is that the Jesuit's authority, like any power, is not exactly one-sided, that "[i]t was a certain kind of power that he exerted and that I was granting him, voluntarily" (227). Thus Wallace suggests that Fogle must make a deliberate choice to commit to something larger than himself (say, civic duty), which will cost him a certain amount of "freedom," in order to overcome his personal nihilism. By extension, the same goes for American politics, in which political infighting and party politics can trump the government's ability to make sound decisions for the betterment of the nation as a whole.

After establishing Wallace's portrayal of the dangers of an American individualism given over to selfishness and nihilism, it is just as important that students explore the positive side of individualism or, more precisely, what Fogle's ability to change his life for the better says about the capacity of the individual self. To this end, I would call attention to the notable Emersonian feel to Fogle's description of his Pauline decision to "[p]ut away childish things" (172) because "there were depths to me that were not bullshit or childish but profound, and were not abstract but actually much realer than my clothes or self-image, and that blazed in an almost sacred way" (187). The sovereign or sacred self that emerges at the moment of decision, or is actually always there to begin with, shares something with Emerson's divinity of the soul. A survey incorporating an Emerson essay, such as "The Poet," "The American Scholar," or an excerpt from *Nature*, as well as selections from Thoreau's *Walden*, can help to establish Wallace's link to the transcendentalists. Emerson's "Self-Reliance" is especially apt as its lauding of the divine self—"[n]othing is at last sacred but the integrity of our own mind" (1165)—and diatribe against conformity pairs creatively with the young "rebel" Fogle's ironic realization that "I was just as much a conformist as he [his father] was, plus a hypocrite" (165). Asking students what Emerson and Thoreau might have thought about Fogle's decision to join the "Service" (as Fogle calls it) with its seemingly institutional conformity prompts them to consider what individualism meant in the nineteenth century and what Wallace thinks it means today. Emerson, after all, claimed that "a greater self-reliance,—a new respect for the divinity in man,—must work a revolution in all the offices and relations of men" (1175), and it is curious to consider Wallace as a post-postmodern Emerson in this respect. Moreover, Thoreau's "Resistance to Civil Government," with its criticism of the ways in which governmental institutions may dominate individuals and its call for a citizen not to "resign his conscience to the legislator" (1858), offers a compelling foil to Fogle's unquestioned belief in the civic good of working for the IRS. Yet who in the modern world is ever free of an institutional affiliation (from one's work to the very university that teaches about individualism) or is completely "off the grid," in today's parlance? In this light, students should look closely at the Jesuit's rallying sermon, which recalls Frederick Jackson Turner's *The Significance of the Frontier in American History*. The Jesuit claims that "accountants . . . are today's cowboys" who are "[r]iding the American range. Riding herd on the unending torrent of financial data" (233). Moreover, "[y]esterday's hero pushed back at bounds and frontiers" and "generated facts," whereas "the heroic frontier now lies in the ordering and deployment of those facts . . . . To put it another way, the pie has been made—the contest is now in the slicing" (232). If this is so, does Fogle provide a model for how to remain an individual within an institution?

The second day spent analyzing Fogle's narrative should focus mainly on the literary techniques and genre conventions that Wallace employs. Fogle's story is clearly a "conversion narrative" and resonates with the tradition of the Puritan sermon. It also shares generic qualities with captivity narratives, such as Mary Rowlandson's, and slave narratives, such as *The Narrative of the Life of Frederick Douglass*, as well as autobiographical texts, such as the first chapter of W. E. B. Du Bois's *The Souls of Black Folk* and *The Education of Henry Adams*, both of which link personal revelation to national discovery. Students can trace the similarities and differences between these narratives and Fogle's, which is distinct from the earlier texts in that it displays a self-consciousness of generic conventions, though it does not, following Wallace's critique of postmodernism, use any metafictional techniques to parody or ironize these conventions. After a short introduction to the conversion narrative, students might complete a short written response to the questions, In what ways does the story illustrate the features of a conversion narrative, and why might Wallace employ the genre?

Having already discussed the "sacred self" with its Emersonian overtones, students should recognize the spiritual aspect of Fogle's narrative and understand Wallace's aim of converting the reader, so to speak, to the pursuit of an aware, responsible, and morally earnest citizenship. Fogle's tale can be put in fruitful dialogue with Jonathan Edwards's "Personal Narrative," an example of a Great Awakening text that reacts to Enlightenment sentimentalism by emphasizing the emotional experience of spiritual awakening. Students might compare and contrast Wallace's religiously tinged yet secular conversion story with Edwards's. That Fogle, for instance, gives a metacritique and a psychological explanation of a onetime Christian classmate's conversion, but does not discount its actual effects, is compelling. In the light of Wallace's aversion to postmodern cool and irony and his desire to stress emotion and feeling in his work, students may be asked to consider the postmodern challenge to Enlightenment ideas of the self and the rational world, the degree to which Wallace's text rejects or accepts Enlightenment values, and the possibility that post-postmodernism might mark a new kind of sentimentalism in America literature. Introducing Paul Giles's argument that Wallace is a "sentimental posthumanist" (291) can help to clarify such questions for the class. Students should debate whether Wallace reworks the conversion narrative in a way that is self-aware enough to refute charges that he is merely naïve or nostalgic for a former, mythic, Emersonian self.

Unlike these generically structured and carefully ordered texts, moreover, Fogle's story exhibits a style similar to the stream of consciousness in Ernest Hemingway's "The Snows of Kilimanjaro" or in William Faulkner's "Barn Burning." T. S. Eliot's "The Love Song of J. Alfred Prufrock" could come into play here too, as Eliot's narrator appears to ramble, offering seemingly disordered reflections that on further study prove to be bound to one another by images, allusions, and symbols. Asking students to distinguish how stream of consciousness works differently in each of these texts helps demonstrate the evolution of this modernist stylistic device. Wallace's story is not merely a catalogue of imbricated senses, emotions, memories, and desires, however. It evinces a kind of meta-aware stream of consciousness in which Fogle attempts, with some success and in keeping with the theme of willful choice, to guide his thoughts, memories, and reflections. It is as if Fogle has become a participant-observer of his own stream of consciousness, marking a kind of meta-awareness typical of an age in which neuroscience has transformed our understanding of the mind, so that consciousness appears paradoxically both more transparent and opaque than even an erstwhile modernist depth psychology, with its Freudian, Jungian, and mythic underpinnings, represented it to be.

Before and beyond Irony

The survey setting can also reveal how one of Wallace's most important themes, the destructiveness of postmodern irony, shares a genealogy with the American preoccupation with innocence and experience. "My Appearance" or "Little Expressionless Animals" may be sequenced with Nathaniel Hawthorne's "Young Goodman Brown," Henry James's "Daisy Miller: A Study," T. S. Eliot's "Prufrock," Flannery O'Connor's "Good Country People," and Jhumpa Lahiri's "Sexy" to create a cluster of texts expressing the theme of lost innocence. In all these stories, characters struggle to overcome skepticism or to accommodate painful knowledge about the world, which sometimes leads them to dire cynicism and other times to guarded optimism.

Such texts simultaneously interrogate the notion of "the American as Adam" that R. W. B. Lewis traced in nineteenth-century American literature and that can comprise one thematic route of inquiry throughout the survey. The optimistic Adam, in following the spirit of the new nation, is a figure usually free of history, personal ties, and obligations. He is the Emersonian individual, whose "moral position was prior to experience, and . . . was fundamentally innocent" (5). Adam is thus part of the larger myth of America as a place of newness, innocence, optimism, and self-invention. Familiarizing students with the Adamic figure will allow them to consider and challenge Lewis's claims in a wide array of works. They may observe that Wallace's critique of postmodern culture is not far from Lewis's complaint, regarding early-twentieth-century literature, that "irony has withered into mere mordant skepticism" and "[t]he new hopelessness is . . . as simple-minded as innocence" (196)—a comparison that helps situate Wallace's battle against irony in the long American tradition of weighing innocence against experience.

A good place to begin exploring the theme of innocence and experience in the shorter survey is "Young Goodman Brown," in which the naïve protagonist adopts a holier-than-thou attitude toward his community, believing he has witnessed the moral hypocrisy of his entire village. Since students often align their views of the Puritan community with Brown's, it is a good idea to ask them why he ends up living an alienated and bitter life as "[a] stern, a sad, a darkly meditative, a distrustful, if not desperate man" (1297) whose "dying hour was gloom" (1298). Students will invariably note how Hawthorne upsets our assumption that innocence is always positive and experience negative. Young Goodman Brown walls himself behind the cynical presumption that human nature is essentially corrupt in order to avoid a transformative experience, only confirming his naïveté. Brown's innocence keeps him from ever testing the claims of his superior morality; thus his supposed knowledge becomes a platform from which he looks down on others. During the class discussion, I suggest employing Wallace's phrase that "cynicism and naïveté are [not] mutually exclusive" ("Westward" 304) to sum up Brown's predicament. By the time the class reaches Wallace at the semester's end, the theme of innocence and experience will have been neatly encapsulated by this phrase (which can also apply to the texts discussed below), and students are likely to identify this theme immediately in Wallace's work.

The theme of experience masking innocence also appears in works by James, Eliot, and O'Connor that portray intelligent characters who view the world from detached, ironic stances, much to their detriment. Since for Wallace, irony (even its postmodern variation) has its time and place ("E Unibus Pluram" [*Supposedly*] 66–68), it is important to underscore for students that irony and cynicism are acceptable modes of defense for characters in these texts. This will help later on when distinguishing Wallace's negative take on such attitudes in his criticism of postmodern society and culture. Nonetheless, what Wallace sees as a cultural problem in the postmodern era can also be read as a common and personal one in many twentieth-century texts. Consider the sophisticated Winterbourne's failed attempts to figure out the naïve Daisy in "Daisy Miller." Although Daisy is equated with innocence and Winterbourne with experience, James breaks down this binary as Winterbourne's so-called knowledge leads him to misread Daisy and to mask, as he later admits to his aunt, his true feelings toward her and thus, ironically, his own naïveté in matters of the heart. One moral of this story that gels with Wallace's work is that, although others are technically unknowable, true relationships require that one must risk being vulnerable to the other.

In the war-shattered world of "Prufrock," knowledge leads not even to a belated, if ineffectual, enlightenment but to inaction and an increased sense of alienation. Prufrock's ironic view of modern life (tinged with nostalgia for a supposedly more innocent time) and his fear that the limits of language prevent him from expressing his subjective emotions trap him in unending solipsistic despair. This debilitating state is similar to that of numerous Wallace characters, from *Infinite Jest*'s Hal to the depressed person in *Brief Interviews with Hideous Men*.

Finally, nowhere does Wallace's assertion about the relation between cynicism and naïveté seem more apt than in "Good Country People," in which the pretentious Hulga bitterly plays the perpetual teenager, torturing her blindly quixotic mother. Yet Hulga, a master of irony and black humor, is humbled after a trickster bible salesman steals her wooden leg and reveals her philosophical nihilism to be merely a cynical armor covering deep psychological wounds. In each of these stories, so-called experience and knowledge lead to a character's ironic attitude and cynical resignation toward the world as they see it, an ultimately destructive behavior. Students will often respond positively to the cynicism of these characters or texts (particularly Hulga's character) because they expose society's hypocrisies. In final preparation for Wallace's critique of irony, then, I recommend pointing out to students that the characters' cynicism, although perfectly understandable, only compounds their problems. This sets the stage as the course moves on to an age in which, per Wallace, irony cannot be reduced merely to an individual's or a character's defensive shield against an untenable reality because postmodern irony itself ultimately helps constitute and sustain this reality and must be faced directly without resort to further ironic modes of disengagement.

Wallace's "My Appearance" and "Little Expressionless Animals" are well suited to tie into the theme of innocence and experience, though the former story is perhaps the better fit. An excerpt of the last paragraph of "E Unibus Pluram" will contextualize Wallace's story vis-à-vis postmodernism, but I advise directing students' attention to the fact that Wallace sees his stance against irony as a moral decision. This frees Wallace's work from being seen as merely a reaction to postmodernism. "My Appearance," which relates a B celebrity's puzzling over how to *appear* sincere while actually *being* sincere on NBC's *Late Night with David Letterman*, illustrates the dangers of treating irony as a mode of being, and Edilyn's struggle to remain sincere in a media-saturated age of irony is something to which a generation of social media users can relate. Edilyn's husband, Rudy, claims that the way to survive *Letterman* lies not in being sincere or insincere but in "being *not-sincere*" (185). But there is a problem with putting on such an act. As Edilyn says to him later, "if no one is really the way we see them, . . . that would include me. And you" (200). Not unlike Winterbourne, Prufrock, and Hulga, Rudy adopts a cynical attitude rather than grapple with the complexities of being—an honest undertaking that would require remaining open and trusting toward others—in a world of appearances. The final irony, however, is that he takes an obvious illusion—a meta-TV show meant to entertain—to be the reality of daily life, a rather naïve mistake that will cost him his marriage at the very least. Edilyn resists this pessimism, however, and realizes that playing along with Letterman constitutes just that, play. The end of the story is not exactly a happy one, but Edilyn manages to keep a strong sense of her own identity and authenticity in a world in which reality and image have imploded. The choice to reject irony and its attendant cynicism as a way of life, Wallace suggests, is difficult but possible.

The sober ending of "My Appearance" also resonates with "Sexy," which updates and inverts the international theme of "Daisy Miller" in its story about a white woman, Miranda, who carries on a failing affair with an Indian émigré, Dev. Miranda's failure to realize the difference between perceiving herself as a sexy mistress and being a truly cared-for lover mirrors her inability to learn about Indian culture in a multicultural America and globalized world. While claiming to offer access to all cultures to those who can afford it, the commodification of those very cultures both incites and hinders any real cross-cultural transmission. As in "My Appearance," authenticity is not what it seems, and an American citizen on American soil can feel as dislocated as an immigrant. Globalization, like the media in Wallace's stories, has clearly transformed the space and place of understanding self and culture, and there is no escape from this. Miranda's decision that her affair with Dev must end signals a tempering of her earlier romanticizing of him—a false form of knowledge stemming from innocence as ignorance—and her acceptance of the reality that she is a mistress and not a true lover. The story's final image of the Mapparium, which resembles the Taj Mahal—the "everlasting monument to love," as Laxmi calls it, in contrast to the fleeting, loveless affair Miranda is engaged in (3254)—is not wholly ironic, as the image creates a peaceful scene against a "clear-blue sky spread over the city" (3264), suggesting that Miranda, like Edilyn in "My Appearance," has not become cynical after her self-realization.

Taken together, these texts allow students to see the ways in which the myth of American self-invention is caught up in a binary of innocence and experience. For many characters, losing innocence means losing optimism, the capacity to be open to others, and faith in the world. Experience thus results in pessimism, solipsism, and an ironic attitude toward life in general. Wallace's work, as "My Appearance" and Fogle's story demonstrate, calls attention to the ongoing moral challenge for the erstwhile American Adam, the Emersonian self, or the individual citizen to avoid accepting a cynical and corrosive view of an admittedly troubled world. This means recognizing the inescapable fact that the individual is dependent on others, yet also recognizing that the individual self must, at times, choose not to participate in a culture in which selfishness and disaffection are the norm. Wallace's post-postmodern Adam, as the cases of Fogle and Edilyn suggest, does not leave the Garden mourning a lost innocence, as it might be argued Young Goodman Brown or Prufrock does, for that would simply be nostalgic or reactionary. Nor does this newly exposed Adam employ irony as a defensive shield or a weapon, as can be seen in "Daisy Miller" and "Good Country People," because that might lead only to solipsism and despair. Instead, Wallace's American Adam must make an earnest decision to fall openly into the world, to embrace sentiment but not sentimentality, and to recognize the difference between received knowledge and lived experience.

What is at stake in teaching Wallace in the survey is nothing less than his critical reputation. If Wallace is to be seen as more than just a postmodernist, then it will be incumbent upon literary critics to make the case for his continued inclusion in the American canon, a highly contested area these days. If you want to know how a battle is really going, outside the maps, the statistics, and the generals' generalizing, getting a look at the ground might be a good way to start. In the battles of canon formation, the trenches are surely in the surveys. How the survey is conceived, taught, and received today will affect literary and cultural transmission tomorrow. Including Wallace in the survey in a truly thoughtful and productive fashion, one that affects both our reading of his work and our conception of American literary history, requires some imagination and a willingness to let Wallace roam outside his, and our, postmodern comfort zone. Doing so will ultimately strengthen the case for the importance of one of the most engaging and transformational American writers of our time.

Wallace as Major Author: Teaching the Oeuvre

Jeffrey Severs

Counting posthumous publications, David Foster Wallace's novels number approximately 2,150 pages, his short stories 1,100, and his collected essays, reviews, and journalism more than 1,000. Printed interviews and a math book add another 600 pages or so. Chris Fogle could tell us how many words that adds up to, and perhaps only an *OED* devourer like Hal Incandenza would seek to read all those pages over the twelve to fourteen weeks of a typical university semester. But the Wallace corpus, I argue, can and should be, for the right audience, taught all together (or almost all together). I have observed considerable appetite among graduate students for seminars centered on Wallace, whose humor, stature in contemporary letters, and restless experimentation make it easy for instructors to sustain student interest and learning over an entire term. Some readers, depending on their teaching context, may even find my remarks in this essay applicable to advanced or honors undergraduate courses on a single author. The significant number of Wallace-obsessed students will be attracted to such a class; if my experience is any indication, a few will have read his corpus once through already, while many more will want to travel new roads after having tried on their own *Infinite Jest* or the most famous essays. Most important, though, students who follow Wallace's development from his Amherst days to 2008 will see him tackling a huge number of questions significant to contemporary literary studies in general, from the nature and viability of postmodernism to the revitalization of avant-garde forms and the interplay of fiction, memoir, and journalism.

With some strategic acts of contextualization (for which, I show, there is both room and necessity in the all-of-Wallace seminar), students can be prepared to map understudied parts of his oeuvre and, using him as a springboard, to construct for themselves larger genealogies of fiction's relation to encyclopedism, neuroscience, film studies, ethics, existentialism, and any number of subjects. The suggestions that follow focus on cutting and configuring a syllabus, providing literary contexts, and helping students make connections in the giant network the Wallace corpus forms, with particular attention to the interface of philosophy and fiction. In the interest of pluralism I describe options for compression and arrangement at nearly every turn, drawing recommendations from my own classroom successes but also suggesting that there are a half-dozen or more good paths through a comprehensive pedagogical take on Wallace. Taking up all the possibilities covered here would swamp a seminar; it is up to readers to use what makes most sense for their students.

To begin, what to cut? When I teach my Wallace seminars, I give four weeks (or twelve class hours) to *Infinite Jest* and two weeks to *The Pale King*. Wallace's masterpiece deserves a solid month in such a course, and had I more time I would give three weeks to the final novel's complexities. Fitting in just the other major fictional works, even without intertexts, is very difficult, and *The Broom of the System* is the Wallace text best to drop altogether from a syllabus if space cannot be found. I have taught my seminar both with *Broom* and without. Wallace's claim that his first novel seemed to him years later to have been written by "a very smart fourteen-year-old" (qtd. in Max 48) is one justification for dropping it, too harsh though this judgment may be. But a stronger case acknowledges that Wallace only really began mounting his systematic critique of predecessors and contemporaries in *Girl with Curious Hair*, which, as critics such as Kasia Boddy (23–24) have argued, constitutes an ambitious array of responses to literary techniques as Wallace found them in the late 1980s. If only a partial cut seems justified here, a teacher might excerpt from *Broom* the encounters between Lenore and LaVache at Amherst: while Wallace would later abandon many of the parodic excesses of Rick Vigorous's voice, the devilish undergraduate philosopher LaVache Beadsman was a rough draft for both Marathe and the Hideous Men, and a taste of LaVache can prepare students for these more powerful portraits as well as the evasiveness of the addicts in *Infinite Jest*. Including all of *Broom* can make for great lines of questioning about Wallace's development as a builder of novels: for instance, how do we compare Rick's many oral stories to *Infinite Jest*'s compendium of AA speeches, or his composition of the Monroe Fieldbinder story "Love" to Wallace's other uses of earnest and affecting narratives in the midst of more ironic writing? But usually something big will have to go, and *Broom* is the best candidate.

Of the story collections, *Brief Interviews with Hideous Men* gains the most from being taught as a complete, integral book, whereas *Girl* and *Oblivion* are easier to excerpt, if needed. Cutting some stories from the first and third collections would leave more time to concentrate on gems such as "My Appearance," "Here and There," "Incarnations of Burned Children," and "Good Old Neon": everyone will have their own least-favorites, but "Say Never," "John Billy," "Oblivion," and "Philosophy and the Mirror of Nature" come to my mind as knotty stories that are least likely to result in robust classroom discussions. These are stories with formal and thematic agendas Wallace executed better elsewhere. A teacher might pair "Westward the Course of Empire Takes Its Way" and "The Suffering Channel" in a single, streamlined week attending to the favorite Wallace form of the novella / longish short story (as well as the favorite Wallace topic of how television deals with grotesqueness). "The Soul Is Not a Smithy" could be added to such a mix and also offers, if placed properly in the course, a useful preview of the concerns of *The Pale King*, into which Wallace initially planned for it to go, according to editor Michael Pietsch (L. Miller et al.).

In addition to cuts, a Wallace seminar benefits from the art of judiciously joining important smaller works with the larger ones they most illuminate. I do not teach the nonfiction collections on their own but instead seek out strong pairings of fiction and essays in which students can see Wallace, in essence, describing his agenda or offering critics a place to begin their own interpretations. The manifesto-like "E Unibus Pluram: Television and U.S. Fiction" and "Joseph Frank's Dostoevsky" are obvious pieces to place early in the course, probably between *Girl* and *Infinite Jest*. Those essays lay out Wallace's mission of displacing irony with moral imperatives and "plain old untrendy human troubles and emotions" ("E Unibus Pluram" [*Supposedly*] 81). Instructors should also raise an important counterfactual question, though: how might we read *Infinite Jest* differently if these essays were not there to guide us, especially on the vexed subject of sincerity? "A Supposedly Fun Thing I'll Never Do Again" and "Getting Away from Already Being Pretty Much Away from It All" offer primers of a sort for *Infinite Jest*'s portrait of hyperconsumption, while the David Lynch essay aligns nicely with horror-influenced elements in *Brief Interviews* and *Oblivion*. And the "Author's Foreword" of *The Pale King* could be shown to be an extension of Wallace's treatment of death-of-the-author theory in "Greatly Exaggerated." That essay ends by quoting "William (anti-death) Gass" saying that the erasure of the author "'may mean many things, but one thing which it cannot mean is that *no one did it*'" (144–45). Do the contorted efforts of *The Pale King*'s "Author's Foreword" to assert the author's living presence jibe with this early essay's conclusion?

Since there is not enough time to study Wittgenstein in detail as a class, alongside *Broom* I have taught "The Empty Plenum" (a probing overview of the philosophical stakes of David Markson's *Wittgenstein's Mistress*) and Wallace's pithy discussions of the *Tractatus* and *Philosophical Investigations* in the 1993 interview with Larry McCaffery (essential to assign in covering Wallace's early career). In *The Pale King*, Wallace was in some respects rewriting "Lyndon" and "Luckily the Account Representative Knew CPR"; thus I sometimes save these stories from *Girl* to use as lead-ins to our study of Peoria office life. If Frederick Blumquist has roots in the heart attack of "Luckily," and if Wallace's attraction to office spaces dates back to the 1980s, what other connections might be found between the early efforts and the seemingly anomalous late work? What kind of lines can we draw, for instance, between Lyndon Johnson and DeWitt Glendenning? In these and other ways, a Wallace seminar needs to be willing to deviate from the strictly chronological in order to expose the author's career-long concerns.

What to do with the space created by compressing and rearranging Wallace? Equipping students in one semester to grasp the wide range of Wallace's allusiveness would be a fool's errand, but a writer so attentive to his postmodern predecessors and peers cannot be studied in a vacuum. I have taught a Wallace seminar that draws fictional contexts almost exclusively from short stories: Donald Barthelme's "The Balloon" (the story Wallace credits with making him want to become a fiction writer [Burn 62]) and "Robert Kennedy Saved from Drowning"; Jorge Luis Borges's "Pierre Menard, Author of the *Quixote*" and "Borges and I" (which I teach along with the Frank Bidart prose poem of the same name, quoted at the beginning of *The Pale King*); and, of course, John Barth's "Lost in the Funhouse," which, together with his "Literature of Exhaustion" and Wallace's

"Westward," makes for a rich week of discussion on the attempt to break with metafictional tendencies. A teacher might include Cynthia Ozick's "Usurpation (Other People's Stories)," quoted at length in "Westward" but critically neglected in Wallace scholarship (for reasons of the gendering of postmodernism that are worth questioning with students). A syllabus can also be enriched by some of the highly compressed stories of Lydia Davis, who, in a collection such as *Break It Down*, builds claustrophobic dreamscapes from the same Kafka-inspired tools Wallace uses in *Brief Interviews'* briefest tales. Davis has also remarked on being directly inspired by Wallace's blank-question format in her story "Jury Duty," from *Samuel Johnson Is Indignant* (Halford).

Because short stories often fail to immerse a student in a writer's vision and prove difficult to talk about in detail when a big Wallace text is the main object of class conversation, though, I have also begun the seminar with a few classic, relatively short postmodern novels (while retaining a few essential stories). Vladimir Nabokov's *Pale Fire* makes an excellent opening and might be offered to students as summer or winter vacation reading, ready to be discussed at the seminar's first meeting. Teaching Nabokov allows me to say that the seminar's unofficial subtitle is "From *Pale Fire* to *The Pale King*" and suggest that students take up Brian McHale's provocative claim that Wallace's title refers to Nabokov's, "though exactly how *The Pale King* might be related to *Pale Fire* is harder to say" (193). A teacher can also suggest to students that *Pale Fire* may provide a template for the account of the artist in *Infinite Jest*, for, like *Pale Fire*, *Infinite Jest* derives its name from a controversial, posthumous, intradiegetic work whose provenance is in question; and the name of Molly Notkin, a critic who tells tales about a dead artist's intentions, is probably Wallace's attempt to evoke the Kinbote/Botkin problem Nabokov readers face (note the rhyme Botkin-Notkin). *Pale Fire's* scholarly apparatus, from commentary to index, also seems one precedent for *Infinite Jest's* endnotes and filmography. Students advanced enough in their studies to be examining Wallace at length are likely to have already read *Lolita* (a key object of parody in Rick Vigorous's sections of *Broom*, as Marshall Boswell points out [*Understanding* 41–42]); and the seminar can keep returning to Nabokov as a reference point on the seductiveness of voice and postmodernist game-playing, on up through *Brief Interviews'* several Nabokovian figures and the "Author's Foreword" of *The Pale King*, seemingly indebted to Kinbote's "Foreword" in *Pale Fire*.

Don DeLillo's *End Zone* is another great, compact choice for leading students toward Wallace, who treated his inheritance from DeLillo with a respect it is useful to play off against the blunt remarks about postmodernist "patricide" in the McCaffery interview (Burn 48). Even when I have chosen not to make space for all of *End Zone* on my seminar syllabus, I have still included an excerpt, De-Lillo's football game in the snow, to read alongside *Infinite Jest's* Eschaton section. From my archival work at the Harry Ransom Center at the University of Texas, Austin, I show the class slides of the younger writer's first letters to his eventual mentor in which Wallace describes the huge influence DeLillo's novels had on him and details the sources for Eschaton in *End Zone* (Wallace, Letter

[11 June 1992] and Letter [15 July 1992]). Considering *Infinite Jest* in the light of *End Zone* can drive discussion in a number of ways. For instance, how does Hal's opening (but chronologically final) breakdown relate to *End Zone*'s final pages, and how might students compare Hal's "[c]all it something I ate" (*Infinite Jest* 10) to Gary's apparent hunger strike? If DeLillo's fascistic, godlike coaches (Emmett Creed, Rolf Hauptfuhrer) seem tied to the Vietnam War and the pressure to join the military that pervades *End Zone*, to what cultural contexts do students tie Wallace's Gerhard Schtitt? How, by extension, should we describe the political values at work in *Infinite Jest*, and what similarities are there between Wallace and DeLillo as political writers? Comparisons of the two writers' use of dialogue and dark humor would also be apt, and a minilesson, or perhaps even student presentations, on the intertwining of games and postmodern literature could work well, using as examples not only tennis and football but also odd creations such as Bang You're Dead (DeLillo 31) and Le Jeu du Prochain Train (*Infinite Jest* 1058).

When it comes to Wallace's influences from outside the American tradition, it would be difficult to slip in a little bit of Dostoevsky, but Kafka's tales can open up many lanes of ongoing investigation. I include Kafka's *Complete Stories* in my course book order and dip into it for a series of required or recommended readings, depending on context. "The Metamorphosis" (with which, again, advanced students are likely to have some familiarity) can underscore the deep existential crises depicted when Hal "taste[s] floor" (12) and Ken Erdedy contemplates an insect near the start of *Infinite Jest*. A teacher might also ask whether Gately's muteness in his hospital bed owes a debt to Gregor Samsa's inability to speak. "The Burrow" or "In the Penal Colony" can also be used to draw out some Kafkaesque features of "The Suffering Channel" or the contortionist boy of *The Pale King*'s section 36. But *Brief Interviews*, as it showcases the encyclopedist's sharp turn to the very short and parable-like story, is the main place to have students interface with Kafka. I have students read Wallace's "Some Remarks on Kafka's Funniness . . ." as well as the parables referred to there ("A Little Fable" and "Poseidon" among them), "Judgement," and the bottomless paradox that is "On Parables." Asking students to sift through their Kafka volume's short-shorts independently for moments that seem to evoke Wallace, I urge them to unearth and bring to the table their own parallels between Kafka and *Brief Interviews*, particularly in the combinations of the "absurd and scary and sad" ("Some Remarks" 63) evoked by "A Radically Condensed History of Post-Industrial Life," "Signifying Nothing," and others.

There is of course no time to cover the bureaucratic nightmares of *The Trial* or *The Castle* as the basis for David F. Wallace's absurd attempts to approach the Regional Examination Center and begin work there in *The Pale King*. But "Before the Law" (included as a parable in *Complete Stories* even though Kafka used it in *The Trial*) can open up issues of impossible access in Wallace's novel as well as the absurd legal subtexts of the death of Chris Fogle's father and the silence imposed by corporations on David Wallace in section 9. In the absence of a common Freudian vocabulary among the students, Kafka's example can also help them develop sophisticated ways of discussing Wallace's dogged attempts to convey the uncanny and to offer readers (as "Signifying Nothing" says) some "weird one[s]" (*Brief Interviews* 75).

Finally, I turn to the all-important issue of making thematic connections across Wallace's career. Once a Wallace-centric course is underway, a teacher can begin to ask big questions, often ones that help students identify good, synthetic topics for final research papers. For instance, in what ways are LaVache, J.D. Steelritter, Michael Pemulis, and the "chicken-sexer" of "B.I. #48" all similar figures? Is moral nihilism their linking trait, or can students detect other shared features of personality in the patterns of their language use? How does Wallace approach authority (patriarchal and otherwise) in "E Unibus Pluram," *The Pale King*, and "Authority and American Usage," which climaxes on an idea of *"technocratic"* authority (122) that illuminates much in the later Wallace? A teacher might ask students, with these essays' precepts about authority in mind, to compare passages describing Stonecipher Beadsman, J.D. Steelritter, James Incandenza, and the fathers of "The Soul Is Not a Smithy" and Fogle's section. Next, one might turn the question from the familial to the administrative and civic: If DeWitt Glendenning is a "successful administrator" who manages "not to *act* in such a way as to be liked, but to *be* that way" in *The Pale King*'s section 39 (435), why do Wallace's notes suggest that he was to become "ineffectual—lost in a mist of civic idealism" (543)? Does Glendenning face problems that the grammarian and technocrat Bryan Garner does not in "Authority and American Usage"? As students attempt to connect Peoria to the larger American predicament, what parallels can be drawn between Glendenning and the John McCain portrayed in "Up, Simba"? And should Johnny Gentle be included in this discussion? In a whole semester devoted to Wallace, students are ideally able to see his mind working on the same intellectual problems across very different narratives and generic forms—another key benefit of mixing together his argumentative essays, journalistic works, and fiction.

There was rarely anything small-bore about the ideas that Wallace explored, and, while it may seem yet another dauntingly huge task to integrate major philosophical issues, a Wallace seminar, especially at the graduate level, cannot do without some. Students in a literature program, I have found, often vary considerably in their preparation in theory and philosophy, and a good, flexible course can make a virtue out of one student's ability to explain how Descartes's "[c]ogito tautology . . . relieved 300 years' worth of neurotic intellectuals of the worrisome doubt that they existed" ("Empty Plenum" [*Both*] 84) while another student rises to the task of summarizing what Wallace means when he refers to "Derrida and the infamous Deconstructionists . . . successfully debunk[ing] the idea that speech is language's primary instantiation" ("Authority" 84). A class will never come away having covered all the bases, but despair not. Wallace said in 2006 that if people saw his fiction "as fundamentally about philosophical ideas," it was a sign that the "characters are not as alive and interesting as I meant them to be" ("Frightening Time"). Wallace's quest to render philosophical ideas in forms that non-philosophers would find attractive can itself become a metasubject for a seminar to consider: how is it that Wallace's characters grant to a community of readers, often with quite different types of intellectual preparation, a useful common vocabulary for seeing the self's pretensions, foibles, and capacities? The answers here are probably connected to the large number of his characters who struggle with various types of abstraction, as well as to the alignment between Wallace's views and philosophical pragmatism, as David H. Evans has shown. Getting the chance to meet over three months or more to discuss Wallace ought to produce in students a self-conscious question about such occasions and what the author would think of them: Where does communal study fit in the dynamic of reading Wallace so often described, its ability to make us "conceive of others identifying with our own" pain and "become less alone inside"? Is it, as Wallace suggests in the McCaffery interview, "just that simple" (Burn 22)?

In addition to the class simply doing its collective best with an overwhelming number of philosophical reference points, I like to focus on a major theme or two as we work through *Infinite Jest*. The gift, a significant object of exploration in that novel, is one such theme. In the middle weeks on the book, as we pass through descriptions of "the U.S.A.'s Experialistic 'gift'" of Reconfigured lands to Canada and of the maxims of Boston AA, in which sobriety "is regarded as less a gift than a cosmic loan" to be paid "*forward*" (58, 344), I assign the opening chapter of Lewis Hyde's *The Gift: Creativity and the Artist in the Modern World*, showing slides of Wallace's annotations of it from my Ransom Center research and making mention of Wallace's glowing blurb on the twenty-fifth anniversary edition. I add to the mix the first chapter of Derrida's *Given Time: I. Counterfeit Money*, pointing out to students that, in defining the giving of a gift as an aporia (the gift, always given with the expectation of return, "is the impossible" [7]), Derrida explicitly contrasts his ideas with Hyde's notion that gifts can be—and must be—"unconditional" (19–20n8). If Hyde and Derrida are two ends of a spectrum on the possibility of gift-driven societies, where should we place Wallace? This is exceedingly difficult material to manage, especially in the context of a complex novel, and admittedly this strand of discussion has not always worked well for me. But, when we eventually get to the challenge of Barry Loach's brother in *Infinite Jest*, *Brief Interviews'* "The Devil Is a Busy Man" stories and "Church Not Made with Hands," and Leonard Stecyk's "pathological generosity" in *The Pale King* (544), these gift theories, revisited, can continue to pay dividends in class discussions.

Wallace-specific literary criticism has proliferated in the years I have been teaching my seminars, and I do incorporate some of these essays into the course reading and require students to assemble bibliographies of such material when situating their final paper claims. But I think the deepest engagement comes from focusing on taking apart the fiction in weekly discussions, leading students to catch Wallace doing that work of transforming foundational philosophical claims into compelling predicaments of character, particularly on what may be the single most important subjects in all of Wallace: choices and the freedom to make them. In a transitional week after *Infinite Jest*, during which some students are writing short papers, I have other students read short excerpts from Kierkegaard's *Fear and Trembling* (Bretall 116–34) and *Either/Or* (Bretall 97–108) and write online posts about those passages in the novel where they think Wallace has Kierkegaard most in mind. "You are in the kind of a hell of a mess that either ends lives or turns them around," writes Wallace in *Infinite Jest*, in a passage that is likely to get attention here. "You are at a fork in the road that Boston AA calls your *Bottom*, though the term is misleading, because everybody here agrees it's more like someplace very high and unsupported: you're on the edge of something tall and leaning way out forward" (347).

When we later discuss "Octet" and *This Is Water*, I refer back to this exercise and ask students to try to sort out Wallace's different modes of valorizing choice and decision making. What brings together the drama of an addict's Bottom, the "[s]o decide" that ends "Octet" (160), and selective attention in the supermarket? Reading Wallace's undergraduate philosophy thesis, later published as *Fate, Time, and Language: An Essay on Free Will*, is almost undoubtedly out of the question due to time constraints (except for a student researching Wallace's relation to analytical philosophy or modal logic). But, in the context of examining choice, students will benefit from hearing a summary of the problem on which the collegiate Wallace saw fit to unleash his analytic powers. The fatalist, as Richard Taylor writes in a passage Wallace's thesis quotes, "thinks it is not up to him what will happen next year, tomorrow, or the very next moment." Thus he thinks it is "pointless for him to deliberate about anything, for a man deliberates only about those future things he believes to be within his power to do and forego" (qtd. in *Fate* 143–44). How much of Wallace's preoccupation with choice and will seems to be born in this moment! Students might be led to round up several characters from the oeuvre who seem designed to puncture the fatalist thesis of the individual's powerlessness.

Focused on a teacher's detailed plans for a class's trajectory, I have not offered here a sense of just how many unpredictable avenues a discussion of any Wallace work will go down—and usually, if a class's basic goals are still met, to everyone's benefit. An all-of-Wallace class is likely to draw strong, dedicated readers, and my students have continually surprised me with the insights our conversations produce: how we should read Orin's phone conversations with Hal in relation to the section on video calls and masking (144–51), how Mario's "bradykinetic" state (78) relates to *Infinite Jest*'s narrative form, or how the anorexia of *Style* interns in "The Suffering Channel" contributes to the story's examination of bodies, to cite just three examples. Wallace's mind touched and made use of seemingly everything, and the student who has studied Buddhism extensively, the one who took a lot of math classes before deciding on an English major, and the one who has seen an astonishing number of films and can recite whole stretches of *Blue Velvet*'s dialogue will each have ample opportunities to shine in a Wallace-centered class and to teach classmates and teacher alike new ways of reading.

If Wallace teaches us anything, it is that we, as citizens of information-glutted societies, have to be somewhat reckless in what we take in and process, even if we are seeking refuge in reading fiction, even when our ultimate goal is, like Wallace in his "Deciderization" essay, to reduce "a very large field of possibilities down to a manageable" load (*Both* 303). I have described several ways in which a teacher facing the Wallace corpus can make the field more manageable, but the big job still remains: truly understanding how Wallace's texts work will always involve a kind of mind expansion that keeps us open to yet another example, a new angle, the four other ways something might be put. So play the Joe Isuzu and Pepsi ad clips that "E Unibus Pluram" refers to. Throw in Barthelme and Borges, Davis and Kierkegaard. Sort through with students the pleasures and frustrations of following a Wallace footnote across several pages, and compare works that seem, at first glance, utterly singular. Try to study it all. One really can do a good job of teaching while giving students everything—and more.

Digital Wallace:
Networked Pedagogies and Distributed Reading

Kathleen Fitzpatrick

David Foster Wallace was a colleague of mine at Pomona College, where he spent the last six years of his life teaching writing and literature courses, and his death was an enormous loss both for our department and for me personally. It feels a bit odd to begin a professional essay with a personal connection like this, but I mention it because everything that follows—both the class I taught and the ways I taught it—was in large part means of coping with that loss.

I was far from alone in seeking such coping mechanisms. In the weeks after Wallace's death, the Internet teemed with articles and blog posts about him, and online communities dedicated to the discussion of Wallace's work, such as the listserv *wallace-l* and the Web site *Howling Fantods*, experienced significant upticks in activity.[1] Many readers, it seems, experienced both a need to return to the writing and a desire to connect with one another in the process of their reading. I've written elsewhere about one of the most interesting sites of such reader-to-reader engagement, Matthew Baldwin's *Infinite Summer* (infinitesummer .org).[2] Baldwin gathered a small crew of bloggers who agreed to work through *Infinite Jest* together over the course of summer 2009, supporting one another through the process of reading and interpreting a lengthy, difficult text, as well as exploring the novel's many personal and cultural resonances that had been amplified by the author's death.

More locally, at Pomona College, I offered a spring 2009 course covering the works of my lost friend and colleague. This course was intended to serve a number of purposes; among them, it was a means of reaching out to the significant number of students who had hoped to work with Wallace at some point in their education but had not had the opportunity. It was also, more selfishly, a means of working through my own grief by engaging with the literary legacy that remained. Is it possible, both my course and *Infinite Summer* implicitly asked, that reading together might help us understand the somewhat outsized loss we all feel? With the passage of a bit of time, however, I recognize a more important question lingering in the course: Is there something in the potential for this shared experience that is a particular outgrowth of Wallace's work? That is to say, is it possible that reading and writing with one another can help students surface many of the issues regarding connection and empathy that run throughout Wallace's writing, finding their way together past the dangers of a dismaying experience of readerly isolation and into a space of discussion and exchange that might begin to serve as the basis for a caring community?

Both *Infinite Summer* and my course put to use a range of networked tools— blogs and wikis, most notably—in order to create a means of reading and instruction that was distributed not just in a technological sense but also in a communal sense. The choice of these technologies and pedagogies was not merely incidental, not simply an adoption of the latest bells and whistles in the search for means by which to interest the so-called network generation. Rather, these tools enabled an engagement with the purposes of reading and writing—trying to know something about the way another person thinks; trying to make the way you think knowable by another—that helped us to home in on several of the core thematic concerns throughout Wallace's writing, including the desperate need for (and acute difficulty of) personal connection and communication in contemporary Western life.

Wallace expressed at several moments across his writing career deep concerns about twentieth-century mass media forms and the alienating, isolating effects they seemed to have on the American self. In his essay "E Unibus Pluram: Television and U.S. Fiction," for instance, television disrupts the possibility of human connection by providing easier, more attractive, but ultimately false alternatives to it: "the more time spent watching TV, the less time spent in the real human world, and the less time spent in the real human world, the harder it becomes not to feel alienated from real humans, solipsistic, lonely" (163).[3] The worst of television, in this assessment, is that it pretends to provide a solution to the problem of which it is in fact a key cause: it transforms an audience that desires (but fears) communication and connection into a passive, isolated body characterized by pure receptivity. The catatonic victims of the Entertainment in *Infinite Jest* are only, in this sense, the logical extreme of Wallace's fears for the televisual audience.

Given that *Infinite Jest* was written from the perspective of the early 1990s, it is unsurprising that the novel's portrait of the next generation of interconnected, screen-based communication devices—personal computers—would develop along similar lines: the networked computer would become, in the novel's projection, a device providing ever-more-individuated forms of entertainment, reducing users' potential field of agency to the choice of what to watch. In part, this portrait derives from Wallace's reading, explored in "E Unibus Pluram," of George Gilder's *Life after Television*, which imagines a network of personal telecomputers providing viewers with immediate access to an infinity of entertainment options. For the most part, however, the communication facilitated by these devices remains one-way, an experience of passive reception of broadcast information, with very few if any options for the individual to contribute to anything resembling a conversation. As Wallace noted in the margin of his copy of *Life after Television*, alongside Gilder's description of the potential for highly individuated programming, "So where is community? Everyone stays home, everyone does his own thing" (35).[4]

There is of course important ground for critique of twenty-first-century, Internet-based communication networks. For instance, some scholars have expressed concerns about the degree to which the Internet may exacerbate tendencies toward the creation of inward-facing communities of the like-minded, resulting in increased failures of communication across ideological boundaries.[5]

This insularity is not attributable to the technology, however, as is suggested by *Infinite Jest*. In contrast with the novel's isolating telecomputers, the networks that actually facilitate online communication today are many-to-many structures, linking any participant in the network with any other. Wallace, reading Gilder, catches this but seems to miss its full import: "In another happy development, transporting images through glass fibers rather than the EM spectrum will allow people's TV sets to be hooked up with each other in a kind of interactive net instead of all feeding passively at the transmitting teat of a single broadcaster" ("E Unibus" 186). The interactivity of that net, however, should not be dismissed; the links among contemporary computers are not just many-to-many but also two-way, permitting their users not merely to receive information but to contribute to the exchange as well. This many-to-many, two-way network structure thus has enabled the potential for users to communicate with one another in a fashion that can encourage the development of the connections Wallace missed.

That these connections, where they exist, develop in the course of reading and writing is not unique to the Internet, but neither is it incidental. The act of reading, even when conducted in complete isolation, has always served on some level as an attempt to connect with and perhaps even understand another human mind—and, in fact, the act of reading has only comparatively rarely in its history been conducted in complete isolation. Reading has far more often been a social activity, an engagement not only with the author but with other readers as well, whether in small domestic groups or in more public-facing social structures.[6] Writing, similarly, even when conducted in relative retreat from the world, has always had an imagined reader as its target (even if that imagined reader isn't real or is only a future self). At the risk of grave oversimplification: writing seeks to make itself understood; reading seeks to understand. This mutual quest may take place with large time lags, as books are published, circulate, and are read over the course of many years or even centuries; or it may take place with near immediacy, as thoughts are produced and exchanged in something approaching real time online. And the quest always runs the risk of failure: failure on the part of the author to make himself understood (a situation we might see in Hal Incandenza, at the opening of *Infinite Jest*, doing his best to speak clearly yet producing nothing recognizable as language), or failure on the part of the reader to understand (an example of which might be found in the critical responses to James Incandenza's films, which often layer thick philosophical analysis over what may have been a far more straightforward attempt to communicate with his son). But the goal of the novel as a form of communication, for Wallace, was always "to give the reader, who like all of us is sort of marooned in her own skull, to give her imaginative access to other selves," with the hope that it might somehow help her to feel "less alone inside" (McCaffery, "Conversation" 127).

Infinite Jest's emphasis on communication, its failures, and the potential dangers presented by its more insidious forms of mediation made the novel my course's obvious centerpiece—and yet its length threw something of a wrench into the course's structure. My intent was for us to work our way through all the book-length published work (fiction and nonfiction) in its order of publication, so that we might build a sense of a career and the ways that ideas developed across it. But, given the extraordinary length of *Infinite Jest*, as well as the degree to which it would overshadow much of what followed if placed in strict chronological order, it seemed prudent to reach another accommodation. I decided to spend a week with the novel in its proper sequence within the semester, paying close attention to its first few sections and setting up its universe, after which I divided up the rest of the term's twice-a-week class meetings, with one session each week focused on continuing to read through *Infinite Jest* and the other session spent working our way through the rest of the texts on our reading list. This enabled us both to avoid a premature conclusion to our discussions about *Infinite Jest* and to read the work that followed in an explicitly intertextual fashion, exploring the development of particular ideas across different texts. As a result, my students found themselves rethinking ideas they'd formed early in the semester about *Infinite Jest*, reexamining their assumptions in the light of the later work and lingering in its complexities a bit longer than usual.

Most of my courses around this time made use of digital writing platforms such as blogs for various purposes, and so I somewhat automatically built a blogging requirement into this course as well.[7] As was common practice in all of my courses, students were encouraged to adopt usernames that were unconnected to any of their existing online personas. Since the identities behind the usernames were known only to class members, students could post publicly while preserving the blog as a space of learning (which is to say, a space in which mistakes could be made without potential long-term consequences). Students were required to post at least one entry each week, before the week's first meeting; the blog posts were expected to serve as reading responses, exploring some issue that had arisen in the texts we were covering that week. These posts were expected to adhere to relatively formal mechanics for quotation, citation, and explication. The students were encouraged to produce other posts as well, which could be as informal as desired, in order to further explore issues from class discussion or to bring the class's attention to material published online that they might find of interest. They were also required to comment at least twice over the course of the week on other students' posts, with the aim of transforming what could have been a forum for the mere broadcast of ideas into a venue that was more genuinely built around exchange. At times, the requirement led to somewhat perfunctory comments of the "that's interesting; here's what I think" variety, but more often than not the comments became spaces in which students challenged one another, adding to one another's interpretations and connecting online exchanges back to in-class discussions. Over the course of the semester, between the intensity of their engagements in class and the continuous nature of their contact outside class, the students developed something of an identification with the course, leading to a spate of posts during the last week lamenting the term's end. This connection grew partly out of the shared experience of

working through three thousand difficult pages of emotionally and intellectually charged prose and partly out of the requirement of doing so in the active,
out-loud, ongoing way that the blog required. As one student noted, "[w]hile I've
grumbled over my keyboard on several Sunday nights, this blog has really helped
me begin to hack away at some of the questions I've gathered from Wallace's
work. Its been fun" (reidau).

It *was* fun, as the best conversations about good books with smart people can
be. But it was also difficult, in several ways. In a course conducted so soon after
the author's suicide, it was difficult to avoid searching the texts for evidence of
the tragedy to come, while nonetheless acknowledging the often bitter emotional
truths which with those texts were concerned. It was difficult in a single-author,
career-tracing course to avoid reading as an exercise in hagiography, even as we
attempted to honor the literary legacy with which we had been left. And it was
at moments difficult to keep the class's focus on seemingly impersonal, public
modes of literary interpretation when the material encouraged more personal
types of introspection. I cannot say that I was wholly successful in helping the
class resist these interpretive traps, but, insofar as we did remain focused on more
critical modes of approach, it was due to a habit of gentle self-correction that we
picked up from the semester's very first readings: W. K. Wimsatt and Monroe
Beardsley on the intentional fallacy, coupled with Wallace's essay on Joseph
Frank's Dostoevsky and his interview with Larry McCaffery. Together, these
texts reminded us to think carefully about exactly whom we meant when we
noted that "Wallace" did or said something, and even more carefully when we
suggested what he might have meant by it.

Moreover, in order to ensure that the course's public, collaborative work remained the focus of the semester (rather than allowing the blog to become an
odd side note in a course otherwise focused on producing the usual single-
authored term paper) and that the students' focus remained on a broader sense
of the engagement between readers and texts (rather than on their own idiosyncratic responses), I asked the class to devise, as their final project, a wiki. The
wiki should, the assignment noted, offer a "collection of reference material for
the study of David Foster Wallace's writing. This material might include explication of particular references in the texts, summaries of the critical arguments
about the texts, or any number of other things." Beyond that, I left content decisions to the class collectively, asking the students to discuss either during or after
class or on the blog their plan for structuring and producing the project. The
goal, I emphasized, was to "present . . . the best possible resource for the study
of Wallace's work." Explaining that "this will be a lasting legacy, our gift to the
field and to future readers," I urged the students to be "thorough and exacting
in both your research and your writing." The project required not only the production of original entries but also the practice of good wiki etiquette in "adding to and improving" classmates' entries, including use of the "Talk" pages to
discuss changes being made to colleagues' work. Grades would be determined
based on a combination of an assessment of the project overall and an assess-

ment of the students' own contributions, accessible through the "user contributions" pages made available by the software ("Term Project").

The discussion attached to the wiki's home page reveals traces of the students' process of negotiation and decision making in planning for the wiki, as well as evidence of their work together along the way ("Talk:DFW Wiki"). It's difficult, at a remove of some years, to reconstruct their thinking from these odd notes, but it's fun to see them once again in the process of wrestling with what it might mean to attempt to summarize a semester in networked form, to capture some of what made the reading compelling, and to create something that might be useful to future readers who don't have the benefit of a group with which to discuss the texts. As the students note on the page that lists a number of thematic approaches through which readers might explore Wallace's work in the aggregate (rather than in a more focused, text-by-text fashion), "these pages represent our combined efforts to make connections that resonate beyond a single text, to bridge together ideas that recur throughout Wallace's oeuvre, with the hope that together, these ideas will carry more significance to the reading experience than they would alone" ("Themes Page").

There are some bumpy spots in the wiki, places where the work of a single editorial hand might have done more to smooth out the project's presentation than could a collective of partially responsible, differently focused participants. And the wiki's overall development is uneven; some pages, produced by more focused or impassioned students, are far more fully developed than others.[8] Ideally, the wiki would have been a starting point for the next iteration of the course, whose students could have been tasked with editing it into something far more polished and complete. Unfortunately, however, this course served for me not only as a memoriam to my lost colleague but also as a farewell to my department; my position, and thus my teaching, were at the end of that semester moved wholly into the department of Media Studies, and so I did not have the opportunity to teach the course a second time. And more: a few years later, I left Pomona College and had to migrate all my teaching Web sites to my personal hosting service, disrupting inbound links and search results that might have led more Internet users to them. But the wiki remains, and several of its key pages have been accessed thousands of times.

In the end, I believe the most important lesson to be derived from my experience with this course to be not about durability but instead about interconnection, especially the richness that in-the-moment networked communication can lend to the experience of literary engagement. While it's clear that the literal act of reading still requires the careful one-on-one attendance of a reader to the work left behind by a now-absent author, the course as my students and I experienced it demonstrates the possibility that reading in a larger sense—processing that work, interpreting it, contextualizing it—need not be a lonely enterprise. A wide range of courses, both those focused on Wallace's work and those engaged in similarly deep readings of other authors, could fruitfully integrate the kinds of networked reading and writing platforms that I used, encouraging students to approach and understand the work of those courses collectively. Readers have long had an array of book clubs and other environments in which the interpretive act could be carried out in a social setting; in the early twenty-first century, the very same electronic media whose isolating effects Wallace worried about can instead be used to create the personal connection that his readers seek.

NOTES

[1] Christine Harkin has explored, in a paper delivered at a 2009 conference entitled Footnotes: New Directions in David Foster Wallace Studies, a wide range of the reactions to Wallace's death published online, indicating the enormity of the response. Matt Bucher, administrator of *wallace-l*, notes that, despite the difficulties involved in finding and joining the list, "we gained ~100 or so members in the weeks after his death"; Nick Manaitis, administrator of *Howling Fantods*, notes that traffic was "absolutely incredible," requiring him to upgrade his service with his hosting provider.

[2] See Fitzpatrick, "Infinite Summer."

[3] Page numbers for "E Unibus Pluram" refer to the essay published in the *Review of Contemporary Fiction*.

[4] Wallace's annotated copy is housed in the David Foster Wallace archive of the Harry Ransom Center at the University of Texas, Austin.

[5] See, for instance, Cass Sunstein's concerns about the failures of deliberation produced by such ideological clusters online: "When like-minded people cluster, they often aggravate their biases, spreading falsehoods" (58). Examples abound: see any number of *Reddit* boards or political blogs.

[6] See, for instance, Elizabeth Long, whose examination of the ideological construct of the solitary reader demonstrates the degree to which the "consequences of construing textual interpretation as a fundamentally solitary practice . . . involve suppression of the collective nature of reading" (107).

[7] The course blog is archived at machines.kfitz.info/166-2009/. It was originally hosted at a Pomona College URL but was migrated to my own server in 2011 when I changed jobs. I have written elsewhere about my early experiments with course blogs; see Fitzpatrick, "The Literary Machine."

[8] See, for instance, the difference between the "Narcissism" and "Solipsism" pages ("Narcissism"; "Solipsism").

After Deconstruction:
Wallace's New Realism

Mary K. Holland

It is difficult to read David Foster Wallace's work without recalling structural-ism's basic insights about the disconnection between words and things, and it is impossible to imagine a Wallace who had not read Derrida. Yet so often we and our students love his fiction precisely because it works so hard to move us out of the realm of failing language and into a space where communication and mean-ing clearly happen, into a conversation. Most delightful, for readers exhausted by the early postmodern literatures of exhaustion, is his work's ability to con-struct this feeling of intimacy with another, to seem to close the gap between word and world, precisely through its acknowledgment of that construction. That is, one way of thinking about the quality that many of us love best about Wal-lace's work, and that draws our students into it, is as a realism that goes beyond traditional Realism[1]—no longer aiming to deliver a lifelike representation of the world but rather aiming to give the reader the feeling of stepping into it through language. This essay will offer methods for exploring Wallace's varied concepts of, reactions to, and innovations in realism in two different course settings—survey and Wallace seminar—as well as ways of teaching traditional Realism in relation to contemporary revisions of it at all levels.

Wallace offered realism as a framework for understanding his fictional aims as early as the 1993 *Review of Contemporary Fiction* interview that has instead led us so often to contextualize his work in terms of its intervention into a highly metafictive postmodernism (McCaffery, "Conversation"). While the term *meta-fiction* all but falls out of his ruminations on his writing after the McCaffery in-terview, ruminations on realism occur in interviews with increasing breadth, as Wallace moves from his declaration in 1996 that "I've always thought of myself as a realist writer" to his 2004 observation that "I don't know many writers who don't think of themselves as realists" (Burn, *Conversations* 60, 108). In so doing, he raises questions that generate significant reconsiderations of genre, period, and technique, when posed to a class: What does it mean to label as realist fic-tion that so clearly diverges from traditional conventions? What is realistic about traditional Realist writing? What is realistic about Wallace's writing? What does it mean for writing to be realistic at all—that is, what can language do to seem to bring the real world near?

These are heady questions that allow classes to move from the realm of de-scriptive literary history—who wrote what, how, and when—to a higher-level in-quiry about the history of literary form and method, and of our understandings and descriptions of those methods over time. Such a framework offers the added benefit of connecting generically wild writers today—such as David Mitchell, Ro-berto Bolaño, Mark Danielewski, Lily Hoang, Steve Tomasula, and Debra Di Blasi—through Wallace and back to traditional Realist writing by way of their shared central goals for fiction—to connect us to the real world and to each other, through language. It also allows us to chart with our students connections, rather than our habitual divisions, between realism, modernism, postmodernism, and millennial literature, viewing each as bringing its own cultural and aesthetic priv-ileges to bear upon our constant attempts to understand the world by represent-ing it in writing. Such sophisticated inquiries are, of course, stars to aim for throughout a semester spent navigating one text and concept at a time. This fram-ing curiosity about Wallace's role in revising realism requires what is for me its primary benefit: constant attention in the classroom to Wallace's own changing form and technique, a focus that seems appropriate for a writer who used a simi-larly formal lens in his own classrooms, whether the text at hand was "Araby" or *The Silence of the Lambs*.

Such a framework can be fruitfully incorporated, with varying degrees of depth, into a variety of syllabi containing Wallace, and so this essay first outlines ways of situating Wallace's work in terms of realism and antirealism, with sug-gested adjustments to accommodate varying course levels and incorporations of Wallace's work. It then proposes methods for teaching specific texts by Wallace in the context of realism in two types of courses: a survey, which moves from nineteenth-century Realism through modernism and postmodernism, in which only one or two class periods are devoted to Wallace; and a course whose focus is Wallace's oeuvre.

A History of Realisms

Whatever the level of a course on this theme, I like to begin by asking my students what they know about realism—in part to gauge how much depth I need to bring to the ensuing discussion, and in part to see what is being taught these days about realism, a topic that has been spawning fascinating scholarly reconsiderations of genre and period for decades and yet often stagnates in our classroom renditions of it. In my experience, students typically paraphrase definitions by nineteenth-century American realists like William Dean Howells—"nothing more and nothing less than the truthful treatment of material"—or of a Norton introduction—"verisimilitude of detail, a norm of experience, and an objective view of human nature" (Baym 911). Both are fine places to start, as is M. H. Abrams's pithy definition in *A Glossary of Literary Terms*, which one might introduce by providing quotations in class discussion or for preparatory reading. Or, for an extended, pre-postmodern treatment of American realism, one might assign René Wellek's "The Concept of Realism in Literary Scholarship" in *Concepts of Criticism*. Students will likely enter this discussion considering realism as "traditional" or "proper" fiction, at obvious odds with the strange experiments of modernist and postmodern writing. Such an opposition relies on a naïve understanding of "truthful," "objective," and "verisimilitude," all of which need to be probed with students in discussion (thus providing an excellent opportunity to introduce core concepts of postmodernism). At more advanced levels, a quick consideration of critical work on American realism from the past few decades will destabilize this understanding of traditional Realism as "objective," "true," and emanating from a single, discernible viewpoint, and as neatly eclipsed rather than continued by modernist and then postmodernist literary techniques. One might excerpt or assign "The Style of American Realism" from Harold Kolb's *The Illusion of Life: American Realism as a Literary Form* (61–129), or the preface to Eric Sundquist's *American Realism: New Essays* (vii–viii), to aid the class in considering realism as a collection of period-specific representation techniques—many of which continue beyond the period—rather than as the essence of fiction.

More recent reassessments that view realism, like metafiction, as always aware of itself as a method of representation can extend this discussion of our changing understanding of realism over time. Pam Morris's *Realism* provides an excellent overview of the impact of antihumanist and poststructural ideas on notions of realism (24–44), and the introduction to Fredric Jameson's *The Antinomies of Realism* provides a brief but impactful depiction of realism as a dialectic between the affective experience and the storytelling impulse that relays it (1–11). Both accounts see realism as inherently bound up with mimesis and necessarily experimental in its techniques (making the popular oppositions of realism and metafiction, and of realism and experimentalism, fraught at best) and suggest that we might more productively explore these terms alongside each other and as interrelated, which Wallace's work—always equally concerned with moving the reader and showing us how he does so—provides an excellent way of doing. Reading Wallace's work in relation to a history of realisms allows us to examine his own complicated relation to Realism, as we see him at times inventing metafictive techniques designed to move fiction beyond what he sees as the limits of Realism, at other times borrowing Realist techniques for those metafictive ends, and even, as in *Brief Interviews with Hideous Men* and *The Pale King*, seeming himself to oppose Realism and metafiction in his larger quest for metafictive meaning. Meanwhile, in an upper-level class, tracing such a history of our understanding of realism, in preparation for exploring the ways in which it is being reimagined by Wallace and other writers today, allows us to raise larger questions for discussion: How might we see literary periods defined by contemporary critical revisions of their works, as much as they are defined by the period's own sense of itself? And—considering Morris's provocative argument that realist texts can best be read through a deconstructive lens—how has poststructuralism, and Derrida's deconstruction method of reading literature, revised our understanding of all literature? For an introduction to poststructuralism and deconstruction to assist in such a discussion (and to open up ways of reading Wallace's work in general), one might (ambitiously) assign source texts like excerpts from Derrida's *Of Grammatology* and Paul de Man's "Semiology and Rhetoric" (both in *The Norton Anthology of Theory and Criticism*); or, for an easily digested introduction, I often rely on Peter Barry's "Post-structuralism and Deconstruction" in *Beginning Theory* (61–80).

Wallace shares, over years of interviews, a clear sense of how his understanding of realism developed, making Stephen J. Burn's *Conversations with David Foster Wallace* instrumental in teaching Wallace's work from this perspective. Assigning interviews by Larry McCaffery, Laura Miller, Mark Schechner, and Steve Paulson will suffice for introducing students to Wallace's ideas on realism. He consistently differentiates "big-R Realism" from realism in general, the first naming mid- to late-nineteenth-century writing whose conventions, when carried over into the late twentieth century, and as perpetuated by MFA program culture, he finds "soothing and conservative" (36), "delusive[ly]" "familiar" (38), no longer "all that real" (108), "hokey," "contrived," and "commercial" (130). In such characterizations, students will likely identify the expected postmodernist disdain for "naïve" nineteenth-century notions of mimesis espoused by Realists such as Howells. Realism in general for Wallace, however, simply denotes what all good fiction should do: it should *feel* real by "trying to convey the way stuff tastes and feels to you" (129) and by reproducing our contemporary experience of being "fragmented" and bombarded by a "symphony of different voices" and "digressions" (132); and it should *be* real by making plain its fictionality, revealing itself as "an illusion of realism" (130).

Such an understanding of fiction's mandate to expose its artifice marks Wallace as a descendant of (rather than dissident from) early postmodernists commonly viewed as antirealists, including John Barth and William H. Gass, whose "The Literature of Exhaustion" and "Philosophy and the Form of Fiction," respectively, can fruitfully be discussed alongside the Wallace interviews. When possible, as other contributors to this volume note, Barth's 1967 essay should be read in its entirety alongside Wallace's manifesto (as articulated to McCaffery), but its influence on Wallace can be clarified by noting some of the quite specific understandings of literature shared by the writers. Not only has Barth already declared that *"all* work is experimental" (64) and noted the necessity of "rediscover[ing] validly the artifices of language and literature" (68), but in interviews Barth also describes these endeavors in terms of a reinvented Realism ("John Barth" 8) and transcending the realism/antirealism divide ("Interview" 8). In the essay that coined the term *metafiction*, Gass also describes the linguistically self-conscious writer's task not as "render[ing] the world" but as "mak[ing] one," and points out that our mistake has been to regard fictions as "ways of viewing reality and not as additions to it": "the sentence confers reality upon certain relations, but it also controls our estimation, apprehension, and response to them. Every sentence . . . takes metaphysical dictation" (24, 25, 14). One might even mention John Gardner's *On Moral Fiction* as a precursor to Wallace's plea for a return to morality, in the form of empathy with suffering, widely seen as inherent in Realism but lacking in the metafiction that seemed to have displaced it.

Full consideration of all these elements and suggested source texts would occupy several class periods, split between opening discussions of realism as conceived over time, and, later in the semester, Wallace's own concepts and techniques. But in a survey course spanning from nineteenth-century Realism to Wallace and beyond, I simply use a short lecture to complicate our working, historical definition of Realism once we arrive in the postmodern period. A handful of projected or distributed quotations from *Conversations* then suffices to frame our discussion of Wallace's work in terms of his revised ideas of realism— all of which can be done in part of one class period. However much time is spent establishing it, this context of changing and multiplying models of realism will allow teachers to encourage students to attend to Wallace's strategies and techniques for rendering the world in fiction, which understanding students can then place alongside a larger comprehension of the evolving forms and functions of fiction, and of our ways of reading and characterizing fiction.

From Realism to Realisms: Wallace in a Survey

In a survey course spanning early-twentieth- to twenty-first-century American fiction, discussion naturally moves from strategies and themes of nineteenth-century Realism to the innovative realisms that erupt through the modernist and postmodern periods. Having discussed Realist concepts and techniques of mimesis, as detailed above, using writers including Stephen Crane and Theodore Dreiser, students are able to return to them as a basis for comparison with every new mimetic and aesthetic theory we encounter, from imagism to metafiction to mixed media. In such a course that moves quickly, and at an introductory level, when I come to Wallace as participating in and pivoting away from postmodernism, I teach "Octet" and "The Devil Is a Busy Man" (the second story using this title in *Brief Interviews*) along with the McCaffery interview. Though it is perhaps overcited in criticism, I continue to rely on the interview as the clearest and most comprehensive introduction to Wallace's diagnosis of fiction as he found it and his agenda for making it productive again. I ask students to read the urgency of Wallace's pleas in the context of a literary world characterized by the disaffection and blank irony of the Barth, Donald Barthelme, Edward Albee, and early Don DeLillo we will have just read. And I ask them to identify not just the passionate appeals to humanity, which they revel in, but also the strategies Wallace proposes for making metafiction newly meaningful, namely, exposing fiction's mediating devices in order to force the reader to engage, and perhaps empathize, with text and writer. Often I use Wallace's framework of diagnosis and cure as a prompt for writing assignments, whether for long essays or for in-class exams, directing students to discuss other writers in terms of that framework, which has led to many discerning essays connecting Wallace backward to writers such as Barthelme and forward to writers including Jonathan Safran Foer, Jennifer Egan, and Mark Danielewski.

"Octet" introduces students to a wide array of Wallace's characteristic themes and strategies (sincerity through irony, the fear of solipsism and narcissism, and writer-reader empathy; footnotes, structural gaps and excesses, and conspicuously shifting point of view) while demonstrating his attempts to put into practice the techniques for making metafiction matter and for creating the reality of contemporary experience in language, through digression, incompletion, and seemingly endless accretion. Along with the quizzes' imperative to judge and their revisions' suggestion that we never have enough information for judging, I ask my students to consider how the story's gaps and failures, along with its interrupting structural excesses (footnotes), make the narrator's voice present, precisely through anti-Realistic devices. Having read John Ashbery's "Paradoxes and Oxymorons" in a previous lesson, we then compare the technique and tonal implications of Wallace's second-person address and writer-reader collapse in "Pop Quiz 9" to those in Ashbery's poem. How do both authors simultaneously undermine stable notions of text, reader, and writer, *and* deliver the comforting reassurance of Realism, by constructing a solid sense of their own connection to text, reader, and the world?

The second "The Devil Is a Busy Man" story is handy because it is contained in the recent Heath anthology, it's quite short, and yet it demonstrates ably the ironized dramatic monologue that Wallace pioneered and launched in diverse effective ways throughout his career. After a quick review of the dramatic monologue and a refresher on the duplicity of Robert Browning's "My Last Duchess" (which most students have encountered before), I ask my students to identify the speaking situation of "Devil," what truth the speaker is trying to hide, and his techniques for trying to hide it. We then look at those techniques—circuitousness, clichés, and omissions, coupled with odd specificities—and observe how all linguistic evasiveness leads to revealed particularity. How, I ask, does tone ultimately become the mask while language, despite its seeming evasiveness, tells the truth? Finally we examine the story's ending line, in which the speaker, who claims to hide his generosity from us, discloses not just the truth of his (false) generosity but also the ugliness of his deeper vanity, or his "dark" and "evil" soul: his need to both reveal that generosity and lie about that need (193). Together with "Octet," "Devil" demonstrates the potential for language to bring to light deep truths, even while seeming to unmask superficial lies, and the impossibility of ever having enough information or access to truth to make stable judgments about either. Such a reading enables students to appreciate the productivity of Wallace's metafiction, as it simultaneously exposes the lie of reductive notions of Realism while achieving Realism's simple goal: despite illustrating that every act of representation is a mask and a falsity, "Devil" communicates real truth through language.

We can then connect Wallace's techniques for representing reality, truth, and sincerity through many layers and sources of truth and linguistic construction to earlier texts we have discussed, even to traditional Realism (and naturalism). Reaching back to the text that begins my American survey, we reconsider the strange third-person stance of Henry Adams's autobiography (using "The Dynamo and the Virgin") as an incipient multiplication of perspective and self-characterization that opens the text to skeptical reading. Even at the beginning of the semester, I can't help but teach Crane's "The Open Boat" as pointing forward to postmodern indeterminacy, with its sustained distancing of third-person narration from the action of the story, its rampant irony, and its characters' desperate attempts to read as meaningful things we know are not even signs (there is no bus, or bicycle, or waving man). In the wake of Wallace, Crane's realism seems an obvious and prescient precursor to poststructural literature. And years before "Octet" does the same with its last commanding word, Dreiser's "The Second Choice," with its egotistical letter from playboy Arthur butting up against the free-indirect-discourse devotion of Shirley, asks us to "decide": whose version of the affair is true, and how do we know? The continuity between Wallace's multiplied truths, registers, and textual pieces, and the uncertainty opened up by modernist and postmodernist blurring of time (as in Elizabeth Madox Roberts's "Death at Bearwallow") and voices (T. S. Eliot's "The Waste Land"), or by the juxtaposition of private and public selves (as in Anne Sexton's "Her Kind"), will be clearer for students but is still worth tracing. I typically end this survey with Foer's *Everything Is Illuminated* and explore the ways in which it fulfills Wallace's agenda for fiction through devices usually considered antirealist, including embedded, linked hypertexts; layers of mediation; and even magical realism. In tracing these occurrences of similar techniques through texts from periods once considered radically opposed to each other, the class can consider how every formal innovation is an extension of a previous technique, informed by changing notions about the relation between language and reality, and fueled by a desire that remains largely unchanged over time: to somehow bring the two together.

Wallace's Changing Realism

While Jeffrey Severs's essay in this volume details methods for teaching the Wallace-centered seminar, here I suggest ways of addressing Wallace's changing techniques for writing realism as one possible aspect of such a course. When I teach an all-Wallace seminar, alongside each work of fiction I have students read interviews from *Conversations* in which Wallace discusses that work, or that were conducted while he was writing that work; as detailed above, doing so will reveal his changing notions about realism. One could introduce the topic of Wallace's realism in earnest while teaching *Infinite Jest* through Andrew Hoberek's "The Novel after David Foster Wallace," assigned in conjunction with the final portion of the novel. Such a discussion will enable students to read the novel's formal innovations as representing sincerity, to connect Wallace's celebrated verisimilitude of voice with Realist representations of class and social difference, to consider the novel's maximalist form as reaching back to the pre-Realist novel's attempts to render social mimesis, and to place Wallace's new realism alongside other contemporary examples by Jonathan Franzen, Jeffrey Eugenides, and Egan.

Having established a framework for reading Wallace as a realist writer, the class can then reflect on earlier fiction (assuming the reading schedule is organized chronologically) and ask whether it employs similar realist techniques. Perhaps assisted by Lance Olsen's "Termite Art," the instructor can ask students to detail the many ways in which Wallace's first novel handles the problem of representing reality in enormously different ways than does the more mature *Infinite Jest*. Indeed, the great distance Wallace's writing travels between *The Broom of the System* and *Infinite Jest* is one of several reasons I would recommend teaching Wallace's early novel in such a seminar; students' pure enjoyment of it is a second. Blatantly Pynchonian, *Broom* seems much more interested in depicting the early Wittgensteinian problem of being trapped in language than in demonstrating how language can connect us to something outside of it. A key example is chapter 17, in which multiplying levels of quotation subsume characters into the tellings of their stories in a clear allusion to Barth's similar technique in "Menelaiad."

Girl with Curious Hair can be read fruitfully alongside the relevant chapter in Marshall Boswell's *Understanding David Foster Wallace*, which reads *Girl* as "pointing *away* from the mediated reality and toward some undepicted, yet still vital, reality" (69). Students might consider how Wallace accomplishes this reorientation of his focal point from language to reality through style and technique, by appropriating Realist narrative strategies for his own metafictive ends. For example, Boswell, citing "Termite Art" (which is also helpful in teaching this collection), reads the deceptively straightforward opening of "Little Expressionless Animals" as not a return to but a "parody of the minimalist style of the 1980s" (70) and describes its new realism, like that of "My Appearance," as the story's preservation of a boundary between text and real world—a boundary that "paradoxically reaffirms the text as a site of human interaction between author and reader" (73).

Infinite Jest and *Brief Interviews* (as discussed above), then, mark a consider-able shift in Wallace's experiments in realism, from a more properly postmod-ern attempt to invoke the real in a textually pervaded space to attempts to use text to seem to move the reader beyond it. Whereas *Infinite Jest* uses a variety of voices to escape monologism, *Oblivion*'s stories create dialogism by multiply-ing both technical point of view and perspective (the difference between which Wallace recognized, though students often do not, so teaching *Oblivion* creates an excellent opportunity for review). When I teach *Oblivion* I usually begin with "Good Old Neon," easily the most widely understood and passionately loved story in the collection. I ask students to identify the "you" of the story, generally lead-ing to confusion and disagreement, which can be resolved by careful attention to the story's last few pages: what seems to be dead Neal, comforting his live self in the moment before death, becomes David Wallace imagining that con-versation in an attempt to understand why such a seemingly heroic individual would choose to kill himself. This shifting or multiplied point of view thus re-veals the central importance of perspective: dead Neal's profound keyhole rev-elation, offered to his live self, is yet another act of solipsism. But, imagined by David on his behalf, it becomes a remarkable act of empathy with the suffering of another that allows David to attend to his own similar suffering—his mind's own anxious monologue—and to silence it.

"Mister Squishy" is a far tougher sell, and thus difficult to teach, but it offers a big payoff in terms of demonstrating the power of Wallace's technique. First, I help students get a handle on the relentlessly boring, corporate-speak-laden story by developing through discussion a reading of Terry Schmidt's character—his naively romantic dreams, his facelessness, his fury—and of the story's cri-tique of corporate and media culture. Then, I ask students to identify the story's point of view. Rarely can a student do so correctly, as the first-person pronoun appears only twice, once in the main text and once in a footnote on the fifty-seventh page. Next, we consider how the entire story changes once we read it from the first-person point of view. I ask them how this point of view invalidates everything we thought we understood about Schmidt through what we thought was free indirect discourse, and how this invalidation changes the story's theme and the subject of its critique. I ask them to consider how the first-person point of view enacts on the story the same total domination that the corporation and media exert in the story and seem to be criticized for by the story.

The perspectival confusion is clearer in "The Soul Is Not a Smithy," which multiplies perspective by multiplying texts and textual registers. The story com-prises two texts—an adult's recounting of a teacher's mental break in his fourth-grade civics class, interrupted by all-caps reports on the trauma—which share the same first-person point of view. Meanwhile, the recounting fractures into four subnarratives: the narrator's description of what happened in the classroom that day, his observations of the world outside as seen through a gridded window, sto-ries he created while looking out the window, and memories of his childhood. To make the complexity of this narrative structure clear, I start by asking students to identify the various textual registers, locate when each begins and ends, and describe what is happening in each (in undergraduate classes, I put my own book, in which I've marked these subnarratives in four different highlighter colors, under the document camera). By considering the thematic content of the narrative strands in the context of their structural interrelation, we can see that it is only through the interplay between the different texts (report and narrative) and between the subnarratives, and among the different subject positions both texts and subnarratives imply, that we and the narrator discover that the real trauma of the story is not the teacher's mental break but the narrator's fear of becoming his self-alienated father. These three stories from *Oblivion* allow a class to discuss the highly technical ways in which Wallace's writing deviated increasingly from Realism while maintaining focus on its traditional bildungsroman themes.

The incompleteness of *The Pale King* prevents us from placing it or its realist techniques in a linear relation to Wallace's other work. But the novel offers an abundance of evidence that crafting new and questioning old ways of writing realism were central to his final project. One of his notes on the manuscript suggests as much: "Central Deal: Realism, monotony. Plot a series of set-ups for stuff happening, but nothing actually happens" (546). A discussion about realism in this novel might start with this note before exploring the ways in which the novel probes this "central deal" through the interrelation of realism, monotony, and the absence of narrative action. First, students can be asked to consider how the contrapuntal blend of traditional Realist and self-conscious/anti-Realist episodes echoes the structure of *Brief Interviews*, identifying examples of each. (Then the instructor might reveal that all and exclusively the significant Realist episodes—sections 6, 16, 22, 33, 35, and 36—were previously published in magazines, and ask students to think about how literary magazines' taste for Realism might shape literary output in general and dictate who thrives in this medium—Franzen quickly comes to mind.) Next, one can guide the class in exploring how Wallace once again works to create a sense of realism through metafiction in the two "Author Here" sections, asking students to identify the various techniques he uses, perhaps having assigned this analysis as homework before class discussion. First, Wallace makes some straightforward meta moves, as his narrator distinguishes himself, the "real" author, from the author-persona (66) and exposes the conventions of fiction and nonfiction, insisting that he writes the latter (73). Students can point to the ways in which the narrator strives to mimic real experience, for example, attributing the jumbled quality of the Exam Center description to the difficulty of taking notes in a moving van (276n25) or listing a moment's competing sensory impressions to imitate our sense-oriented memories (289).

Then students can consider how Wallace more inventively creates a heightened sense of realism by using the metafictive sections to criticize the novel's Realist sections, and even themselves, in a kind of meta-metarealism. Note, for example, how the "author," David Wallace, deflates the Realism of the Chris Fogle section—itself a stunning example of epiphanic bildungsroman—by admitting later that this seemingly "true" story, supposedly Fogle's own account for a documentary, was "heavily edited and excerpted" (257). And how might we read section 15, which documents Sylvanshine's "fact psychicness" (118), as a wry comment on the absurdity of a traditional third-person omniscient point of view? As in "Octet," much of the realism of the metafictive sections comes from their repeated insistence on their failure to narrate realistically, as when the narrator declares that "it's probably best to keep the explanations as terse and compressed as possible, for realism's sake," but then continues his dense, detail-packed description for pages, "none of [whose] truths yet existed, realistically speaking" (296, 297). As dead Neal laments in "Good Old Neon," "certain distortions are just part and parcel of linear English" (283). How can we see Wallace trying to circumvent these problems of language by acknowledging them? How does he do so similarly and differently in "Octet" and *The Pale King*? And—as an interesting side note—what does it mean that the character-narrator who attempts to use language to articulate and then negate the problems of getting to something real in language is twice named David Wallace, the name Wallace continued to use for himself, even after the literary world came to know him as David Foster Wallace?

Finally, I would ask students to consider the realist strategies that are least clearly articulated in *The Pale King* but have emerged as clear themes in the novel and in Wallace's oeuvre—and are perhaps the novel's most intriguing answers to the dilemma of how to represent the real. One strategy is expressed by an unnamed interviewee for the same documentary, who describes an "unperformable" but "totally real, true-to-life play" in which a wiggler (the narrator's term for an IRS auditor) sits working until the audience has given up and left, at which point "the real action of the play can start . . . except I could never decide on the action, if there was any, if it's a realistic play" (106). In a discussion of the speaker's equation of "realistic" with "unperformable" and actionless, you will probably touch on the Lacanian Real, while reaching back to compare this idea of realistic art to that demonstrated by many of James Incandenza's films in *Infinite Jest*. But ultimately I think one of the most revealing questions we can ask about *The Pale King* is how it shows Wallace striving to move beyond the Lacanian and metafictive strategies of his previous work. How might we relate this idea of the unperformable play to Chris Fogle's insight—supported rather than critiqued by the rest of the book—that the "realest, most profound parts of me involved not drives or appetites but simple attention, awareness" (187)? In what ways do we see this book, and its notes, striving to create through language *this* realism—an invocation of the real, perhaps of the Real, through provocation of our own attention? Might sections of the book intend to act like the wigglers' 1040s, invoking the boredom necessary to turn our attention away from its narrative and theories of narrative and back to something inarticulably real?

Looking at Wallace's work as a whole, a seminar might consider a final aspect of his new realism that emerges: however we might judge the success of any particular anti-Realist attempt to use language to get beyond language, it's impossible to read Wallace's fiction without registering those attempts and the urgency behind them. Inevitably when reading Wallace we feel the "Author Here," making his own fiction some of the most powerful evidence we have that the early postmodern death of the author is, as he argued, "Greatly Exaggerated."

NOTE

[1] Here and throughout this essay, I use *Realism* to stand for traditional, nineteenth-century realism, or the "big-R Realism" that Wallace specified in his interview with Larry McCaffery as the mode of writing he was working against.

Beyond the Limit:
Teaching Wallace and the Systems Novel

Patrick O'Donnell

> The amount of organization and toiletry-lugging he has to
> do to get secretly high in front of the subterranean outlet
> vent in the pre-supper gap would make a lesser man quail.
> Hal has no idea why this is, or whence, this obsession with
> the secrecy of it. He broods on it abstractly sometimes,
> when high: this No-One-Must-Know thing. It's not fear,
> per se, fear of discovery. Beyond that it gets all too abstract
> and twined up to lead to anything, Hal's brooding. Like
> most North Americans of his generation, Hal tends to
> know way less about why he feels certain ways about the
> objects and pursuits he's devoted to than he does about the
> objects and pursuits themselves. It's hard to say for sure
> whether this is even exceptionally bad, this tendency.
>
> —Wallace, *Infinite Jest*

In the 1960s and early 1970s in the United States, the word *system* had the gravitas of a cultural "keyword," what Raymond Williams has defined as belonging to "a shared body of words and meanings" that reflect "the practices and institutions which we group as *culture* and *society*" (15). Among many other things, *system* connoted everything that was wrong with government, capitalism, and war. If, on a fair day in May, 1970, four students were killed during a peaceful antiwar demonstration taking place within the bucolic confines of a state university in Ohio, the system was to blame. If entire Los Angeles neighborhoods went up in flames in the hot summer of 1965, the system was the culprit. If, in 1974, the nineteen-year-old heiress to a publishing empire was melodramatically transformed into a gun-toting revolutionary after being kidnapped by the members of a black revolutionary movement, any contradictions in the story were attributable to the system. The first published work of anarchist Abbie Hoffman, cofounder of the Youth International Party and a leading defendant in the Chicago Eight conspiracy trial, was entitled *Fuck the System* (printed in 1967, it bore the pseudonym of George Metesky, whose activities in the 1940s and 1950s earned him the moniker the Mad Bomber of New York City). Artists from the Bob Dylan of "Masters of War" (1963) to the Beatles of "Revolution" (1968) were addressing the system as a monolithic, interlocking network of governments and economies that were conspiring, even as rivals, to sustain the conditions of the Cold War.

It is of significant literary historical interest, then, that this was also the age of the "systems novel," in Tom LeClair's revealing terminology, or novels that induce "communications loops ranging from the biological to the technological, environmental to personal, linguistic, prelinguistic, and postlinguistic, loops that are both saving and destroying, evolutionary spirals and vicious circles, feedback variation and mechanistic repetition, elegant ellipses and snarling complications" (xi). LeClair presents the early novels of Don DeLillo (*Great Jones Street* [1973], *Ratner's Star* [1976], *Running Dog* [1978]), Thomas Pynchon's *Gravity's Rainbow* (1973), William Gaddis's *J R* (1975), and Robert Coover's *The Public Burning* (1977) as symptomatic of a "shared body . . . of meanings" adhering to systematicity in 1960s and 1970s America. In LeClair's analysis, narrative systems and social systems are described as being either open or closed, containing opportunities for reader interaction (and, taken to the streets, political action) or demonstrating the claustrophobia and tautological limitations inherent in the pretense of narrative omniscience and godlike oversight. The same open/closed dynamic, as LeClair demonstrates, is extended in the important novels of the period to systems of all kinds: scientific, linguistic, mechanical, psychological, cybernetic.

LeClair's formulation of the systems novel has had a significant impact on our understanding of contemporary narrative at the end of the twentieth century, and it can easily be seen how it is reflected both in the historical events I have already mentioned and in key publications of the period from multiple disciplines. Works such as Geoffrey Bateson's *Steps to an Ecology of the Mind* (1972), the translations into English of Jacques Derrida's *Of Grammatology* (1976) and of Simone de Beauvoir's *The Second Sex* (1974), Douglas Hofstader's *Gödel, Escher, Bach: An Eternal Golden Braid* (1979), and Anthony Wilden's *System and Structure: Essays in Communication and Exchange* (1983) can be viewed as having produced a collective discourse on systems, good and bad, open and closed, that has anchored our understanding of contemporary culture. LeClair's characterization emphasizes the encyclopedic nature of the systems novel with its investment in bringing together and connecting diverse forms of knowledge as critical elements of the story, thus enacting a narrative world that simulates the complexity, epistemological entanglements, and open- or closed-ended possibilities of the real one, or ones. In effect, such novels are constituted as encyclopedic systems of history, knowledge, experience, and affect that offer large-scale contemporary mappings of the imaginary onto the real, and vice versa.

This is the backdrop for understanding a crucial aspect of what has transpired in the development of the contemporary novel at the end of the twentieth century and into the opening decades of the twenty-first. When I teach the fiction of David Foster Wallace, it is important to provide information about this background for students unfamiliar with it, not only because it critically informs Wallace's novels, but also because Wallace himself was a serious student of the philosophy, literature, and theory of 1960s and 1970s America. His writing is infused with his reading of Pynchon, with his investigations into the linguistic philosophy of Ludwig Wittgenstein (equally an influence to be discerned in Pynchon and Derrida), and with his wary understanding of deconstruction, poststructuralism, and postmodernism, especially as these forwarded the debate over what

Roland Barthes termed the "death of the author."[1] In order to illustrate this background, I assemble an anthology of brief excerpts from the sources cited above, including the introduction to *In the Loop*, the "metalogues" "Why Do Things Get in a Muddle" and "Why Do Things Have Outlines" from Bateson's *Ecology*, portions of the "Achilles and the Tortoise" dialogues from *Gödel, Escher, Bach*, Pynchon's short story "Entropy," and aphorism 60 of Wittengenstein's *Philosophical Investigations*. Students are asked to read these and to respond, following brief introductory commentary, to the question of what concepts of system emerge from their reading. Throughout the ensuing discussion of Wallace's work in the course, students are encouraged to return to this background information, as well as to note passages when Wallace's text refers to systems or systematicity of any kind, in order to understand more fully his renditions of system as a way of knowing and navigating the world.

As is the case with the systems novels of John Barth, Gaddis, Pynchon, and others, Wallace's "loose, baggy monsters" (*The Broom of the System, Infinite Jest,* and *The Pale King*) enact large narrative systems that engage with an array of intersecting systems underlying multiple disciplines while simultaneously performing a critique of systematicity.[2] In *The Broom of the System*, everything from the tunnels underlying the city of Cleveland to the matrix of patois, vernacular, slang, and slur articulated by a talking cockatiel named Vlad the Impaler undergirds the bildungsroman narrative of Lenore Beadsman, who embarks on a quest to find her great-grandmother, escaped from a nursing home, while orchestrating her own escape from an addictive, self-effacing relationship with a deranged, neurotic boyfriend. In *Infinite Jest*, addiction, as it is both managed by and fomented within political, educational, and rehabilitative systems, is the central issue, but one hedged by Wallace's broader interest in narrative systems and genres as vehicles for the relation of history and experience. In *The Pale King*, necessarily a partial, fragmentary narrative that inculcates the incompletion of life and art, "potholed throughout by narrative false starts and dead ends" (Alsup), the oft-reviled system of the United States Internal Revenue Service forms the backdrop for the novel's plot trajectories. Systems of all sorts are thus integral to Wallace's novels: they structure affect and experience; they enable a mapping out of intersecting lives and serve as the sites of enacted desires which inevitably resist systematic boundaries and constraints. At the same time, systems in Wallace, as in Gaddis, Pynchon, and others, are satirized and criticized for their rigidity, their brutality, and their adversarial relationship to multiple forms of identity and expressivity. Teaching Wallace inevitably involves helping students navigate this paradox and understand the ways in which the systems novel demonstrates the homology of narrative and social systems.

Students of Wallace's fiction can be directed first to the rhetoric, discursive materiality, and form of the novels to study the ways in which his use of figures of speech, his representations of thinking, and his generic mashups inform the themes permeating his work. In Wallace, figures of speech illuminate the tensions and contradictions that exist between human need and necessity (often manifested in the form of addiction) and social institutions (schools, hospitals, halfway houses, rehab clinics, businesses, government bureaucracies) that instantiate systems of control and domination about which Wallace's protagonists, like those of Pynchon or DeLillo, are inevitably paranoid.[3] Correspondingly in his novels, abstract systems of thought, logical chains, and language systems are often played off against the regime of the body, a material entity governed by the chaotic fluctuations of need and desire and often represented as being entirely out of control, as is the case with the enormously obese Norman Bombardini of *The Broom of the System* or the tragically addicted Don Gately of *Infinite Jest*. Structure (or lack thereof) mirrors language and thought in the novels. They are unwieldy, recursive, and replete with digressions, riffs, interruptions, and asides, or, in longer form, the notorious rambling footnotes of *Infinite Jest* and the shaggy-dog dreams of *The Broom of the System*. The inchoate, to a large degree, is Wallace's game; his fiction at every level reflects an antipathy toward systems (social, linguistic, narrative) paired with an anxiety about what can happen if one entirely loses the forms of organization and control upon which systems are founded. At the same time, and perhaps contradictorily for those new to Wallace or more comfortable with realism, linearity, and logical progression in the novel, his fiction demands from the reader attention to rhetorical and generic patterns that emerge at heightened moments (often, long moments) in which the narrative language itself seems divided between form and formlessness, system and chaos.

Teaching Wallace is thus a matter of teaching fiction in pieces. In his compelling close reading of *Infinite Jest* within multiple historical, literary, and critical contexts, Stephen J. Burn observes "the complications that can emerge from trying to map [the] larger world" of a novel that so clearly "depends on the reader reconstructing a larger narrative from a number of subtle hints and apparently incidental details"; a "sufficiently detailed map" of the novel, Burn states, "would . . . probably be even larger than the intimidating 1079-page terrain that already makes up the work" (*Reader's Guide* 33–34). Indeed, *Infinite Jest* is a fragmentary novel of many scattered parts, an intricate jigsaw puzzle in which at least half of the pieces are missing and must be reconstructed or reimagined as elements within continually shifting contexts. The reader of Wallace's novels must be prepared to be both fascinated by the text and, at times, frustrated by the work required to fully engage it; hence, the following teaching techniques have proved useful, especially for newer readers: first, allowing students to openly confront the frustrations and difficulties they may encounter in reading Wallace, enabling them to see what assumptions they may have about the novel as a genre, and how Wallace contravenes these; second, encouraging symptomatic reading by paying attention to the implications of a limited passage or riff of a novel such as *Infinite Jest* as a recursive element echoed by other passages scattered throughout the novel, without undue attention to how a given part fits into an unmapped whole.

One such passage that illuminates Wallace's use of rhetorical figures to illustrate the complications inherent in systematicity occurs in *Infinite Jest*, where Michael Pemulis, rival and friend of the novel's titular protagonist, Hal Incandenza, conducts an extended conversation with Idris Arslanian, a younger student at the Enfield Tennis Academy. The one-sided conversation concerns a complex physical process called "annular fusion" that Arslanian is attempting to understand as a student in the outlandish physics class taught at the academy, which has twelve-year-olds engaging in advanced theories of nuclear physics and quantum mechanics. Blindfolded by his tennis coach as a training exercise and hoping to be guided to a lavatory, Arslanian listens patiently to Pemulis's elaborations. Pemulis, knowing he has a captive audience, insists on explaining the process in detail while extending the range of its analogous presence in contemporary politics, waste disposal, and social relationships. Pemulis's discourse is labyrinthine and open-ended—like the novel itself, it seems as if it could go on forever or stop at any time—and it promises to continue as Arslanian lurches toward the bathroom, bodily urgency at last trumping logorrhea. What Pemulis is attempting to explain to Arslanian is how the disposal of radioactive products from fusion has led to the Great Concavity, a huge and ever-growing waste disposal site that takes up hundreds of thousands of acres in O.N.A.N., or the Organization of North American Nations, the volatile political alliance of Mexico, Canada, and the United States in the novel's near-future setting.

According to Pemulis, getting rid of the nuclear waste produced by fusion involves an "anathematic" process in which toxic materials are used to convert waste into fuel, a method of disposal and "recycling" that produces endless rotations of barren wastelands where nothing can survive, with verdant jungles teeming with mutant life, "rapacial feral hamsters and insects of Volkswagen size and infantile giganticism" (573). In this hyperbolic form of waste disposal as crop rotation, Pemulis explains the rapid transformation or "catapulting" of the ecosystem as an instance of "[a]ccelerated phenomena, which is actually equivalent to an incredible *slowing down* of time. The mnemonic rhyme . . . to remember here is 'Wasteland to lush: time's in no rush'" (573). In stating the paradox of this system of energy production and waste disposal, Pemulis underscores its functional circularity and redundancy, for the "annular theory" of fusion deployed in the environmental practice of the American republic in the novel's early twenty-first century is one "that can produce waste that's fuel for a process whose waste is fuel for the fusion" (572).

This example can stand for others in Wallace's fiction in which systems are explored for their inherent contradictions. The theory of annular fusion, put into practice, has resulted in cycles of artificially induced environmental catastrophe and sped-up evolutionary mutation ever encroaching upon the landscape around it, since the process of fuel-to-waste-to-fuel-again can continue only if the black hole of the Great Concavity can grow beyond its bounds. The "system" upon which Pemulis expounds involves at once a quickening of biological life and a deceleration of time; it is both entropic—extracting more energy from the universe than it gives back, hence the need for ever-increasing amounts of space for its functioning—and hypertropic as it produces ever-larger versions of life in its verdant cycle; it is territorially open and philosophically closed. Wallace encourages his readers to consider figures such as that of annular fusion on several levels. Published at a time when the consequences of global warming were finally beginning to be perceived by a larger public, the novel is clearly parodying the idea that the by-products of the devastation induced on planet Earth by technological advances could be viewed as "solutions" to the problems of pollution and waste produced by those same advances. Not only does Wallace explode the fantasy of scientific theories providing, in theory, an adequate rejoinder to the worst excesses of the ensuing practices issuing from them; he also extends in such passages as Pemulis's long-winded explanation a critique of any number of narrative logics that serve as a cover for that which is self-contradictory, self-destructive (for cultures and worlds, as well as for individuals), and irrational. Students of Wallace's fiction can be encouraged in such instances to explore assumptions about what narratives, theories, and explanations are supposed to do, and upon what principles they operate. They can not only consider the insights and limitations of thinking systematically, but also use such occasions to reflect on systems in general, which in Wallace's novels are conflated entities (body, mind, school, nation, world are homologous) that can be viewed, like the waste-fuel cycles associated with annular fusion, as alternatively destructive and energizing.

The epigraph to this essay offers another perspective on the representation of systems in Wallace's fiction, particularly as they illuminate how humans relate to the material objects of a reality that for Wallace is a mosaic of overlapping systems. In his essays, stories, and novels, Wallace often depicts the spatial arrangement of objects in the world—constructed or natural—as, perhaps anthropomorphically, intention-bearing, such that the relation between people, space, and objects involves questions about affect, human purpose, and the dividing lines between animate and inanimate matter.[4] In the cited passage, we learn of Hal's elaborate machinations as he makes a daily journey to the Enfield Tennis Academy's underground Pump Room, where he can get high in complete secrecy, then return to the upper world via a series of tunnels into an "unoccupied men's room and brush his teeth with a portable Oral-B and wash his face and apply eyedrops and Old Spice and a plug of wintergreen Kodiak and then saunter back to the sauna area and ascend to ground level looking and smelling right as rain" (53–54). Hal's movements are ritualistic and programmed, taking place as a traversal of confined architectural spaces that offer a route to isolation and privacy, fulfilling his obsessive, undefined need for secrecy. A specific set of spatial arrangements and a determinate array of objects seem to offer Hal a form of comfort that his secret identity is intact and his presence above ground apparently normal. In effect, despite the immense void that exists between inner and outer selves in Wallace's novels, systems of objects, spaces, and actions allow Hal to maintain the illusion that both secret and visible selves can coexist, entirely separate from each other, and that one can move between them at will as long as the rituals are observed.

This passage and others like it in Wallace's fiction—those depicting a psycho-geographic and pharmacological tour of Boston in the footnotes of *Infinite Jest*, the navigation of the telecommunications tunnels in *The Broom of the System,* or the cartographies of *The Pale King*—offer students a unique opportunity to consider how the passages map both reality and fiction, for finding one's way through the plethora of stories, scenes, and characters that fill Wallace's novels is key to the pleasurable work of reading them. Wallace encourages his readers to interactively engage with his novels as open-ended worlds that depend a great deal on the reader's attention to and navigation of their word-objects for their envisioning and comprehension as partial systems. As Burn suggests in his reader's guide to *Infinite Jest,* the kind of readerly interaction that Wallace promotes is inevitably directed outward, toward a reality that is as frayed, complex, and in need of mapping as that of his novels: "Like Richard Powers' narrative model, where the purpose of fiction is ultimately to reawaken the reader 'to the irreducible heft, weight, and texture of the entrapping world' ("Literary Devices" 15), part of Wallace's aim seems to be to break the closed circle and direct the reader outside the book, to find what has escaped the encyclopedia" (29). Student assignments for reading a novel such as *Infinite Jest* that would heighten attention to this aspect of reading Wallace might be to produce a map of the Enfield Tennis Academy,[5] develop a list of the brand-name objects mentioned in the novel (especially since time itself is subsidized in the novel's near future, the years sequenced in a pattern of rotation and named after national brands, such as the Year of Glad or the Year of the Whopper), or collect and anthologize the novel's scattered jokes, dreams, and hallucinatory fantasies. There are numerous additional ways in which mapping *Infinite Jest,* or any of the novel's parts, might proceed, but the exercise will offer students insight into how much Wallace's fiction is given over to thinking about how to map a world of material, corporeal, and linguistic objects, and how all maps are illusory in their totality. Mapping the novel illuminates, as well, the kinds of investments that the reader must make in order to manage its inventory, navigate its fictional spaces, and link its contents to the "heft, weight, and texture" of the contextualizing reality to which the novel bears reference.

The concept of a reader who must "find what has escaped the encyclopedia" suggests yet another aspect of Wallace's interest in systems—the archival and taxonomic systems to be found in an encyclopedia. As noted earlier, like the systems novels of the '60s and '70s, Wallace's novels are encyclopedic, especially in regard to genre: each is a multigeneric pastiche of narrative types to be encountered both within the local contexts of the novel being read and within the global contexts of the history and provenance of a specific generic kind. In Wallace's novels, the reader encounters an enjambed array of hallucinations, dreams, shaggy-dog stories, extended dialogues, extended internal monologues, (famously) footnotes and footnotes to footnotes, cartographic descriptions, mythological parodies, philosophical discourses, action sequences (such as the tennis matches described in *Infinite Jest*), skits, jokes, word games—the list is seemingly endless. Teaching Wallace can be, in effect, a way of teaching genre, and a way of demonstrating how genres interact both within a specific novel and across literary history.

For Wallace, systems such as genre are a way of framing, mediating, and routing knowledge, information, and vision. A particularly revealing example of Wallace's use of genre as a form of knowledge, and as a means of formulating knowledge, occurs in *Infinite Jest*, where scattered passages document a continuing dialogue that takes place between two key characters in the novel, Rémy Marathe and Hugh Steeply. The conversation—frequently interrupted by the many other interpolated narratives of *Infinite Jest*—takes place on a desert outcrop overlooking the city of Tucson, Arizona, and involves a protracted discussion of the revolutionary and nationalistic political positions taken by the two parties. In the shadow game of their conversations, Marathe and Steeply not only exchange political views and share secrets and pseudosecrets, they also undertake a serious dialogue about responsibility for one's actions and the consequences of fanatically buying into one ideology or another. While seeming merely to parody politics in the acronyms and spy-versus-spy machinations inherent in these scenes, Wallace in effect uses the Platonic dialogue—a genre of conversation leading to knowledge and enlightenment through a series of formal queries and responses—in order to illuminate the complex set of connections that exist between discursive and political systems.

At one point in the novel, Marathe and Steeply are vigorously debating the differences between libertarian views of community and identity (Steeply) and, broadly speaking, socialist views of community and identity (Marathe) that adhere to their political views as, respectively, a pro-US nationalist and an anti-O.N.A.N. terrorist revolutionary. Familiar with Jesuit pedagogy and its indebtedness to both Platonic and catechetical dialogic traditions, Marathe introduces into the conversation the example of a single-serving can of Habitant Soup, the canned version of a traditional French-Canadian pea soup. In the meandering discussion that follows, the interlocutors debate the question—as, in the example, both of them are voraciously hungry and the can offers only one serving—about who should be allowed to consume the soup: Steeply, who has been arguing that American history and national identity are inexplicably tied to the pursuit of individual liberty and happiness, or Marathe, who has been arguing that the individual pursuit of happiness inevitably comes at the painful expense of one or several other individuals. The intricacies of the debate are too labyrinthine to recapitulate here, but for the reader the philosophical consequences of the dispute are painfully clear: favoring either individual or communal choice, the good of the one or the good of the many, necessarily involves the suffering of others. Wallace uses the form of dialogue between these two characters to ferret out the ways in which political ideologies that adhere to notions of liberty and freedom, and operative concepts such as enlightened self-interest and messianic self-sacrifice, are aligned with fundamental matters such as survival and desire that have their basis in biology as much as politics or philosophy. In the fashion of self-questioning Platonic discourse, there is no simple "right side" to the debate between Marathe and Steeply, only an unearthing of assumptions that can be raised by questions that arise from the assumptions themselves. The Marathe-

Steeply conversations of *Infinite Jest* thus offer occasions for students to engage with Wallace's dialogues as a means of self-understanding through dialogue. While initially artificial, dividing a class studying this novel into "pro-Marathe" and "pro-Steeply" camps, then asking each group to formulate the arguments that support the respective positions inherent in a collective politics and an individual politics, can illuminate the specificities of Wallace's text and the notion, implicit in the Marathe-Steeply dialogues, that for Wallace both views can exist simultaneously as contradictions to be not resolved but held in balance.

There are many other examples of such discursive logics operating in the interstices of Wallace's generic mashups that provide students with opportunities to understand how genres, once recognized, can be used to illuminate one of the primary questions that occurs throughout his work, fictional and nonfictional: how do we think and feel, and why do we think and feel that way? In *Infinite Jest*, Hal and Mario's debate about lying, or Avril Incandenza's monologue on sadness; Lenore Beadsman's excursus on the poetics of antinomy in *The Broom of the System*; the autobiography of sweating in *The Pale King*—all can be read both separately and in the context of the novels as instances where Wallace uses form and kind to illuminate a tortuous set of connections between emotion, thought, and the social order. Wallace offers systems to his readers—generic, linguistic, philosophical, social, technological—not so much as answers to the central question I've just raised, but as the means by which such questions can be formulated in the first place. He wants his readers to think both inside and outside systems as they evolve their own system of reading him. The requirements for doing so he leaves up to the individual, and it is, perhaps, the independence and responsibility that he confers upon the reader to make sense of his world and ours that make teaching David Foster Wallace a distinctive challenge and pleasure.

NOTES

[1] See Wallace's essay "Greatly Exaggerated" for his commentary on this issue.

[2] The famous phrase is that of Henry James, and occurs in the preface to *The Tragic Muse*, where he criticizes Thackeray, Dumas, and Tolstoy for writing undisciplined narratives that contain too many "elements of the accidental and the arbitrary" (*Art of the Novel* 84).

[3] In a contemporary register, Wallace thus reiterates one of the consistent themes of American literature, according to Tony Tanner—the contestation between the internal freedom of the individual and the constraints of the social order. In *City of Words*, Tanner suggests how contemporary American fiction stages this contestation as one taking place between narrative form and linguistic freedom, a strategy also deployed by Wallace, conflating literary, linguistic, and social forms in the process of breaking them down.

[4] For an in-depth discussion of how Wallace, influenced by Wittengenstein, regards language itself as composed of object and, thus, views language systems as composed of separable objects arrayed within the space of a sentence just as solar systems are composed of separate planets arrayed within a "space" we are still at odds to fully understand or

define, see Boswell, 21–28. As glossed by Burn, 109–110, this suggests the extent to which Wallace regards individuals as at least partially composed by their relation to objects, including language objects.

[5] The idea for mapping the Enfield Tennis Academy derives from Carlisle's *Elegant Complexity*, a fascinating but somewhat chaotic inventory of *Infinite Jest*'s many parts. Carlisle provides a discussion of the spatial organization of the academy, along with a heart-shaped map of its buildings. Readers of *Infinite Jest* who develop their own mapping systems may come up with an entirely different representation of the academy's, and the novel's, spatial organization.

Twenty-First-Century Wallace:
Teaching Wallace amid His Contemporaries

Robert L. McLaughlin

The variety, richness, and complexity of David Foster Wallace's work offer challenges to teachers and students. They also offer infinite possibilities. Wallace is a central figure in the transition from the high postmodern fiction of the 1960s and 1970s to a new kind of fiction of the 1990s and the twenty-first century. In his essays and interviews he reassesses postmodernism and makes the case for a fiction that cares less about language games and more about connecting with the reader. In his fiction he bravely struggles with these issues, recognizing the formal and stylistic innovations of postmodern fiction and the linguistic turn of poststructural theory but nevertheless seeking to write through them so as to touch something real outside language. My approach to teaching Wallace's work is to place it in two contexts: the reaction against postmodernism that arose in the 1990s and the fiction of other writers of his generation in the United States.

I teach Wallace in an undergraduate survey course on contemporary literature of the United States and in several graduate seminars, some of them surveys, some more focused. In all my classes I strive to minimize lecturing and to foster discussion, using a range of techniques: seating the class in a circle; having three to five students per class responsible for preparing talking points—questions, areas of confusion, or points of interest; assigning each student a topic for a research presentation; with graduate students, making each student responsible for leading the discussion for one class meeting. My goals are to establish contexts and to create opportunities for students to articulate and argue their own answers to questions such as the following:

> How does Wallace understand postmodernism? From what you've learned about postmodern literature, to what extent do you agree with his assessment?
>
> What is Wallace's critique of postmodernism? Why does he see its usefulness as having reached its end?
>
> How does his critique agree with or challenge the views of other authors, critics, and theorists we've read?
>
> To what extent does Wallace's own fiction match the kind of fiction he calls for?
>
> In what ways do you see Wallace's contemporaries responding to or reacting against postmodernism? How is their work like Wallace's, and how does it differ?
>
> Taking Wallace and his contemporaries together, can you articulate conclusions about the state of fiction written in the United States in the

twenty-first century? How is it like the postmodern fiction of the second half of the twentieth century, and how is it doing something different?

Depending on the course, I can ask the students to go into these questions in more or less detail. In the undergraduate survey course, having spent the bulk of the semester on postmodern literature, I have only three or four weeks to spend on millennial fiction, enough time to introduce the students to the questions but not enough time to develop full answers. In a graduate seminar focusing on twenty-first-century fiction, I can spend the whole semester encouraging the students to develop their answers to these questions; the more theory, criticism, and fiction they read, the more complex their understanding of the new century's fiction grows.

Regardless of the course, I pursue the previously mentioned questions by drawing on readings from three areas: contexts, criticism, and fiction. If the course allows time, we read in these areas in some depth. If not, we all read what strike me as the most important texts; others are assigned as research presentation topics or are suggested as future reading.

Contexts

I include in this group texts, mostly from the 1990s, that assess the state of postmodern fiction near the century's end and suggest new directions for fiction. The most important texts, for me, are Wallace's essay "E Unibus Pluram: Television and U.S. Fiction" and his interview with Larry McCaffery, both originally published in the *Review of Contemporary Fiction*. In these pieces Wallace argues that postmodernism's rebellious promise, so necessary in the 1950s and 1960s for questioning authority and challenging master narratives, had been reduced, by the 1990s, to an all-purpose irony that tears down every positive assertion, mocks all sincerity, disrupts the possibilities for human connection, and fosters an intense loneliness that for Wallace is the most urgent problem in the millennial United States. He calls for the next generation of fiction writers to be *"anti-rebels,"* who "eschew self-consciousness" and irony; he asks them to shock the world, as the early postmodernists did, but this time to shock with sincerity ("E Unibus Pluram" [*Supposedly*] 81). I ask students if Wallace's take on postmodernism matches their own. Does his emphasis on irony, or double-coded language, pass over other important aspects of postmodern fiction?

It's valuable to put Wallace's arguments into dialogue with two essays by Jonathan Franzen: "Why Bother?" (originally titled "Perchance to Dream" when it appeared in *Harper's*) and "Mr. Difficult." Franzen's diagnoses of contemporary societal ills are similar to Wallace's: fragmentation, loneliness, "atomized privacy" ("Why Bother?" 70). Franzen doesn't blame postmodernism for this state of affairs, as Wallace does; rather, he argues that postmodern fiction no longer speaks to the world most Americans live in. He sees literature as having the potential to forge connections in a culture that encourages isolation and calls on fiction writers to rediscover "old-fashioned storytelling" ("Mr. Difficult" 259).

I ask students to note the similarities and identify the differences between Wallace's and Franzen's ideas about isolation, loneliness, and postmodern fiction. I tell them that Wallace thought not only that he and Franzen agreed but that he had persuaded Franzen to agree with his ideas (Wallace, "Quo Vadis" 8). I ask students to consider whether Wallace's literature of antirebellion, of shocking sincerity, is the same as Franzen's return to content and context.

I find it useful to bring in parts of Don DeLillo's *Paris Review* interview, both because DeLillo served as influence, mentor, and something of a father confessor to both Wallace and Franzen and because his fiction works in the cusp between the postmodern complication of language and representation and the millennial desire to connect to a real outside language. Discussing the state of the novel, DeLillo talks about the need for fiction that is "equal to the complexities and excesses of the culture" and that can resist being absorbed "into the ambient noise" (qtd. in Begley 96–97). He calls for "the writer in opposition, the novelist who writes against power, who writes against the corporation or the state or the whole apparatus of assimilation" (97). I ask students how DeLillo's concern about the state of the novel compares to Franzen's. Both authors worry about the relevance of the novel in the age of media-inspired distraction, but in arguing that the novelist needs to write against power, DeLillo seems more committed to writing as a political act than does Franzen or, for that matter, Wallace. Is it possible to generalize that postmodern fiction criticizes and intervenes in ideological, economic, and cultural systems more powerfully than does twenty-first-century fiction?

I also introduce an important scholarly voice from the 1990s. Fredric Jameson's *Postmodernism; or, The Cultural Logic of Late Capitalism* insisted on a reconsideration of the liberatory understanding of postmodernism offered by such theorists as Ihab Hassan, Brian McHale, and Linda Hutcheon. For Jameson, postmodernism is all about surfaces. It reduces history, style, and affect to a deadened flatness, which serves not the purposes of opposing power but the needs of the economic-ideological status quo. Postmodernism, despite its facade of rebelliousness, is essentially reactionary. I usually assign only the first chapter of Jameson's book and remind the students that Wallace too saw postmodernism, at least as it became manifested in the 1990s, as encouraging stasis. I ask the students to compare the arguments by Jameson and Wallace about postmodernism's conservatism.

Instructors can doubtlessly find other books, essays, and interviews to replace or augment the ones I've suggested here. My general purpose, before the students get deeply into the fiction, is to help them engage a variety of views on the exhaustion of postmodern fiction in the United States and to develop some ideas on how Wallace enters into dialogue with them.

Criticism

Most of the readings mentioned above were written near the end of the twentieth century in response to the perceived twilight of postmodernism. The criticism I discuss in this section was written after 2000 and assesses both the arguments about the end of postmodernism and the work of fiction writers who seem to be moving beyond the postmodern. Many scholarly voices could be included in this section; I've chosen the ones I find most useful or most challenging. In class I bring these materials in after the students have some millennial fiction under their belts so that they can better see how the critics are responding to the fiction and thus engage the critics in dialogue. Thereafter, I assign fiction and criticism together to foster an ongoing three-way conversation between the fiction, the criticism, and the students.

Among the readings that address the sea change in recent fiction in the United States, Stephen J. Burn's "A Map of the Territory: American Fiction at the Millennium," the first chapter of his book on Franzen, provides an excellent introduction. It both summarizes the 1990s' critiques of postmodernism and notes what seem to be the primary characteristics of millennial fiction, which he calls post-postmodern, including dramatized roots within postmodern fiction; ambitions for encyclopedic masterpieces; characters grounded in the temporal process of history; reduced reliance on metafiction; and a more secure sense of a reality beyond language (19–26). This last point strikes me as especially important because it exists as an implied or explicit thread in much of the other criticism and because it provides a useful position from which students can assess the fiction of Wallace and his contemporaries. (I don't assign my students my own work, or I might suggest my essay "Post-Postmodern Discontent" as a companion piece to Burn's.) A very different take on postpostmodernism is offered by Jeffrey T. Nealon. Following and updating Jameson's *Postmodernism*, Nealon argues for an understanding of postpostmodernism that links the cultural, political, and economic; as he writes, "it's one logic, smeared across a bunch of discourses . . ." (23). For Nealon, postpostmodernism is a mutation of postmodernism, "something recognizably different in its contours and workings" but "not something that's absolutely foreign to whatever it was before" (ix). He sees an intensification of Jameson's postmodernism, in which life since the 1980s has become increasingly corporatized, privatized, and globalized, with a resulting upward distribution of wealth and power. He seeks to understand how the claims and logic of one area (e.g., culture) can be seen to be working in another (e.g., economics). Nealon's focus is much less on literature and the aesthetics of millennial fiction than most of the other readings I use, so the connections may be harder for students to articulate. Nevertheless, some students may be interested in thinking about Wallace's and Franzen's critiques of contemporary American life in terms of Nealon's economic analysis, or in using his ideas as a frame through which to analyze some of the fiction they're reading.

Although they don't use the term *post-postmodern*, Mary K. Holland and Christian Moraru join Burn in seeing millennial fiction in the United States as developing away from postmodernism. In *Succeeding Postmodernism* Holland addresses the argument made by Wallace and others that postmodern fiction, viewed through the lens of its contemporary, poststructural theory, absorbed the world into language that by its very nature could not assert meaning about anything outside of language. Suggesting that this assessment of postmodern fiction is not entirely fair (she writes that postmodernism is "a movement that aimed and aims to do something meaningful using language" [16]), she argues that millennial fiction, written within and through the assumptions of poststructural language theory, seeks nevertheless to create "meaning, communication, empathy, and the relationships and communities that can result from such things." She calls this shift from the perceived antihumanism of postmodernism "new humanism" (3). After reading her introduction, students can be asked to use Holland's arguments as a frame through which to look back at the postmodern fiction they've read and to consider the ways in which more recent writers, especially Wallace, seek to create meaning, relation, and community. They may also want to compare her arguments to Franzen's call for literature to create community by repressing its poststructural awareness. Moraru, in his book *Cosmodernism*, agrees that postmodernism is not dead yet but argues that it has become trapped in its own box, on the one hand arguing for fragmentation, indeterminacy, and antitotalization, while on the other universalizing its method, making the world over in its postmodern image (308). He posits that one way forward from this trap is what he calls cosmodernism, a paradigm made possible by the end of the Cold War and its attendant binaries. Cosmodernism imagines the world through relatedness: our ability to understand ourselves is tied to our seeing ourselves through another's eyes; our ability to understand our nation is tied to our seeing it in "a cultural geography of relationality" (5). Thus cosmodernism is both a critical project and an ethical one. Students who read Moraru's prologue and epilogue might use it as a frame through which to look at the concerns in Wallace's fiction about the difficulty of human relations, and at fiction by such authors as Don DeLillo and Junot Díaz that seeks to redraw the United States' relation to the rest of the globe.

Jeremy Green and Christopher Breu both consider postmodernism in a context of the material conditions that account for its production and consumption. In *Late Postmodernism* Green argues for the continued usefulness of the term *postmodernism* but with the caveat that "we are no longer postmodern in quite the same way as when the concept was first set loose" (1). Some of the things that account for this change include the nature of millennial capitalism and, within that, the processes by which literature is produced, published, and disseminated; the rise of a number of technological innovations that contributed to literature's loss of cultural authority and a transformation of the public sphere; and the writer's confidence in her or his usefulness and ability to reach a dwindling readership. Students might put Green's introduction into dialogue with

Franzen's arguments and with Nealon's critique of millennial capitalism. They might also make use of Green's terms *citra-postmodern* and *ultra-postmodern*, signifying more and less accessible fiction respectively, as they read novels that cover a range of accessibility (14). Breu, in *Insistence of the Material*, theorizes the nature of contemporary materiality more complexly. He is less interested than the other critics I've discussed in defining what kind of literature follows postmodernism; instead, he asks us to reconsider postmodernism once it's disengaged from the linguistic-cultural turn that denies a real outside language. He posits a material turn so as to discover "the forms of materiality that resist, exceed, and exist in tension with the cultural and linguistic" (3). He proposes rethinking what we have called postmodern literature as the late-capitalist literature of materiality, which uses "language experimentally to engage the increasingly obscured yet ever proliferating material underpinnings of everyday life in the era of late capitalism" (26). He connects this literature to biopolitics by arguing that postmodernism developed as both response and resistance to the increasing administration of forms of life. After reading Breu's introduction, students might put his arguments into dialogue with Green's and Nealon's as well as with Wallace's call for a literature that breaks out of its linguistic box.

Unlike many of these other writers, who link the desire to connect to a world outside language with the need to write more accessibly, Lance Olsen, a novelist and critic, is unapologetic in his support for difficult, experimental literature, offering what he calls a poetics of illegibility ("Flash" 246). Citing Wolfgang Iser's continuum of reading, with boredom owing to predictability on one end and overstrain owing to incomprehensibility on the other, Olsen calls for texts "that edge as close as possible to the latter end . . . , those that continuously make their readers conscious (and conscious of being conscious) of their being suspended among ongoing interpretive possibilities designed to raise fundamental questions" ("Flash" 249). Such literature disorients the reader and, in so doing, disrupts the processes by which "dominant cultural mechanisms . . . read/write/think/feel us" (248). Students might compare his argument with Breu's and both arguments with DeLillo: is this what DeLillo means by writing in opposition? In *Architectures of Possibility*, his collection of interviews with innovative writers, Olsen offers in his headnotes an interesting critique of the state of the publishing industry, arguing that its economic concerns encourage a more accessible, easier-to-digest literature. His points here might be connected to Green's and Nealon's arguments. They might also inspire students to consider whether they see a difference between the fiction published by the commercial conglomerates and the fiction published by smaller, independent, and nonprofit publishers.

Other instructors may draw on different critics from the ones I assign. The essays and books I've discussed here have been useful to me in helping students develop their understanding of critical conversations about the end of postmodernism and the literature that follows it. These materials should help students articulate their senses of where critical consensuses are forming and where the key areas of disagreement lie.

Fiction

When the students encounter the fiction, after having read and discussed the contexts and at least some of the criticism, I propose several questions that both encourage discussion and support exploration of the foundational questions I listed earlier. These new questions include the following:

> Where do you see formal and stylistic experimentation, and how would you compare it to the experimentation of the high postmodernists?
>
> Which texts rely on self-referentiality and double-coded language, and which strive for a more transparent style?
>
> Which texts seem to represent the world mimetically, and which do so less straightforwardly?
>
> To what extent are the worlds represented in the texts stable or objectively knowable?
>
> How, if at all, do the texts represent their critique of contemporary society?
>
> To what extent do the texts seem to pursue accessibility?

With these questions in mind, I try to choose texts that, when put into relation, will challenge the students to develop thoughtful and layered answers.

When I teach Wallace in a survey course, I usually assign *Brief Interviews with Hideous Men*, because it contains many of his ongoing thematic concerns—the inability of contemporary humans to escape the cage of ego and connect with others, the critical fascination with pop culture, the challenge of writing or speaking sincerely, the difficulty of escaping language—and it makes use of many of his literary techniques—a highly stylized narrative voice, multiply embedded narratives, dialogue/interview format, footnotes. In a seminar I assign *Infinite Jest* or *The Pale King*, often paired with Franzen's *The Corrections* or *Freedom*. Reminding students that Wallace and Franzen diagnose contemporary America's ills similarly, that Wallace said that they agree, but that their ideas where fiction should go after postmodernism seem to diverge, I use the above-mentioned questions to help students explore the ways the paired novels are alike and different. I'm not surprised when they usually find them quite different, with Franzen generally approximating traditional realism and Wallace seemingly writing in something approaching a postmodern mode. If we think of this difference as a spectrum, where, I ask the students, might we place the other millennial authors we read: closer to Wallace or closer to Franzen; doing something different from both; serving as examples of late postmodernism, post-postmodernism, new humanism, cosmodernism, or some other critical paradigm? By the end of the semester, I hope that the spectrum will become for them a matrix for generating an encompassing structure for the variety of millennial fiction in the United States.

My overall goal, then, is to provide my students with a context in which the criticism and fiction they read can be found to form different relations, with each new critical inquiry and each new work of fiction recasting those relations and reshaping the resulting arrangement. Each student's matrix will serve as an in-process structure that can help make sense of a particularly complex moment in fiction.

Of course, there are hundreds of contemporary authors one could use to create such a matrix, and the result will be different depending on the texts chosen. I'll suggest here some texts that I have found particularly teachable, that are particularly apt for my goals, or that I'm particularly fond of. Wallace's critique of his postmodern forebears can be linked to the underappreciated novel *Silver*, by Mathew Remski. The novel begins by following a World War II foreign correspondent named Tyrone Pynchon but soon brings in a host of fictional and historical characters, including Leni Riefenstahl, the murdered *Playboy* Playmate Dorothy Stratten, Klaus Barbie, and Jesus Christ, and traces the tendrils of fascism in contemporary America. Mary Caponegro, who studied with such postmodernists as William Gaddis, John Hawkes, and Robert Coover, in recent years has tempered her baroque and surreal narrative techniques to treat her themes in a more accessible way. I often assign her story collection *All Fall Down*, which contains an interesting mix of her styles.

Many of Wallace's contemporaries address in various ways the postmodern obsession with language, the question of indeterminate reality, and the problem of accessibility. I frequently assign Rick Moody's *The Diviners*, a narrational tour de force about the attempt to make a miniseries based on a nonexistent novel, with *Bush v. Gore* in the background. Jonathan Lethem has a range of novels to choose from, from his genre pastiches of the 1990s to his recent, more mimetic fiction. I usually assign *Chronic City* for its blend of a fairly traditional narrative style with an unstable, indeterminate, and dystopian Manhattan setting. Junot Díaz's narratively inventive *The Brief Wondrous Life of Oscar Wao* writes Dominican history and immigrant experience over the dominant, white narrative of the history of the United States and calls attention to the universalizing momentum of pop culture. Colson Whitehead also explores the effect of pop culture in constructing the contemporary subject, particularly the African American subject. *John Henry Days* traces the evolution, assimilation, and transformation of the title folk character, and *Zone One* pastiches the zombie-apocalypse narrative. Karen Russell, in *St. Lucy's Home for Girls Raised by Wolves*, offers a generally transparent narrational style, through which she represents surreal enclaves of an otherwise increasingly homogenized America. Richard Powers brings a polymath intelligence and a virtuoso range to his fiction. *Galatea 2.2* conflates the novelist's biography with his narrator's life, all as prelude to an attempt to create a neural net that can pass the master's comps in English. Its narrational ambiguity and its intense intertextuality support an exploration of what it means to be human in a supposedly posthuman age.

I sometimes bring in fiction that stretches the parameters of the matrices students can develop based on texts like the foregoing. Don DeLillo is especially interesting to assign because, as I indicated earlier, his work straddles high postmodernism and its millennial successor. In a course focusing on large novels I will pair *Underworld* with *Infinite Jest*; in a survey course I use *Falling Man*. As we saw from his criticism, Lance Olsen's fiction continues the stylistic and formal experiments of the postmodernists. *Theories of Forgetting* tells the story of two generations of a family in three distinct narrational styles, each occurring on nearly every page of the novel. Students are forced to create a strategy for reading the book that includes deciding where to begin it. Ishmael Reed is another of the great postmodernists, and his twenty-first-century fiction makes no concessions to the trend toward accessibility. *Juice!*, about the O. J. Simpson trial, conflates fact and fiction, collapses historical moments, and considers the relevance of postmodern art in the new century, all in the service of criticizing claims for a postracial United States. Texts like these make it difficult to simply assert the death of postmodernism and so challenge students to think harder about the place of postmodern fiction in our twenty-first-century world.

Despite claims of its cultural marginalization—of which authors are most aware—serious fiction in the United States, fiction that grows out of and responds to the postmodernism of earlier decades, is remarkably robust and rewarding. Wallace's fiction is central to this lively moment in literary history, not just because of the high quality of his work or the critical industry that is springing up around it but also because of its point in common with the work of all the other authors I've discussed. I've thus found Wallace's work indispensable in providing students with a home base to ground and orient their explorations of millennial fiction. My hope is that they will both develop a useful intellectual matrix and also recognize that that matrix will change with each new novel and scholarly article they read.

Wallace and World Literature

Lucas Thompson

This essay sets forth a teaching approach that centers on David Foster Wallace's diverse engagements with world literature. It outlines a module for a senior-level undergraduate course devoted solely to Wallace—ideally one that surveys a range of critical approaches. At just three weeks in length, the module equates to roughly one-quarter of a twelve- to fourteen-week course. It aims to give students a sample of Wallace's transnational literary engagements and to reveal some of the ways in which his work is embedded within broader networks and traditions. In doing so, it allows students to see the interpretive possibilities associated with reading Wallace's work in the light of world literature. However, far from undermining other ways of reading surveyed in the course—which may well explore more proximate texts that position Wallace in relation to American cultural phenomena—this teaching framework sets forth a complementary, adjacent approach. This is because Wallace's engagements with world literature invariably feed back into his idiosyncratic critique of American culture. Ultimately, the module encourages students to see Wallace's texts—and by extension American literature—as embedded within a global network of texts and ideas.

Traditional accounts of Wallace's significance, both in the classroom and beyond, have taken the seemingly parochial remarks scattered throughout his nonfiction and interviews at face value. Such accounts also adduce certain biographical details, such as Wallace's midwestern affiliations and his 1998 admission that he did not hold a current passport (Wallace, "Gus Van Sant"), to justify this approach. For these and other reasons, Wallace's interpreters have tended to emphasize his work's Americanness. In hindsight, it is thus possible to see the many subtle ways in which Wallace's work was uncritically ushered into interpretive paradigms that perpetuate versions of American exceptionalism. However, what has become clear in recent years—particularly with the opening up of the archive, and with the emergence of previously unpublished and little-known pieces—is the extent to which his work was in fact intimately engaged with various world literary traditions. Although Wallace at times may have appeared to be concerned almost exclusively with American cultural phenomena, it has become increasingly apparent that he perceived his work as operating within a global network of texts and ideas.

It is important to pass this new understanding on to students, whose first impulse will likely be to read Wallace in the light of their preexisting understanding of American literature. In all likelihood, students will anticipate studying Wallace as a resoundingly American figure, with classes exploring his idiosyncratic perspective on American culture and literary history. These expectations should hardly come as a surprise, since, as Pascale Casanova points out, "the study of literature almost everywhere in the world is organized along national lines" (xi).

But, while there is some justification for this approach, it is important to emphasize the subtler, more outwardly focused aspects of Wallace's work, registering the various ways in which his fiction continually asks to be read in the light of far broader literary traditions. At this particular moment of reception, when nationally focused readings seem largely to have been exhausted, it is critical to trace the worldly aspects of Wallace's project. We need to place his work within a more expansive, global frame that reveals the ways in which his texts are embedded within wider literary traditions and movements. While the current critical consensus explains Wallace's genealogy with reference to first-wave American postmodernism—embodied by figures such as John Barth, William Gaddis, Thomas Pynchon, and William H. Gass—in reality his work draws on vastly more diverse strands of global literature. In my view, restricting Wallace's fiction to a narrowly nationalistic domain of interpretive possibility severely limits the kinds of things we are able to perceive in his work. It also perpetuates outdated notions of nationalistic partition and ultimately generates an oddly territorialized account of his significance. Instead, it is crucial to show students the value of situating Wallace's work within a larger frame. The scholarly domain of world literature, with its emphasis on the migration and circulation of texts within a global system of exchange, provides us with the necessary tools to do exactly this.

Week 1: Preliminary Investigations, Wallace's Nonfiction

An ideal way of encouraging students to begin thinking about Wallace in relation to broader literary traditions is to assign a selection of his nonfiction pieces that discuss literary figures from outside the United States. Because world literature is likely to be an unfamiliar notion to many students, instructors can begin by taking a slightly indirect approach, having students look at evidence that shows Wallace looking beyond an exclusively American tradition. Five such pieces should be assigned in the first week of the module: "*Mr. Cogito*," "Some Remarks on Kafka's Funniness," "Joseph Frank's Dostoevsky," "Borges on the Couch," and "Tragic Cuban Émigré and a Tale of 'The Door to Happiness.'" These texts are all relatively short—the longest is just over eight thousand words—and will not take students long to read and annotate over the course of the first week. (Depending on the broader unit, it is possible that one or two of these pieces might have been used in an earlier module; if so, instructors may wish to make their own substitutions or else take the opportunity to recast them in a different light.) Each of these essays and reviews reveals Wallace's admiration for a particular global author or text. Moreover, these occasional pieces give a sense of how Wallace oriented himself toward external literary traditions, since they contain oblique references to his own artistic project. They also reveal the author in the process of thinking through a range of important literary and aesthetic questions.

"Mr. Cogito," Wallace's effusive piece on Zbigniew Herbert's poetry collection of the same name, is an ideal object of study at this point, since it immediately reveals Wallace's interest in diverse literary forms and traditions—in this case Polish avant-garde poetry. Though very brief, this enthusiastic account of Wallace's "favorite book of the year" clearly indicates a broader knowledge of European literature and can be set alongside two or three of the collection's poems that instructors feel Wallace may have been particularly drawn to. ("Mr. Cogito and the Pearl" [9], "Hakeldama" [42], and "What Mr. Cogito Thinks About Hell" [53] all work well here, since they each combine the "ironic absurdism" and "earnest emotion" that Wallace admired [*"Mr. Cogito"* 122].) A useful strategy at this point is to encourage students to think about the significance of Wallace's somewhat unexpected choice (a far more predictable selection, for instance, would have been William Gaddis's *A Frolic of His Own*, which won the National Book Award in the same year) as well as the specific qualities of Herbert's work he praises. Class discussion should look at the potential overlaps between the aesthetic agenda Wallace articulated in earlier essays—such as "E Unibus Pluram" and "Fictional Futures and the Conspicuously Young"—and this text, focusing on Wallace's characterization of the collection's "bravely earnest" central character, who is depicted as being somehow "both intellectual and not too bright" as he "grapples with the 'Big Questions' of human existence" (122). How might Herbert's poetic creation fulfill Wallace's call for "new literary rebels" capable of "eschew[ing] self-consciousness and hip fatigue" in order to treat age-old human questions with reverence and seriousness? And how might Herbert offer an unlikely model for the kind of art that attempts to communicate in meaningful ways with the reader? The text also allows students and instructors to consider the ways in which Wallace viewed *Mr. Cogito* as indicative of a wider Eastern European literary tradition that has the potential to reinvigorate American literature. Toward the end of his piece, Wallace makes the extraordinary claim that "only writers from Eastern Europe and Latin America have succeeded in marrying the stuff of spirit and human feeling to the parodic detachment the postmodern experience seems to require" (122). He then suggests that such a marriage is also possible in American literature, given the right set of political circumstances: "Maybe as political conditions get more oppressive here," he predicts, "we Americans'll get good at it too." By closely examining this diagnosis within class discussions, students can begin considering the ways in which Wallace approached texts from external literary traditions.

The larger claims that close Wallace's reflections on Herbert lead helpfully into "Some Remarks on Kafka's Funniness," an address that was later collected in *Consider the Lobster.* Here Wallace again seems to be thinking about Eastern European literature—though, admittedly, of an earlier period—in his implicit claim that Kafka's highly idiosyncratic brand of comedy has greater existential weight than contemporary American forms. It is telling that Wallace runs through several canonical American writers in making this argument, citing "Pynchonian slapstick," "Rothish priapism," and "Barthish metaparody" (62–63) as instances of literary comedy that fundamentally operate as escapes from reality. By contrast, Wallace saw Kafka's humor as "depend[ing] on some kind of radical literalization of truths we tend to treat as metaphorical," a strategy that frequently combines grotesquerie with comedy (63). For Wallace, this technique allows Kafka's fiction to generate "a religious humor" that spiritually interrogates the reader, denying escapist relief and using laughter to address truths that cannot be accessed by other means (64). During class discussions on this text, instructors should bring in examples from Wallace's fiction that embody precisely this form of comedy. There are many such examples, which fall into two categories: minor comic riffs and extended literalizations. In the former category are the videophone section of *Infinite Jest*, which riffs on the expression "to project a certain image of oneself," as well as the description of the pitiable Ennet House resident Dave K. Bearing a surname that makes obvious reference to many of Kafka's fictional creations, K. painfully and literally "hit bottom" during "some insane drunken limbo-dance challenge" wherein his spine became contorted into a permanent "limbo-lock," such that he "scuttles around the Ennet House living room like a crab, his scalp brushing the floor and his knees trembling with effort" (824). There are also many sustained instances of comic literalization, in which Wallace extends an idea in a way that allows him to rehabilitate proverbial and codified expressions. Marathe's account of meeting his wife, Gertraude, is an important example of this technique (774–82). Here Wallace touches on many of the themes of choice, self-sacrifice, and duty expressed in his conversations with Steeply, in an account that is an extended, literalizing riff on the expression "to sweep someone off their feet." As I have suggested elsewhere, this passage highlights numerous incompatibilities between American and Quebecois ideological positions, particularly around the meaning of romantic love and personal freedom (Thompson 151–52). Such passages align with Wallace's interest in rediscovering the potentialities lurking within proverbial forms of speech and in reanimating truths that have either been forgotten or deadened through overuse.

Instructors should also present students with various other samples of Wallace's theorizations on comedy, such as the revealing authorial aside in "Octet"— in which Wallace-qua-narrator chides himself for writing a vignette that is "too cartoonish, such that it looks as if it's trying to be just grotesquely funny instead of both grotesquely funny and grotesquely serious at the same time" (127)—along with his claim that comedy can function either as "a wake-up call" or as a kind of "anaesthetic" (Interview with Miriam Böttger, 3:19–21). Such inclusions enable students to begin considering the specific ways in which Wallace was looking beyond American literary traditions for techniques and strategies he could transpose within his own fiction.

Instructors might also introduce Gilles Deleuze and Felix Guattari's notion of "minor literature" at this point, in order to think through why Wallace might have been particularly drawn to the work of geographically "deterritorialized" writers such as Kafka ("Some Remarks" 64). This introduction can be expediently done by offering a brief summary of Deleuze and Guattari's central thesis

(18–19) and by setting two or three paragraphs from the opening chapter of *Kafka: Toward a Minor Literature* as in-class reading. Instructors can then encourage students to consider the reasons behind Wallace's linkage of Eastern Europe and Latin America, discussing the ways in which the notion of deterritorialization plays into various postmodern tropes and concerns.

"Joseph Frank's Dostoevsky" is an essay that demonstrates Wallace's intensely personal investment in the work of global writers. It also provokes discussion around the author's recurring impulse to find direct cultural analogies across vast spatio-temporal distances. Wallace's review goes to great lengths to stress the commonalities between the intellectual and cultural milieu of mid-nineteenth-century Russia and that of late-twentieth-century America, making direct analogies between the two. For instance, he equates Russian materialism with late-capitalist consumption, connects the "ideological Nihilists of Dostoevsky's time" (271) with the postmodern literary nihilists of the 1990s, and suggests that critical theory is the modern analogue to socialist ideology in Dostoevsky's Russia. Students should be encouraged to think about the underlying motivation behind these comparisons, as well as the ways in which Wallace is advocating a perhaps counterintuitive precedent for the kind of "morally passionate, passionately moral" contemporary fiction he is calling for (274). At this stage of the module, it is important to get students thinking critically about this strategy of Wallace's. In what sense is he justified in superimposing his own era on Dostoevsky's? What might be artistically productive about this form of cultural comparison? And in what ways is it problematic? Helpful texts here include "A Supposedly Fun Thing I'll Never Do Again" (since we know from the archives that Wallace was making his way through Frank's voluminous biography of Dostoevsky while onboard the cruise ship) and *Infinite Jest*, which Timothy Jacobs has shown to be intimately linked with *The Brothers Karamazov*. As I have revealed elsewhere, "Good Old Neon," the "Irrelevant" Chris Fogle section of *The Pale King* (156–254), and several stories in *Brief Interviews with Hideous Men* also bear palpable traces of Dostoevsky's influence (Thompson 104–11).

"Borges on the Couch" reveals a similarly strong investment in the short stories of Jorge Luis Borges, which Wallace argues are "designed primarily as metaphysical arguments" (288). At the same time, the review hints at many of the qualities that Wallace most valued in fiction, with several passages verging on self-description. When teaching this text, instructors should ask students to identify overlaps with Wallace's own work, drawing on some of the short stories and novels that have been covered in earlier parts of the course. One such passage is Wallace's claim that "[Borges's] fiction is always one step ahead of its interpreters," but there are many others for students to consider. In addition, this review provides yet another opportunity to discuss Wallace's characterization of Latin American and Eastern European literature as being uniquely capable of melding the formal techniques of postmodernism with "the stuff of spirit and human feeling." Here students should be encouraged to imagine themselves in Wallace's position, trying to reinvigorate what he perceived as an exhausted American literary inheritance by looking abroad. What advantages might there be in locating a geographically distant figure to try and emulate? And how might a writer such as Borges have the ability to cast central postmodern concerns in an unexpected light? Such questions allow students to think in more materialist ways about the process of writing fiction and to consider from their own points of view the animating questions for Wallace at this stage of his career.

The final portion of the first week should be spent discussing Wallace's *Philadelphia Inquirer* review of Reinaldo Arenas's *The Doorman*. This brief review sets the stage for later discussions on Latin American experimentalism and artistic appropriation. Early on, Wallace sketches the tragic arc of Arenas's biography and situates him within a broader tradition of Cuban fiction, suggesting that Arenas is "probably the best Cuban-born writer since Alejo Carpentier" ("Tragic Cuban Émigré"). As with Borges, students should here be invited to consider what Wallace found appealing about Arenas, discussing—among other things—Wallace's characterization of the novel's dense symbolism and the way that it deploys an outsider's perspective on American culture in order to construct "a dark parable on the very possibility of community." Revealingly, at one point Wallace compares the protagonist's estranged relation to the United States with Franz Kafka's *Amerika*, noting an important overlap in the way these two texts explore "the nation's bright promise and sad reality." Here classes might consider Wallace's emphasis on the way that international authors approach American culture from estranged perspectives and unusual angles, and think about whether his own fiction attempted to replicate such viewpoints. Subsequent discussions might focus on Wallace's observations of *The Doorman*'s powerfully cross-cultural perspective, as in his claim that "[m]uch of *The Doorman*'s weird moral force concerns Arenas's idea of America as a false door, presenting itself as a utopia for huddled masses who, once they arrive, find either brutal exploitation, or the 'freedom' to start doing their own exploiting . . . which of course is still slavery." Students might here be invited to think about the ways in which Wallace's characterization of American illusions of freedom and "false doors" relate to other passages within his work. Discussions here could center on Joelle's memorable description of the *Infinite Jest* cartridge, which she describes as being either "a cage or a door" (230), or Wallace's intriguing metaphor for Kafka's fiction as "a kind of door" that opens "outward" ("Some Remarks" 65).

Instructors should conclude week 1 by encouraging students to make connections between the five set texts, looking for both overlaps and disparities in the ways in which Wallace frames their value within an American literary domain. In this way, the following week's more abstract, theoretical material will be firmly grounded in the singularities of Wallace's own reading practices, giving students a firm base from which to understand Wallace's relationship to the disciplinary concerns of world literature.

Week 2: World Literature Theory

Having looked at a number of specific encounters, instructors can then zoom out and introduce students to the academic field of world literature. It is helpful to begin by providing a brief genealogy of world literature, starting with important early theorists such as Johann Wolfgang von Goethe and Karl Marx, before tracing its development through to the present day. While many concise historical introductions are available, a particularly accessible genealogy can be found in the opening chapter (1–64) of Sarah Lawall's *Reading World Literature: Theory, History, Practice*, which instructors can assign as part of week 2's readings.

Having traced this lineage, classes should then examine some of the scholarly insights that have emerged in recent years. There are two crucial ideas that students need to be introduced to during this section of the module: textual alterity and the material conditions of textual circulation and reception. These headings can be used to cluster the required readings for this subsection, with instructors assigning extracts from larger works in a course reader. In this way, the reading requirements will not be particularly onerous, and students will still gain a clear understanding of these disciplinary insights, which they can later use to inform their analyses of Wallace's work.

In terms of textual alterity, students should be given extracts from the introduction of John Pizer's *The Idea of World Literature* (1–18) and the first chapter of David Damrosch's *How to Read World Literature* (1–6). Pizer's chapter makes a compelling case for preserving the cultural gap between reader and text, arguing that interpretations of world literature should "sustain textual alterity in its discrete particulars and in its plenitude" (20). Pizer also glosses Goethe's important defense of translation, suggesting that Goethe's mode of cross-cultural reading has "as its highest ideal the movement of the self toward the Other, not a dominion over the Other or a levelling of the Other." Pizer views this approach as being centered on an intentional self-estrangement: the reader is offered an "embrace of alterity . . . that forces the self to become foreign to itself, serv[ing] the twin causes of intercultural dialogue and respect for the foreign" (28). This account offers an oblique definition of an ethical global reading practice. Instructors might lead students in discussing the nuances of Pizer's—and by extension Goethe's—argument, thinking through specific examples of how such an approach might play out. At this point, it is also helpful to encourage students to consider whether Wallace himself was reading global texts in this way, asking classes to draw on evidence from the previous week's readings in making their cases. (A classroom debate would work well here, since there are important arguments to be made on both sides.) In a similar way, the Damrosch extract helps students begin to theorize the "perils of exoticism and assimilation" that are ever present when reading world literature (18).

Classes should think through Damrosch's injunction to avoid both the fallacy that foreign works are intractably mysterious, "naïve and illogical," and the mistaken belief that global authors are "*just like us*, playing by the same rules and [with the same] cultural assumptions" (13). These critical texts—together with seminar discussions that flesh out their particularities—will give students a sense of the complexities surrounding world literary texts, as well as the interpretive rigor that such texts demand.

It is also important to give students a sense of world literature's emphasis on material phenomena, stressing the quantifiable ways in which we can trace the circulation of texts across borders. The "Kafka Comes Home" chapter from Damrosch's *What Is World Literature?* (187–208) works well in this context, as does Rebecca Walkowitz's article "Unimaginable Largeness: Kazuo Ishiguro, Translation and the New World Literature," which should be assigned in full. Another useful text to assign is an extract from the opening chapter of Paul Giles's *Antipodean America* (19–23), which makes the case for focusing on moments of transnational "friction" (20), a helpful strategy when examining Wallace's global encounters. Giles's argument is a useful corrective to the utopian leanings within some accounts of world literature, which emphasize intangible—and occasionally dehistoricized—modes of intellectual exchange. Giles warns against "being seduced by the impossible chimera of a purely multilingual and interchangeable world culture" and instead suggests that "a more materialistic version of comparative literature would focus also on those points of friction where national and transnational intersect with each other in uncomfortable ways, and where cross-border translations either succeed only partially or fail" (20). Following this critical survey, instructors should challenge students to think about which perspective they found most appealing and which one they think makes sense of Wallace's literary practice. Do Wallace's own intersections with global texts invariably entail certain kinds of failure? Are they attempting to be as ethically rigorous as Damrosch's and Walkowitz's accounts demand? Is Pizer's ideal replicated within any of the essays and reviews considered thus far, or are there more pragmatic aesthetic encounters taking place? Introducing these theoretical positions allows students to consider Wallace's engagements in a systematic way and provides a critical lexicon that will be essential for the module's final assessment.

Weeks 2 and 3: Case Study: Manuel Puig

In the remainder of week 2 and moving into week 3, classes should together carry out a critical case study that combines various theoretical perspectives with a detailed examination of Wallace's work. In this section of the module, students work collaboratively to uncover five highly specific linguistic strategies that Wallace appropriated from the Argentine novelist Manuel Puig. These strategies include the use of ellipses to signal charged silences and extraverbal forms of communication; the incorporation of found texts; embedded apostrophes to textually absent interlocutors; a redacted question-and-answer format;

and a reliance on transcribed speech, presented without context or explanation. Students may well locate others, but these are the main devices. Assigned extracts should clearly show these appropriations. I suggest the following sections, which are taken from numerous novels and short stories and together amount to fewer than forty pages: from Puig, *Eternal Curse on the Reader of These Pages* (55–67, 25–30), *Betrayed by Rita Hayworth* (182–84, 24–25, 37–39), and *Heartbreak Tango* (185–88); and, from Wallace, *The Broom of the System* (25–28), *Infinite Jest* (40, 140, 160), and *Brief Interviews with Hideous Men* (14–15 [from the short story "B.I. #14"]).

Ideally, students should come to class having closely read and annotated these extracts so that they can discuss their observations in small groups. Discussion should initially focus on identifying the techniques and representational strategies that Wallace lifted from Puig and then consider the reasons underlying these appropriations. Did Puig's strategies resolve particular stylistic or representational problems for Wallace? Do they reproduce certain aspects of postmodern experience? And how might these appropriations relate to Wallace's project of invoking—rather than exhaustively describing—emotions and central themes? Such questions can lead students to see Puig's substantial influence on Wallace's fiction, allowing them to make their own discoveries about this literary debt.

Circling back to Wallace's characterization of Latin American fiction in "Mr. Cogito," classes should think through how these five techniques relate to his broader account of Eastern European and Latin American experimentalism. While acknowledging the perhaps surprising extent of Wallace's stylistic borrowings, discussions might also consider the potentially revealing omissions. Why, for instance, was Wallace not particularly interested in the political dimension of Puig's fiction? Many scholars have pointed out that Puig's stylistic innovations were invariably linked to forms of political engagement; for example, Leonard Cheever noted that Puig's techniques were intended to serve expressly political ends, "emphasiz[ing] not only the surrealistic nature of Argentine politics, but also the nature of the lunatic world that might be produced if . . . 'leftist Peronists' manage to have their way" (69). In other words, Puig's formal innovations are directly tied to political circumstances, particularly the Peronist ideology that was then dominating Argentine politics. (It is not necessary to unpack this complex period in Argentine history for students, simply to emphasize that Wallace's reading of Puig is fundamentally apolitical.) Using some of the theoretical ideas canvassed earlier in the module, students might discuss the possible reasons behind Wallace's elision of Puig's novels' political content and consider why he may have been primarily attracted to Puig's unusual engagement with postmodern textual concerns. Throughout this comparative analysis, students have the opportunity to trace the tangible impact of an international figure on Wallace's work, while also thinking about the ways in which his practice either aligns with or departs from theoretical accounts of transnational exchange.

Research Essays: Sustained Examinations

Following the specificity of the Puig-focused section of the module, the next sub-section gives students the opportunity to explore the intersections between world literature and Wallace's work that are of most interest to them. Ideally, this should be done in the module's final assessment task, in which students carry out a detailed examination of one such intersection. In the context of the broader course, instructors might allow students to focus on a particular critical approach, writing an essay that makes use of some of the theoretical material covered earlier. In this way, students have the chance to explore a critical methodology, metaphor, or set of terminology they find appealing. Instructions for the final assessment task should be open-ended enough to allow for a diverse range of essays, but not so vague that students struggle to know where to begin. An ideal way of framing this task is to assign an essay of 3,500–4,000 words on Wallace's relationship to an international author or text of the student's choosing. Such essays will draw on students' knowledge of the texts that have been examined throughout the course, but they will also require additional reading and research.

By focusing on a particular stylistic or thematic correlation between Wallace and a representative of world literature, students will develop a range of research skills and learn how to apply world literary theory in a close textual analysis. One option is for students to flesh out one of the engagements covered in the first week of class, exploring in greater depth Wallace's fascination with Herbert, Kafka, Dostoevsky, Borges, or Arenas. In this case, essays might focus on the techniques and preoccupations Wallace appropriated from such figures, using a comparative analysis of two or more texts. While such analyses require detailed knowledge of at least one representative text, in many cases the necessary reading need not be overwhelming. In terms of a Kafka-Wallace comparison, for instance, students might explore the ways in which the literalization strategies within a short story such as "The Penal Colony" find echoes in Wallace's fiction or examine how what Wallace describes as Borges's ability to explore philosophical abstractions within narrative forms is replicated throughout Wallace's work. Likewise, students may choose to compare the central character in Dostoevsky's relatively brief novella *Notes from the Underground* with one of Wallace's similarly ironic and detached narrative personae—"Irrelevant" Chris Fogle from *The Pale King*, perhaps, or Neal, the narrator of "Good Old Neon." Likewise, shorter comparative texts can be isolated from Arenas's and Herbert's bodies of work. As well as exploring the terms of these artistic negotiations, students can use the critical texts surveyed in the second week of the module to consider how Wallace's engagements either conform to or depart from scholarly accounts of global literary exchange.

Alternatively, students may choose to explore Wallace's connection to a figure they have encountered elsewhere in the course. Some might be intrigued by, say, references to figures such as Albert Camus, Søren Kierkegaard, or Leo Tolstoy throughout Wallace's fiction and interviews, or want to compare a translated text with Wallace's original. Still others might take a more materialist approach, mapping the ways in which Wallace's work has been received by audiences around the world.

A course on Wallace and world literature also provides teachers with an opportunity to examine not only the various difficulties and challenges associated with reading texts in translation but also the productive ways in which texts can—in Damrosch's formulation—"gain in translation" (*What* 281). Individual classes might survey a range of contemporary perspectives on translation (with readings from scholars such as Susan Bassnett, Emily Apter [*Against*; *Translation*], Azade Seyhan, and Gayatri Chakravorty Spivak [*Aesthetic*; *Death*; *In Other Worlds*]). Wallace was deeply ambivalent about whether his own work could be adequately rendered in other languages, telling one interviewer that "I don't like translations of my work" (E-mail message to Martina Testa) and claiming in another setting that his short story "Incarnations of Burned Children" was "almost impossible to translate, mostly because of the large number of non-standard and very English-specific punctuation and syntax devices" (Greco 98). Yet, as someone who read only English and French, he relied heavily on translated versions of many texts. The overwhelming majority of Wallace's encounters with world literary texts were therefore mediated through translators, giving teachers and students the opportunity to reflect on the reasons why particular global authors might be translated and marketed to American literary audiences. During this part of the course, instructors might draw on students able to read translated extracts of Wallace's fiction in other languages, asking them to present their findings to the class. Concurrently, English-speaking students could survey some of the interviews given by Wallace's translators, homing in on the strategies with which these translators have handled particular cultural transpositions, but also noting—in many cases—their accounts of working with Wallace himself. There are also several key archival documents that could be introduced at this point, including some highly revealing correspondence with translators. Wallace had tetchy exchanges, for instance, with at least three of his Italian translators, while he steadfastly refused to offer assistance to Ulrich Blumenbach, the German translator of *Infinite Jest* (DeMarco). In fact, he confessed to feeling bemused as to what his work could possibly have to offer an international audience: "I question why any foreign publisher would want to try to translate my work anyway. The whole thing seems very mysterious to me" (E-mail message to Adelaide Cioni). In spite of such palpable cynicism, however, Wallace's work has in fact gained in all kinds of important ways through various networks of translation. Classes might reflect on the ways in which Wallace has found a truly global audience—with his work now being translated into numerous other languages—and how these new audiences might be approaching his work.

Teaching Wallace's fiction and nonfiction in the light of world literature offers students a productive and generative way of understanding his work. Part of the value of this approach lies in the implicit challenges it poses to nationalist frames of interpretation; yet another important part lies in the countless global inter-texts and influences that it suddenly brings into focus. As the open-ended nature of my assessment ideas suggests, students may very well wish to take up particular lines of interpretation that have been gestured toward throughout the module. Such explorations can be extremely fruitful, both in expanding our sense of Wallace's artistic and intellectual precursors and in allowing us to see new things in his work. Teachers who are hesitant to reconfigure entire course modules along these lines can still find value in encouraging students to consider the ways in which our interpretation of Wallace's work can be limited and forestalled by restricting his work within a national frame. In units dealing only briefly with Wallace's fiction, carefully worded essay questions could give interested students the opportunity to explore one or two of these transnational points of intersection, and lecturers might find ways to give students a sense of the interpretive possibilities associated with viewing Wallace's work as world literature. When Wallace is being studied alongside other contemporary American novelists and short story writers, instructors might devote some of their time to showing students how similar authors can also be productively situated within larger frames of reference. Even merely hinting at Wallace's profound engagement with world texts can open up new lines of inquiry for students, allowing them to see beyond illusory national boundaries and thus reimagine global literary space. This teaching emphasis also affords the chance to gain a richer understanding of the operations of literary influence, and gives students the tools to trace the way that many texts migrate across national borders.

As Wallace's work continues to find new readers through various networks of translation (*Infinite Jest*, to take just one example, has already been translated into German, Italian, Portuguese, Spanish, and French), it is crucial to continue to examine the gains in meaning that his fiction will accrete as it is placed within new cultural and linguistic contexts. Although Wallace cynically—and somewhat self-deprecatingly—imagined his readership to be "mostly white, upper middle class or upper class, [and] *obscenely* well educated" (Lipsky 82), recent history has proven him wrong. As we teach Wallace to diverse groups of students, and as his work continues to find new communities of readers around the globe, it is crucial to emphasize the global dimensions of his project. Positioning world literature as a critical lens with which to read Wallace's fiction reveals many new interpretive possibilities and, ultimately, gives students an invaluable perspective on his work.

Early Wallace and Program Culture

Andrew Warren

"Like a Dryer with Shoes in It"

"'With Dan, he was not the star of the class, as David was, as were one or two others who were really quite good . . . Dan was good,' he finally admitted, as if for the sake of politeness. 'But in a much quieter way'" (Storrs). The Dan here is Dan Brown. The David is David Foster Wallace. The person relating the story is Alan Lelchuk, a writer in residence at Amherst College from 1982 to 1984 who taught Dan and David creative writing.

Straining to imagine those two writers as undergraduates—doing the same assignments, reading and discussing each other's work—is a mental exercise I never seem to tire of. It's also the place where I begin my course on Wallace. I relate Lelchuk's comparison of the two writers and then place some sentences from *Infinite Jest* alongside some from *The Da Vinci Code*, each using a variation on the word *heart*.[1]

Infinite Jest	*The Da Vinci Code*
He said she had a face that'd break your heart and then also break the heart of whoever like rushed over to your aid as you pitched over sideways grabbing your chest.(1015)	Sir Leigh Teabing's heart practically stalled to see Rémy aiming a gun at him. *What is he doing!* (141)
Gately's heart is now somewhere around his bare hairy shins, at the mention of Federal crewcuts. (827)	Heart racing, Sophie ran to the woodshed and got the spare key her grandfather kept hidden . . . Heart pounding, she placed her finger in the slot. (118)
The guy was like totally legless. Orin's rising heart went out. (598)	
Mario loves Hal so much it makes his heart beat hard.(890)	Her heart raced as she realized what it must be. *A necklace!* (445)
His shoulder beat like a big heart, and the pain was sickeninger than ever. (590)	Teabing's heart turned grave, then resolute. (473)
My chest bumps like a dryer with shoes in it. (5)	

Thinking and talking through the differences between these sentences is a direct line into many of Wallace's concerns and anxieties: the nature and uses of cliché; the porous border between irony and sincerity; polished versus ugly (deliberately unpolished) writing; what signals something as genre or literary fiction; the author's relationship to an implied reader—how much work he expects the reader to do. Such big questions, I suggest to my students, are simplified if we can figure out how these sentences conform to or diverge from the principles young Dan and David learned in their creative writing classroom: "Write What You Know," "Show Don't Tell," "Find Your Voice."[2]

Teaching Wallace's vexed relation to the practice, culture, and ideals of MFA programs isn't easy. It involves developing students' skills in analyzing rarefied literary techniques while also providing a historical context for why particular techniques were privileged, impugned, or singled out at all (such as, in his case, the frequent use of name brands). Getting students up to speed in what are often taken to be opposed critical methodologies—formalism and historicism—is hard, but it can also be wildly productive, particularly since Wallace explicitly works to show how or why certain formal techniques, like irony, dovetail with certain generations' preoccupations, like exploding hypocrisy or appearing cool and noncommittal. We see that critical labor in his essays and interviews, but also in the tissues of his own fiction, so often in secret dialogue with that of his peers, predecessors, and teachers. Of course, this avenue of inquiry sets up the far more interesting question of which techniques Wallace felt were most called for in his (and our) time.

In this essay I discuss some ways to teach Wallace's early writing—that is, the work that came before *Infinite Jest*, much of which was written for or about different creative writing programs. My principal focus will be the collection *Girl with Curious Hair.* As I do in class, I contextualize Wallace's fiction with a look at the essays and interviews where he explicitly discusses MFA programs and the institutionalization of literature. Fiction's institutional support and conditions of production have received much attention of late, both in academia and in the popular press, and I address that debate, giving particular attention to Mark McGurl's *The Program Era: Postwar Fiction and the Rise of Creative Writing.*[3]

Teaching Wallace from a writerly perspective early on helps make the headier aspects of his work feel more natural. By the same token, Wallace's absorption of and resistance to creative writing protocols are often best conceived in the context of his dynamic understanding of how fiction, authorship, and reading work. In *Girl with Curious Hair* (and perhaps in Wallace's work more generally) we see theory and program—two key institutions in Wallace's development—mutually informing and working against one another. Setting up this productive tension at the beginning of the term opens up the later work to discussions that veer away from what have become default interpretations.[4] In *Girl*, Wallace felt himself doing fresh, original, urgent work. One of my signal tasks in teaching the early texts is to communicate how he approached this task and why he felt it was necessary. Since Wallace was only a few years older than many of my students when he wrote them, the stories in *Girl* often seem more approachable than his later works. Showing how those pieces were composed within an academic context not radically different from their own helps strengthen the connection between their sensibilities and the young Wallace's. That connection is all the more tangible when I begin the course with *Broom of the System* (his senior thesis) or his college story "The Planet Trillaphon as It Stands in Relation to the Bad Thing."

The remainder of this essay is broken up into three parts: the first contextualizes my teaching of early Wallace within the course; the second outlines how I teach Wallace's institutional context; and the third describes in greater detail how and when I teach individual stories from *Girl with Curious Hair.*

David Foster Wallace and Environs: Overview of the Course

My course began as an upper-level seminar of about eighteen highly motivated undergraduates and has since become a lecture for about sixty (also highly motivated) students.

The syllabus presents three large-scale and open-ended questions:

> What roles do earnestness, sincerity, and attention play in a world that trades in irony, insincerity, and inattention? Or, put another way, how do our idealizations of human communication match up to its apparent realities?
>
> How does the self sift through the "tsunami of available fact" (Wallace, "Deciderization" 312) presented to it each day, hour, minute, second? How should it?
>
> What does fiction have to do with any of this? How do you present these problems (much less their solutions) in fictional form? What is fictional form, now? What good is it?

If these are the course's unanswerable topoi, its official goals—as an English course—are more specific:

> To introduce Wallace's myriad styles, ideas, and concerns. Though the syllabus varies from year to year, we read the lion's share of Wallace's published work in roughly chronological order.
>
> To ask, with Wallace as our example, what exactly an "author" is today. That is: How does a collection of texts, written and revised across a lifetime, constitute an author's corpus or oeuvre? What strategies can a reader or critic use to make sense of that body of work? How is the work shaped

by an author's intentions, biography, and social context—including the literary marketplace? How far out does an "author" extend—to the "major" works? to the diaries and marginalia? to artistic influences and to writers influenced in turn?

To give a sense of Wallace's generation and of the generations that came before and after him. Given the quantity (more than 2,500 pages) and complexity of the Wallace texts we tackle, this goal is downplayed. I teach a range of texts alongside Wallace's and have students present (in seminar or in sections) what I call "prose comparisons," which close-read Wallace's style against that of another author. Each week I also assign five-page excerpts from authors such as James Joyce, William Gaddis, Don DeLillo, Ralph Ellison, Fyodor Dostoyevsky, Dave Eggers, Jennifer Egan, Aimee Bender, Jonathan Franzen, Junot Díaz, Jhumpa Lahiri, or George Saunders. These prose comparisons are meant to give a feel for the craft in contemporary American fiction and to bring Wallace's own prose technique into relief against that background.

In practice, this aspect feels a bit like a creative writing workshop, with students weighing the worth and feel of individual words. I model the prose comparisons by juxtaposing descriptions of luxury goods in "Girl with Curious Hair" with those in Bret Easton Ellis's *American Psycho*[5] and the maximalism of Thomas Pynchon's *The Crying of Lot 49* with the minimalism of Raymond Carver's "What We Talk about When We Talk about Love."

I try to show, for example, how Pynchon's syntax ebbs and flows between vastly different possibilities, how his sentences' grandeur hinges on tentative declarations of uncertainty:

> Somewhere beyond the battening, urged sweep of three-bedroom houses rushing by their thousands across all the dark beige hills, somehow implicit in an arrogance or bite to the smog the more inland somnolence of San Narciso did lack, lurked the sea, the unimaginable Pacific, the one to which all surfers, beach pads, sewage disposal schemes, tourist incursions, sunned homosexuality, chartered fishing are irrelevant, the hole left by the moon's tearing-free and monument to her exile; you could not hear or even smell this but it was there, something tidal began to reach feelers in past eyes and eardrums, perhaps to arouse fractions of brain current your most gossamer microelectrode is yet too gross for finding. Oedipa had believed, long before leaving Kinneret, in some principle of the sea as redemption for Southern California (not, of course, for her own section of the state, which seemed to need none), some unvoiced idea that no matter what you did to its edges the true Pacific stayed inviolate and integrated or assumed the ugliness at any edge into some more general truth. Perhaps it was only

> that notion, its arid hope, she sensed as this forenoon they made their sea-
> ward thrust, which would stop short of any sea.   (48)

The radical undecidability—of the nature of the reality she lives in, of the relation between language and that reality, of the border between self and world, of
the existence of the Tristero conspiracy—that Oedipa encounters in *The Crying of Lot 49* is built into the syntax of the text itself. Oedipa's experience of uncertainty in her world is thereby mirrored in the reader's experience of uncertainty in reading the text, and this, I argue, is what makes the book interesting
and its sentences difficult and beautiful. Against this I pose some of Carver's
sentences, highlighting the way they punch out staccato, single-syllable words
to describe a brutal scene:

> Terri said the man she lived with before she lived with Mel loved her so
> much he tried to kill her. Then Terri said, "He beat me up one night. He
> dragged me around the living room by my ankles. He kept saying, 'I love
> you, I love you, you bitch.' He went on dragging me around the living room.
> My head kept knocking on things." Terri looked around the table. "What
> do you do with love like that?"
>   She was a bone-thin woman with a pretty face, dark eyes, and brown
> hair that hung down her back. She liked necklaces made of turquoise, and
> long pendant earrings.   (138)

That unflinching brutality is offset by the extended syllables (*necklaces, turquoise,
pendant earrings*) drawn out at the passage's end that hint, like Pynchon's own
extended clauses, at the possibility of a different life.

   Due on the second day of class, the first assignment asks students to read a
short selection (typically "My Appearance" or the opening pages of "A Supposedly
Fun Thing") and "find a word or phrase or stylistic tic that points to something
crucial or revealing or puzzling about the selection. Then write a short essay, no
more than one single-spaced page, about how that word or phrase or tic works
to reveal that crucial thing."[6] Perhaps even more than its pathos or themes, what
first draws students to Wallace's writing is his ability to find the mot juste. I find
that slowing students down and forcing them to isolate and describe Wallace's
stylistic choices—a style they intuit at the speed of reading—alongside the
stakes of those choices helps stabilize the frenzy of plot, idea, character, and voice
already robustly present in *Girl* and in the essays. This attention to craft and writerly detail in the early work also helps set up one of the course's key ends: considering *Infinite Jest* as a work of art rather than a merely technically accomplished constellation of difficult ideas and strong feelings.

Weird Achievements and Tangled Relations: Wallace's Institutional Context

Of course, MFA programs' alleged anti- or unintellectualism has become a cliché. "The trope about CW students not reading, or being encouraged to be sort of ahistorical and New Agey—I don't see that," said George Saunders in 2010 (31). Whether "that" is true, and who decides what counts as "that," is perhaps best left for class discussion (what "not reading" means is a vibrant topic). My purpose in this section—and in teaching—is less to say something new about MFA programs' relation to the contemporary literary scene (how could you?) than to reveal how and why Wallace thought through it as a concrete social, aesthetic, and personal problem. I want to balance Wallace's investment in the creative writing program against his similar investment in theory or continental philosophy, two newish institutional forces an outmoded American literary scene had to confront. It's my contention, here and in class, that what Wallace assimilated from the program and from theory cannot be neatly separated, either in the early work or in what came later. Perhaps *Girl with Curious Hair*'s weirdest achievement is its melding of the program's attention to literary form with theory's rigorous questioning of it. The result was Wallace's first real vision of how a writer might communicate, today, with a reader—a tangled relation that he never ceased to render with his own kind of spiritual urgency.

Wallace clearly felt both drawn to and repulsed by the program and by institutions more generally. A child of the academy, Wallace joined institutions (quiz and sports teams, college clubs, Arizona's MFA and Harvard's philosophy programs) as a matter of routine. They provided much-needed structure (and money and health care), even if the persistent drive to master those structures so often led to crises of achievement like the ones thematized in the Enfield Tennis Academy of *Infinite Jest*. Hence the later work's devotion to "unmasterable" institutions—Alcoholics Anonymous in *Infinite Jest*, the world of business in *Oblivion*, the media in *"Consider the Lobster" and Other Essays*, and the Internal Revenue Service in *The Pale King*. These organizations cannot be mastered but demand mastery, or self-mastery. System and individual are always involved in a vexed dialectical play. Its two limits are Hal's apparent solipsism in *Infinite Jest* (a problem caused by his reaction to systems) and *The Pale King*'s vision of total immersion, where a character named "David Wallace disappears—becomes [a] creature of the system" (548). That these extrema are so closely associated with the act of writing (Hal *does* "communicate" with the reader, David Wallace is the "author here" in *The Pale King*) is crucial.

Despite his youthful intransigence, Wallace taught undergraduate creative writing courses that were traditionalist in emphasizing the building blocks of fiction. The weekly sections for his Literary Analysis course, for example, are "Plot," "Point of View," "Character," "Setting," "Irony," "Tone," "Theme," and

"Symbol" ("English 102"). For a class in writing fiction, Wallace's "Guidelines for Writing Helpful Letters of Response to Colleagues' Stories" address similarly basic concepts and techniques.[7] But the students are also guided to ask more fundamental, personal questions: "What has the writer set out to do?" and "Has the writer actually done what she set out to do? Can you see the gaps between what she thought she was doing and the way the story actually comes off?" Although such problems lie at the heart of stories like "Octet" or "Westward the Course of Empire Takes Its Way," we academic critics tend not to ask them out loud, an omission challenged by Wallace's critical sophistication.

This tension between writing's personal, institutional, and critical valences has recently been historicized in McGurl's *The Program Era*. I assign selections from it (pp. 1–49 and 399–410), both for its readability and for the vocabulary it gives students for talking about Wallace. Its diagrams are particularly useful. McGurl's depiction of creative writing's standard "autopoetic process," for instance, neatly unfolds key issues in Wallace's work and teaching and opens a channel between style or technique and idea or theme (23). McGurl's diagram shows the complex interrelations between "experience," "craft," and "creativity" stressed in creative writing programs and associates three writerly mantras— "Write What You Know," "Show Don't Tell," "Find Your Voice"—with these aspects of creative writing. What is important is less that writers follow these commandments to the letter than that they attend to the ongoing process between their personal history, the literary tradition in which they find themselves, and their freedom to transform that tradition and transfigure their history through writing. Autopoetics, a term McGurl borrows from systems theory, names this recursive process whereby an author makes a work. It normalizes something many students take as uniquely postmodern, or even uniquely Wallaceian: recursion. All art, even a realist story—indeed all life—is self-reflexive, says systems theory.

Many readers in 1989 would have been aware that *Girl* was written largely within an MFA program's environs. In her acute *New York Times* review, Jenifer Levin remarked that "the pieces that don't work ('Luckily the Account Representative Knew CPR' and a ponderous novella, 'Westward the Course of Empire Takes Its Way') come off as the sort of inside jokes that might play best in a creative writing seminar." And even her praise is couched in workshop language: "When showing rather than telling, Mr. Wallace allows his characters to function in both a symbolic and a living context. When showing rather than telling, he is tender enough and strong enough not to shy away from love—whether he's attempting to define it or (better yet) simply daring to expose it." When I teach Levin's review alongside *Girl*, I point out how in her eyes McGurl's dogma of craft ("Show Don't Tell") frees Wallace up to be authentic—to "Find [His] Voice" and "Write What [He] Know[s]." My point isn't that this three-body problem of craft, freedom, and authenticity explains Wallace's fiction—early, middle, or late—but rather that it was a key rubric under which he worked and was interpreted.

Teaching Girl with Curious Hair

Girl with Curious Hair is on all counts a difficult, demanding text. Its method and telos are expressly apocalyptic: to clear a space for Wallace's future fiction and perhaps for American fiction more generally. I have suggested that stressing its historical, institutional, and biographical contexts can mitigate some of its demands, but even so it is likely to exhaust even the most well-intentioned undergraduate—particularly one who feels the weight of a 1,079-page novel pressing down from a few weeks off. I therefore try to balance teaching Wallace's works chronologically with giving the clearest, most energizing introduction to his styles, hopes, and ideas.

Week 1: Getting a Feel for Wallace's Styles

This week is designed simply to make students comfortable with Wallace's writing and thinking. By the time we properly begin (following the pagination of *Brief Interviews*, I call the first few classes "Week 0"), the students will have read and written about the story "My Appearance," and I in turn will have lectured on the first pages of *Broom of the System*, *Infinite Jest*, and *The Pale King* to give them a sense of Wallace as a developing writer. Instead of diving straight into *Girl* (or *Broom*), we begin with some essays: first, those where Wallace develops his journalistic persona ("Getting Away from Already Being Pretty Much Away from It All," "A Supposedly Fun Thing I'll Never Do Again," and "The View from Mrs. Thompson's"), and then "E Unibus Pluram: Television and U.S. Fiction." The key word here is *irony*, and I ask whether Wallace's characterization of it in "E Unibus Pluram" fairly describes how it actually works in "My Appearance" or the narrative essays.

Week 2: Sixties Counterculture and Black Humor

The goal here is to give a fuller taste of the previous generation's fiction that Wallace describes in "E Unibus Pluram," in particular to show how compelling and sophisticated it can be. I typically assign some combination of Pynchon ("Entropy," "The Secret Integration," *The Crying of Lot 49*, or the preface to *Slow Learner*) and Barth (selections from *Lost in the Funhouse*), juxtaposed with Raymond Carver. This is also a good week to teach "Lyndon," where Wallace effectively maps the emotional, artistic, and political crises he feels in the 1980s back onto the '60s.

Week 3: Technique and Form in the Short Story from Wallace Back to Joyce

The last two times I have taught the course, I have devoted a full week to what I call "narrative boot camp," designed to get everyone reading critically and suspiciously. I ask students to read the story "Girl with Curious Hair" carefully and to think about the reliability of its narrator in relation to brief passages from

Ellis's *American Psycho*. The basic question is how and whether Wallace, at the level of the sentence, creates ironic distance from the hypercapitalism he's trying to criticize. This week everyone also reads Joyce's *Dubliners*. Each student picks a story to be an expert on, which involves writing a detailed response paper outlining the argument from a chapter in Margot Norris's *Suspicious Readings of Joyce's* Dubliners that introduces them in a very pragmatic, intuitive way to the basic tenets and vocabulary of narrative theory.

Week 4: How Wallace Negotiates the Pressures of His Precursors and His Present

Now we dig deeper into *Girl with Curious Hair*. Given the amount of time I devote to teaching *Girl*'s stylistic, intellectual, literary, and historical context, I typically do not assign students the entire collection. For instance, I have not found a tried-and-true way to teach "Westward the Course of Empire Takes Its Way," the self-protesting metafictional novella about MFA students that concludes *Girl*. In lecture, I mine "Westward" for apposite quotes about the goals and methods of writing fiction,[8] but I find that I can make similar points with shorter, more efficient pieces from *Girl*, thus conserving much-needed energy for *Infinite Jest*. Specifically, I give lectures on details in "Little Expressionless Animals" and voice in "Here and There." I conclude with "Fictional Futures of the Conspicuously Young," the *Review of Contemporary Fiction* interview with Larry McCaffery, Levin's *New York Times* review, and a tour de force close reading of "Everything Is Green."

People appreciate that two-page story's Carver-like economy, holding it up as an example of what Wallace was capable of when he held himself—and his millions and trillions of thoughts and feelings—back. Like the unfinished *Pale King*, which it resembles, it projects a world and a potential beyond itself. Of course, *Infinite Jest*'s ending, which "can be projected by the reader somewhere beyond the right frame," does this too (qtd. in Max 321n19). But for many readers the uncertainties of "Everything Is Green" feel right or necessary, while *Infinite Jest*'s feel unnecessary. Part of this attitude has to do with a culture that values restraint and observation over expressive risk in its high art, perhaps as a corrective to its popular entertainment. But there is a more practical aspect. You can read and reread and keep all or most of "Everything Is Green" in your head to judge whether or not its gaps and ambivalences seem right and inevitable. Meanwhile, only Wallace's head, wrapped tightly in a bandana, could contain *Infinite Jest*'s multitudes—one would have to take on faith the necessity of its aesthetic decisions. Wallace insisted that writing either "clicked," or it didn't; and *Infinite Jest*'s ending clicked for him, "musically and emotionally" (Burn, *Conversations* 37, 51, 72).

For me, the lion's share of teaching literature involves inciting a productive play between these different capacities—the head, and the heart, and the nerve endings. The process is Wallaceian insofar as it asks students to notice how and why they're noticing what they're noticing, to install a feedback loop in their reading. But first they must notice *what* they're noticing—a word, mood, image, tone, rhythm. If *Infinite Jest* is a summer camp in how to read a novel, "Everything Is Green" is a workshop. It is exemplary as a piece of eighties-style minimalism as endorsed by the University of Arizona's MFA program, but it also twists and submerges theoretical problems treated more overtly in the rest of the collection, particularly the author-reader relationship. Once again Wallace locates himself vis-à-vis the questions his generation is asking about its connection to literature: that is, to what extent it is a craft to be learned in writing programs, or an unstable text to be questioned in theory classrooms, or an aesthetic object to be appreciated in a chair by a sunny window.

"Everything Is Green" is obviously all of these things. However you read the mysterious final line, "Say her name" (*Girl* 230), Wallace has pulled you in and implicated you in the story's stakes. Wallace discovered even in realist minimalism a form that could contain the deep issues that interested him across his life. Ending a piece with an ambiguously performative utterance is also a technique he uses across his career—"So decide" ("Octet" 160), "Are you immensely pleased" ("E Unibus Pluram" [*Supposedly*] 82), "Not another word" ("Good Old Neon" 181), "Read these" (*The Pale King* 6). Though doing so entangles students in a host of theoretical problems, I have found that beginning my course with a careful attention to craft can also open up texts that had seemed closed off. In the early work we see Wallace, that creature of the system, trying to open up the program to its own potentials. And teaching the early work—slowly, contextually—can open up students to their own potential as readers—a goal not far, as I understand it, from Wallace's hopes in writing it.

NOTES

[1] In my final lecture, I add passages from *The Pale King* such as the E. M. Cioran reference "to the human heart as 'God's open wound'" (399).

[2] These mantras appear as chapter titles in Mark McGurl's *The Program Era*, which I discuss further below.

[3] I also teach Chad Harbach's *MFA vs. NYC* and Rick Moody's "Writers and Mentors."

[4] Marshall Boswell's call for papers for the *Studies in the Novel* issue on Wallace asks for "essays that move beyond the well-trodden themes of irony, postmodernism, solipsism, and addiction."

[5] I suggest, for instance, that Ellis's repetitions and lists of products create a feeling of unintended irony, while Wallace's build on each other to exaggerate the ludicrousness. Contrast Ellis's "I check my Rolex while I'm buying scruffing lotion at the Clinique counter, still in Bergdorf's, to make sure I have enough time to shop some more before I have to meet Tim Severt for drinks at the Princeton Club at seven. . . . I run into Bradley Simpson from P & P outside F.A.O. Schwarz and he's wearing a glen-plaid worsted wool suit with notched lapels by Perry Ellis, a cotton broadcloth shirt by Gitman Brothers, a silk tie by Savoy, a chronograph with a crocodileskin band by Breil, a cotton raincoat by Paul Smith and a fur felt hat by Paul Stuart" (*American Psycho* 178) with Wallace's "I wear English Leather Cologne which keeps me smelling very attractive at all times.

English Leather is the men's cologne with the television commercial in which a very beautiful and sexy woman who can play billiards better than a professional makes the assertion that all her men wear English Leather or they wear nothing at all. I find this woman very alluring and sexually exciting. I have the English Leather Cologne commercial taped on my new Toshiba VCR and I enjoy reclining in my horsehair recliner and masturbating while the commercial plays repeatedly on my VCR" (*Girl* 55).

[6] The prompt continues: "Think of a 'stylistic tic' as anything that happens repeatedly and does some sort of persuasive or logical or emotive work in the piece. Writing, for example, in dialect or using slang at certain moments; addressing the reader in the second person; using footnotes or italics; reusing sentence structures; crazily scientific jargon juxtaposed with something else. The point is to show how Wallace's style or word choice opens up or facilitates or complicates a point he's trying to make, a stance he's trying to take, or an effect he's trying to evoke."

[7] For example, "Is the writing natural and interesting? Does the story's narrator sound human," or does the prose sound "too 'written'? . . . Does the story's plot seem to move toward some climax, epiphany, or other unfolding of meaning? Or does it seem slow and static (or maybe rather random and chaotic)?" (*David Foster Wallace Reader* 620–21).

[8] I pair another quotation about hearts ("Please don't tell anybody, but Mark Nechtr desires, some distant hard-earned day, to write something that stabs you in the heart" [332]) with one about how an author cannot aim directly at his or her target's "heart" (293–94).

Wallace and Philosophy

Allard den Dulk

> "*It* is a level of psychic pain wholly incompatible with
> human life as we know it. . . . *It* is also lonely on a level that
> cannot be conveyed. There is no way Kate Gompert could
> ever even begin to make someone else understand what
> clinical depression feels like . . . because a person in such a
> state is incapable of empathy with any other living thing."
> —Wallace, *Infinite Jest*

While David Foster Wallace's writing has a clearly philosophical dimension, its exploration of philosophical themes, rather than being conceptual or theoretical, is driven by a clear desire to express, and thereby allow the reader to experience, some of the most existentially urgent and painful aspects of contemporary human existence. The possibility of conveying these problems in this way is what motivated Wallace's occupational switch from philosophy to literature. In Wallace's work, longstanding philosophical debates—Does language describe the world accurately? Can I explain myself to others? What are the values and dangers of self-consciousness? How can I lead a meaningful life?—are shown to be pressing existential concerns that haunt the texts and their characters, such as *Infinite Jest*'s Kate Gompert. As expressed in the above quotation, for Kate, words like "*clinical depression*" or "*unipolar dysphoria*" do not signify anything: Kate, "down in the trenches with the thing itself," knows her pain only as "*It*"; and she can't convey what this pain is to anyone else (she cannot even see those others as "independent of the universal pain that is digesting her"); she is locked into the terror that is her own consciousness; for Kate, the indescribable pain is the "essence" of her existence, to which "there is no solution" (695–96).

These philosophical themes of Wallace's work—that is, the medium of language (as a bridge to the world and to others), the role of consciousness and the question of meaningful existence—and affinities with specific thinkers have been widely recognized in Wallace scholarship. Some studies (including my own) even take the analysis of this philosophical dimension as their main focus in understanding Wallace's oeuvre. It follows that such philosophical perspectives also constitute a fruitful, perhaps even indispensable approach to teaching Wallace's works.[1]

Wallace himself studied philosophy from 1980 to 1985, focusing on mathematical logic and philosophy of language, and writing his undergraduate thesis on the problem of fatalism (Ryerson 3–5). But Wallace subsequently abandoned philosophy—at least, in its conventional, academic form, and as his primary pursuit—and decided to focus on literature. Wallace later explained that he had no longer felt the "click" he initially experienced in technical philosophy, but had found it again in fiction (McCaffery, "Conversation" 139): literature "felt like it was using 97 percent of me," compared to philosophy using only "50 percent," Wallace said (Lipsky 261).

This statement by Wallace about literature and philosophy raises the question of the relation between the two and, specifically, how his work might be seen to combine them. His writings display an affinity with thinkers who blur the lines between literature and philosophy, as in the aphoristic style of Ludwig Wittgenstein's later writings, Søren Kierkegaard's literary portrayals of different life-views, the oft-praised literary qualities of William James's writings, and Jean-Paul Sartre's expression of philosophical ideas via novels and plays. Additionally, these thinkers all ascribe to literature an inherently philosophical dimension. The ideas that philosophy and literature are partially overlapping activities, and that some philosophical problems are best approached through literature, underlie Wallace's work—and could be seen to underlie his abandonment of technical philosophy—and inform the approaches to teaching Wallace and philosophy offered in this chapter.

Below I will offer outlines for teaching Wallace's work in the light of the three above-mentioned philosophical themes: language (specifically the issues of solipsism and skepticism, in relation to Wittgenstein), consciousness (contrasting excessive self-consciousness with awareness directed toward the world, by way of Sartre), and meaningful existence (opposing attention and even boredom to alienation and despair, in the light of James and Kierkegaard). For each theme, passages from relevant philosophical texts and from different works by Wallace will be briefly explained and questions offered to guide students toward illuminating comparative readings. Though the themes can be taught separately, I will also briefly point out the connection between them.[2]

The discussion of these themes works well both in courses that focus primarily on one or more Wallace texts (e.g., *Infinite Jest*), integrating the themes along the way, and in courses that take the philosophical themes in Wallace's oeuvre as the organizing structure and match up different texts for comparative reading. What is offered below can be shaped into these different teaching formats.

Language: Wallace and Wittgenstein

The connection between Wallace and Wittgenstein is well documented: Wallace explicitly acknowledged the influence of later[3] Wittgenstein on his own thoughts about language (e.g., McCaffery, "Conversation" 144; Wallace, "Empty Plenum" 218), and it has been an important topic in the Wallace scholarship so far.

One of the best ways to address the connection between Wallace's and Wittgenstein's views of language is through their shared understanding of the problems of skepticism and solipsism. According to Wittgenstein, both problems are rooted in the misguided idea that language acquires meaning by referring to something outside itself (an object, a thought); subsequently, any doubt cast on the possibility of bridging this referential gap leads to skepticism (I do not know whether what I say actually corresponds to the world) and solipsism (I only have access to my own experience and cannot assume that others think or feel as I do) (see also Hacker 25–26). Wittgenstein shows that this referential failure is actually *irrelevant* to the meaningful functioning of language and instead describes language as always part of a "life-form," as embedded in the communal structures of groups of individuals (*Philosophical Investigations*, 7e). Wittgenstein's later philosophy can be seen as a series of descriptions meant to therapeutically cure us of the thought-habits that lead us to misunderstand language. Wallace's work can be said to do something similar by showing characters who are in the grip of a misguided view of language and of the resulting problems of skepticism and solipsism (e.g., Lenore Beadsman in *The Broom of the System*, most addicts in *Infinite Jest*) and pointing to potential ways out.

To compare Wallace's and Wittgenstein's therapeutic descriptions of these problems, I suggest assigning sections 28 and 293 from Wittgenstein's *Philosophical Investigations* on "ostensive definition" and "private language," respectively. These sections can each be coupled with several readings from Wallace, but below I will elaborate two relatively self-contained examples, namely, the "Eschaton" section from *Infinite Jest* and the story of the woman with the tree toad from *The Broom of the System*.

Skepticism and Ostensive Definition

Through ostensive definition—"giving the meaning of a word by pointing to an exemplar" (McGinn 42)—"we seem to pass beyond the limits of language and to establish a connection with reality itself," Wittgenstein writes (qtd. in Baker and Hacker 36; see also Hacker 99). But in section 28 Wittgenstein shows this is mistaken. In discussing this section with students, it is important to let them gradually bring out its implications: what goes on when we explain a word by pointing to an object? In itself, a word pronounced while pointing at something can mean a lot of things. Doesn't this fundamental possibility of misinterpretation mean that language fails to unequivocally connect to reality, leading us to skepticism? If our attempt to ostensively define a word (moving beyond linguistic description, connecting it directly to the world) requires further supplement (moving back into language, offering explanation), we have to conclude our attempt has failed.

However, students should be encouraged to see that this problematization, above all, serves to reveal a misunderstanding of how language actually functions. What about examples (ask students to provide these) of successfully pointing at something to explain what we mean? How are such explanations possible? Students will readily point to the importance of the specific "context" of each utterance but should be prompted to specify what that means, how such contexts function. For example, is the context in question linguistic or extralinguistic? If it is the latter, we are back at our previous problem (how is it connected to language?); if it is the former, students should try to explain more precisely how language provides a context to itself.

Wittgenstein answers as follows: I have to know how a word is being used, what the grammatical structures are that surround the word, because these structures are responsible for its acquiring its specific meaning. The rules of language are not determined by reality but result from the communal structures of groups of individuals: "language-games" (4e), as Wittgenstein calls specific forms of language use, presuppose a group of people who relate to each other and to the world in a certain way (a life-form). That does not mean that language and the world are unrelated. On the contrary: language-games determine the meaning we confer upon reality as well as how we relate to it. Wittgenstein concludes that language, to acquire meaning, does not seek or need a referential connection to the world; thus the threat of skepticism supposedly resulting from such a (failed) connection is refuted.

This threat of skepticism, of a failure of language (leading to an endless doubting of truth and reality), and the Wittgensteinian response to it, can be seen to be portrayed in the "Eschaton" section of Wallace's *Infinite Jest* (321–42). First of all, let students observe that the nuclear war simulation game Eschaton is described to have clear rules and demarcations (see, e.g., 322–24). But when it starts to snow a violent debate breaks out among the participants about the relation between reality and representation—namely, about whether the snow falling on the tennis courts affects the nuclear war simulated thereon. Here it is important to ask students what motivates the debate. The characters initiating the debate might be seen as praiseworthy philosophers, doubting unquestioned assumptions. However, Wittgenstein is highly critical of the *"theorizing* or *theoretical attitude"* (McGinn 16): according to him, philosophical problems arise when philosophers remove linguistic utterances from their connections to a certain practice in order to scrutinize them, creating situations in which "language *goes on holiday"* (*Philosophical Investigations* 16e). So, in *Infinite Jest*, the initiators might also be seen to cast unwarranted doubt on the functioning of the game, fostering skepticism toward it.

The Eschaton debate can be seen to refer to Borges's fable "On Exactitude in Science," about a map that completely coincides with reality, causing reality to gradually disappear, leaving just the map—a fable that, by way of Jean Baudrillard's *Simulacra and Simulation,* has come to symbolize the skeptical, postmodernist view that reality has disappeared (is not accessible) and we are left with mere artifice (i.e., language that cannot be connected to the world and therefore might be seen to lack meaning). However, students should be encouraged to question whether this assessment applies to the Eschaton situation. Keeping in mind Wittgenstein's critique of the theorizing attitude, Eschaton's distinction between reality and representation might in fact be seen to be quite clear. As the character Michael Pemulis says, "It's snowing on the goddamn *map*, not the *territory. . . .* Real-world snow isn't a factor if it's falling on the fucking map!" (334–35). Invite students to compare the arguments Pemulis uses to counter what he characterizes as "equivocationary horseshit" with Wittgenstein's refutation of skepticism (337). Briefly put: Eschaton presupposes the reality in which it is played ("it's like *pre*axiomatic") and, in order to play the game, participants have to commit to its rules, which imply a certain relation to reality; it is not possible when "asswipes . . . run roughshod over the delimiting boundaries that are Eschaton's very life blood" (338, 335).

Solipsism and Private Language

Similar to his treatment of ostensive definition, Wittgenstein's "private language arguments" show the impossibility and irrelevance of the suggestion that language acquires meaning through reference to an accompanying mental intention.[4] Of these arguments the "beetle-in-a-box" thought experiment (section 293) is perhaps the most famous.

The beetle-in-a-box thought experiment illustrates that, if we regard the meaning of words as determined by private, mental images (the "beetle'" in "my box"), we admit the possibility that everyone could have very different mental images (for how can I know whether others have the same image in their heads as I do?) for the same word. This might seem to open up the possibility—of which many Wallace characters are convinced—that we all mean different things with our words, and that we are thus not really communicating: if private images determine the meaning of our words, it would seem impossible for us to understand each other, resulting in solipsism.

Subsequently, encourage students to question this conclusion and see that Wittgenstein's point extends further. If private images determine the meaning of our words, what does this mean for my own understanding of my words? The implication of Wittgenstein's beetle in a box is, in fact, that it would also be impossible for me to have a consistent understanding of my own images and therefore of my own words. Why? Because I would not be able to uphold a criterion of correctness to my own words. Against what would I test my definition? My judgment of whether or not the feeling I have right now is pain—Wittgenstein's favorite example, frequently echoed in Wallace's work—depends on the whims of my memory, which decides whether the feeling resembles what I felt before and decided to call pain: "whatever is going to seem right to me is right. And that only means that here we can't talk about 'right'" (78e; see also Hacker 97, 101). In conclusion, private, mental images are irrelevant to the meaningful functioning of language, because an individual could never maintain a private definition of, for instance, pain. Instead, our ability to use a word in a meaningful way presupposes grammatical structures that are already in place in language.

Wallace's *The Broom of the System* takes such solipsistic misunderstandings of language as one of its own main topics. For example, Lenore Beadsman's anxiety that she does not really exist because she is determined by language implies the assumption—an inversion of Wittgenstein's thought experiment—that public language mismatches with what an individual is, internally, privately. This assumption doesn't make any sense, Wittgenstein has shown: a person's self-understanding can never be private.

One of the novel's stories, told to Lenore by her boyfriend, Rick Vigorous, can be read as an explicit variation on the beetle in a box. It tells of a woman who "has a pale-green tree toad living in a pit at the base of her neck." The woman completely identifies with this anomaly and thereby cuts herself off from the world: "The tree toad is the mechanism of nonconnection and alienation, the symbol and cause of the [woman's isolation]." The story suggests a solipsistic universe in which members of a group (the woman and her family) all possess a different creature and define themselves on the basis of this difference: "the mother has a narrow-tailed salamander, one brother has a driver ant, one sister has a wolf spider, another has an axolotl, one of the little children has a sod webworm. Et cetera et cetera." The story symbolizes a situation in which everybody possesses something different (in his or her beetle-box) and thus cannot know what others are experiencing (187–89).

Let students explore how Wallace's story and the rest of his fiction illustrate the solipsistic problems caused by the misguided tendency to regard our so-called internal processes—thoughts, feelings, and so on—as objects and ourselves as the exclusive owners of those objects. One fruitful approach could be to focus on the perception of pain, especially by depressed and addicted characters in Wallace's fiction: for example, "the depressed person" in the eponymous story in *Brief Interviews with Hideous Men*, and Kate Gompert, Geoffrey Day, and Orin Incandenza from *Infinite Jest* (to name just a few) regard their suffering as unique, inaccessible for others, and they are thus locked in a solipsistic worldview. Students could compare these characters to *Infinite Jest*'s Mario Incandenza, who is unable to feel pain (and therefore cannot misunderstand his own conception of it as based on some private sample) but nevertheless understands it and is always perceptive of other people's suffering.[5]

Consciousness: Wallace and Sartre

Skepticism and solipsism are strongly connected to the theme of consciousness. Wallace's fiction portrays many excessively self-reflective characters: their constant introspection fosters the misunderstanding of the relation between thought, world, and language. In its portrayals of processes of consciousness Wallace's work displays a clear affinity with Sartre's phenomenological view: for both, consciousness should always be directed outward (see, e.g., Smith 264–68; Ramal 179–80).

Wallace's and Sartre's shared critique of self-consciousness and emphasis on awareness directed toward the world can be fruitfully examined by reading Sartre's early essay *The Transcendence of the Ego*[6] in combination with, for example, the Erdedy section from *Infinite Jest* (17–27) and the story "B.I. #20" from *Brief Interviews with Hideous Men*.

The title of Sartre's essay makes for a good opening question: what does it mean? Sartre means that the ego, or self, does not reside in consciousness but transcends—is constituted beyond—it, in the world.[7] The essay starts with this specific claim. But the underlying notion that students need to grasp first is that of intentionality. According to Sartre, consciousness has no substance; it is solely a relation, an awareness of something other than itself—in other words, it is sheer intentionality. And Sartre goes on to claim that it is this intentionality (not some sort of internal self or ego) that unifies consciousness. What does Sartre mean by this assertion, that through intentionality, by "going outside itself," consciousness "unifies itself" (6)? He means that consciousness unifies and identifies itself by not being its objects. From this relational, nonsubstantial nature of consciousness Sartre concludes that there is no self (ego) internal to consciousness, unifying it.

Sartre goes on to argue that, when we look at everyday situations that constitute the majority of our conscious states, we can see there is no I present in these experiences. Instead, our consciousness is immersed in the world, focused on the objects of consciousness (and not on consciousness itself). Sartre writes: "there is no I on the unreflected level. When I run after a tram, . . . there is no I. There is a consciousness of the tram-needing-to-be-caught, etc." (13). Let students exchange experiences of situations like this, in order for this idea to sink in. Sartre subsequently offers a progression of the levels of consciousness, up to self-reflection, in which consciousness explicitly directs its attention to the I. But what is this I, then, if it is not an immanent structure of consciousness itself? Sartre acknowledges that we exist as individuals and ascribe an I to ourselves. He holds, however, that this is not the result of something that inhabits, and resides over, consciousness. On the contrary: he regards the I, the self, as a secondary phenomenon that we derive from our experience of "the unity of our representations" (3).

Sartre concludes that self-reflective introspection, aimed at the discovery of a core self at the heart of consciousness, is "a perpetually deceptive mirage" (39). Self-reflection tries to turn consciousness into an object that has a certain essence (an inherent self), while, according to Sartre, consciousness is sheer intentionality and thus has no substance or essence. Such self-reflective objectification is the basic dynamic that underlies bad faith behavior, which consists of trying to give oneself an essence (Sartre, *Being and Nothingness*, 70–95). In *The Transcendence of the Ego*, Sartre describes that such forms of self-reflection—remaining in an objectifying (as if external) perspective on one's own consciousness—can even lead to psychological disorder, to "various types of psychasthenia" (47).

Excessive Self-Consciousness

Wallace's work is filled with excessively self-conscious characters, many of whom suffer from addiction, depression, or both, and the above can thus be related to almost all of his writings. The Erdedy section from *Infinite Jest* portrays its character's hyperreflexive mind as it spirals to the point of his actual psychological breakdown. Students can be invited to map out the different motifs that are tied to Erdedy's self-consciousness and eventual self-destruction, for example: addiction (marijuana, which simultaneously feeds and is meant to shut down Erdedy's self-consciousness), obsession (most obviously, with the woman who said she would bring marijuana), paralysis and passivity (Erdedy cannot phone the woman, cannot put his mind to rest by checking the color of his bong, because of the possible counterproductive effects his mind can think up for each act), secrecy (no one can know he is an addict, because he does not want to see himself as such; self-reflection is an internalization of the external gaze), self-deception (Erdedy has used the same "grueling final debauch" strategy countless times already [27]), and self-disgust (he recognizes his own dependence on something of which the pleasure has become questionable). All these motifs are produced by an objectifying, self-reflective stance, an internalized look that, in Sartre's words, distances itself from the "spontaneity" of experience and "poisons" it through the attribution of conflicting motives to actions: "it is the point of view I have adopted towards them that has poisoned them" (20). Slowly, this leads to an alienation from one's own thoughts and feelings: "[Erdedy] thought very broadly of desires and ideas being watched but not acted upon, he thought of impulses being starved of expression and drying out and floating dryly away, and felt on some level that this had something to do with him and his circumstances and . . . would surely have to be called his problem" (26–27). Other passages on Ennet House and Alcoholics Anonymous (AA) illustrate that this hyperreflexivity leads to a total alienation from the self, where "the cliché 'I don't know who I am' unfortunately turns out to be more than a cliché" (204).

Awareness Directed toward the World

Sartre's suggestion that, instead of inward self-objectification, consciousness should be directed outward, can also be found throughout Wallace's fiction. An interesting, complicated case is provided by the story "B.I. #20." In it, a highly self-conscious, manipulative interviewee narrates how he was affected (moved to change) by an "anecdote," told by a woman whom he had seduced, about how she had avoided being murdered by a sexual psychopath through "self-forgetful," empathetic attention (*Brief Interviews* 245, 252). The woman's "anecdote" clearly contains elements that are to be taken as positive, virtues we might see as being supported by Wallace's fiction in general. But, in reading the story as a whole, it is important to evaluate with students how the role of the narrator complicates a straightforward interpretation of the story as expressing the virtue of attention. After all, it is framed by the narrator, and students could track the many cues to doubt the reliability of his retelling of the "anecdote."

In line with Sartre, "B.I. #20" makes clear that we should not see attention in the way its narrator—at least initially—sees it, namely as a naïve attitude that uncritically ignores information about the world. In the story, we are told to "envision" the woman's focused, empathetic awareness as an "intense concentration further sharpened and intensified to a single sharp point, to envision a kind of needle of concentrated attention whose extreme thinness and fragility were also, of course, its capacity to penetrate" (257). This fragile, single-point attention has a clearly critical and ethical dimension. Likewise, students should respond to the story's request to pay careful attention to its characters and ideas. The need for ethical attention that the story presents to us via the woman is not realized in the narrator's supposed retelling, which is in fact emblematic of the hyperreflexive objectification critiqued above. Instead, the story might be seen to work as an appeal to the reader to realize such attention in the act of reading the story.

This reading of the need for outward-directed awareness can be supplemented with passages from *Infinite Jest*, such as the section detailing Mario's empathetic behavior (312–17) or the AA section portraying "Identification" with other addicts as vital to recovery (343–75), or from *The Pale King*, such as the long section in which Chris Fogle narrates his conversion from self-reflective ("wastoid") absorption to ethical attention (154–252).[8]

Meaningful Existence: Wallace, James, and Kierkegaard

Examining alienating self-reflection and the subsequent need for outward-directed awareness leads to the theme of meaningful existence. Most of Wallace's characters suffer from alienation and despair, and some of them find a way out, through attention and choice, to meaningful existence. These philosophical trajectories can be fruitfully discussed in relation to Søren Kierkegaard and William James. Marshall Boswell's essay in this volume characterizes Kierkegaard's critique of the aesthetic life view as a model for Wallace's portrayal of irony and addiction, and the novel's descriptions of recovery by surrender to AA's Higher Power as based on James's descriptions of religious experience. I offer James's discussion of "The Sick Soul" and "The Divided Self" (lectures 6–8 from *The Varieties of Religious Experience*) as an additional influence underlying Wallace's portrayal of addiction and depression (including his use of the term *anhedonia*) and connect Kierkegaard's *Either/Or* with Wallace's recurring emphasis on enduring boredom (and the importance of attention) in *The Pale King*. These discussions will also provide an opportunity to return to the question raised in the introduction, of how literature and philosophy relate to each other.

Wallace and James: The Sick Soul

Before students read the three above-mentioned lectures from *Varieties*, explain to them James's distinction between "once-born" and "twice-born" individuals (introduced in lecture 5 and taken up throughout lectures 6–8). According to James, the once-born have "no metaphysical tendencies" and are "not distressed by their own imperfections" but cannot be called "self-righteous," because "they hardly think of themselves at all." James ascribes to such individuals a "childlike quality" (79) and a sort of "congenital anaesthesia" that seems to cut them off from "even a transient sadness" (82). Based on this, students should be able to explore the parallels with Wallace characters such as Mario Incandenza and Shane Drinion. Most important, invite students to critically compare the function of such characters (often criticized as too unrealistic to provide a model for meaningful existence) in relation to most other Wallace characters (all prone to addiction and depression) with the existential function James ascribes to the once-born: that while the source of their happiness is congenital, and thus inaccessible for the twice-born, their behavior constitutes an exemplar, a reminder of "grace" for all others—"It is to be hoped that we all have some friend . . . whose soul is of this sky-blue tint," James writes (79).

James describes the twice-born—the more common type of individual—as experiencing a "certain discordancy or heterogeneity" in his or her existence (156). James quotes the poet Louise Ackermann (1813–90), whose realization that her existence is "by accident" and the "globe" without purpose leads her to experience her life as "being in a dream" (64). This realization of meaninglessness is the basic constituent of the postmodern world portrayed in Wallace's work: the critical strategies internalized by contemporary Western culture reveal the world as an unreality. Let students trace this connection in one of the AA / Ennet House sections from *Infinite Jest* (689–98): therein, the "sophisticat[ion]" of the "millennial U.S.A." is equated with "'world-weariness'" and is described as a loss of meaning, of "being really human" (694–95). Additionally, let students reflect on the dreamlike quality of this section—for example, how the narration weaves together different locales and characters—and of the novel in general.

James describes "morbid melancholy" (depression) as an exacerbation of "this sense of the unreality of things" (64). He describes the "peculiar form of consciousness" of these "sick souls" as a "prison house" (128)—compare the imagery of imprisonment and cages associated with addiction and depression in *Infinite Jest*. Moreover, the assigned section from *Infinite Jest* distinguishes between the same "kinds of pathological depression" listed by James; namely, "anhedonia"—described as "mere passive joylessness" (136) by James and as "low grade," "simple melancholy" in *Infinite Jest* (692)—and the "worst kind of melancholy," that is "panic fear" (James 149), or "the Great White Shark of pain" in *Infinite Jest* (695). Moreover, Wallace also includes, in slightly paraphrased form, some of the patient descriptions that James quotes of these different kinds of melancholic experience. For example, consider the description of anhedonia James presents from Father Gratry, a Catholic philosopher:

> Happiness, joy, light, affection, love—all these words were now devoid of sense. Without doubt I could still have talked of all these things, but I had become incapable of feeling anything in them, of understanding anything about them, of hoping anything from them, or of believing them to exist. (138)

Compare this description with the following passage from *Infinite Jest*:

> . . . *happiness, joie de vivre, preference, love*—are stripped to their skeletons and reduced to abstract ideas. . . . The anhedonic can still speak about

happiness and meaning et al., but she has become incapable of feeling anything in them, of understanding anything about them, of hoping anything
about them, or of believing them to exist as anything more than concepts.
(692–93)

James illustrates "panic fear" with a description he later admitted came from his
own experience: gripped by "horrible fear" he had a vision of a patient, a "black-
haired youth with greenish skin," "knees drawn up against his chin," "moving
nothing," and had felt: "*That shape am I*" (149–50). *Infinite Jest*'s description of
Kate Gompert evokes this "panic fear" passage: a doctor observes Kate with "her
knees drawn up to her abdomen," "fingers laced around her knees," her "black
bangs [visible]" and the other half of "her face obscured by the either green or
yellow case on the plastic pillow" (68; see also Evans 187–88).

Given these parallels, let students discuss the connections between James's
and Wallace's respective philosophical and literary approaches. For example, note
that James quotes extensive examples, in effect offering ministories, in different
voices, an aspect comparable to *Infinite Jest*. Furthermore, let students reflect
on the highly personal nature of both authors' writing. Above all, compare the
ways in which James and Wallace insist their audiences try to imagine the experience of depression—see the "burning high-rise" and "electric current" examples in *Infinite Jest* (696–97).

James also asserts that "happiness" can follow this "radical pessimism" (135),
as "the normal evolution of character chiefly consist[s] in the straightening out
and unifying of the inner self" after such dividedness (158). This, in turn, might
be connected to *Infinite Jest*'s portrayal of recovery through AA, which is also
described as the establishing of (or return to) a self (694–95, 860).

Wallace and Kierkegaard: Boredom as Bliss

How to become such a coherent self and realize a meaningful existence, amid
the fragmented plurality of the contemporary Western world, is one of the main
themes of Wallace's work. The connection between enduring boredom and
meaningful life, raised most explicitly in *The Pale King*, can best be understood
in the light of Kierkegaard, in particular "Rotation of Crops" from *Either/Or,
Part I* (281–300).

It is important to let students note that in "Rotation of Crops" it is the aesthete A who is speaking—a narrator embodying the life view Kierkegaard
criticizes—and who famously states, "Boredom is the root of all evil" (285). The
aesthete is only interested in pleasure—in letting himself be led by fantasy and
desire—and, therefore, boredom is the "[evil that] must be held off" (289).
This is also what is expressed in the passage from *Either/Or* quoted in *The Pale
King*: "*Strange that boredom, in itself so staid and solid, should have such
power to set in motion*" (385).[9] In *Either/Or*, this line is followed by: "The effect
that boredom brings about is absolutely magical, but this effect is one not of

attraction but of repulsion" (285). Let students discuss the meaning of these lines. Kierkegaard's aesthete is constantly looking for ways to distract himself (from possible boredom); boredom has "power to set in motion" because the aesthete is repulsed by even the idea of being bored. Invite students to connect this to the different addictions in *Infinite Jest* symbolizing a deep need for distraction from potentially difficult, existential issues.

Subsequently, ask students how the story of Lane Dean, Jr., in *The Pale King* can be read in contrast. In "Rotation of Crops," the aesthete A advises readers to "[n]ever become involved in *marriage*," because "one falls into a very deadly continuity with custom," and to "[n]ever take any *official post*," as one becomes a "little cog in the machine of the body politic" (296–98). Lane, as part of his redemption, can be seen to go directly against this advice. Let students discuss Lane's initial anxiety (36–43) and his subsequent decision to take responsibility through marriage and employment, thus accepting boredom, instead of fleeing from it. Subsequently, let students discuss Lane's situation and possible fate. His job with the IRS is characterized by extreme tedium. How can this possibly constitute meaning, or "bliss" for that matter? Isn't Lane in fact driven to madness and suicide? For Kierkegaard, meaningful existence is not readily achieved: it is subject to uncertainty and requires sustained, endless commitment. That a ghost appears to Lane might be read as a (negative, hallucinatory) result of the boredom he experiences. At the same time, the ghost could also be seen to direct Lane toward the ethical dimension of boredom, that "[*boring*] meant something that drilled in and made a hole" (378). Lane initially interprets this as boredom creating a hole inside, "hollowing out" (384). However, it also points to what elsewhere in *The Pale King* is called "single-point concentration" (293): attending to something and understanding, entering into it (students could potentially connect this back to "B.I. #20"). This latter reading is supported by Lane subsequently thinking of the "Frenchman pushing that uphill stone throughout eternity" (384), a reference to Camus's *The Myth of Sisyphus*. Students are likely to be repulsed by Lane's situation and conclude that it constitutes a negative portrayal. But invite them to reflect on how this might constitute an aesthetic response. The text does not describe Lane's fate, so the reader has to imagine it, and the reference to Camus might prompt us to remember the final line from *The Myth of Sisyphus*: "One must imagine Sisyphus happy" (111).[10]

The inconclusive presentation of Lane's fate (and that of Wallace's other characters) could be compared with Kierkegaard's "indirect communication" (*Concluding Unscientific Postscript* 252). Kierkegaard uses pseudonyms and fictional narrators to philosophically express different life-views from within. Students could explore how this approach to philosophy compares to (Wallace's) literary fiction, and specifically to Wallace's regular use of *exformation*—leaving out crucial information in the course or at the end of a narrative. Most importantly, students should bring out the affinity between Wallace and Kierkegaard, and the other philosophers discussed in this essay, in their requirement that the reader "put in her share of the [work]" to acquire an understanding of the texts and work through the philosophical problems presented therein (McCaffery, "Conversation" 138). According to Kierkegaard, the reader, in order to reach self-understanding, has to confront the different perspectives offered in the philosopher's writings, which cannot directly present the truth of that self-understanding, as this can only be reached, subjectively, by the reader. Wallace's fiction, too, is aimed at generating such self-understanding in its readers, and not so much at offering conclusive truths about its characters (cf. Baskin 143–44, 146). In that sense, Wallace has never ceased doing philosophy, and his work requires that, as readers, neither do we.

NOTES

[1] This chapter therefore derives part of its content from some of my previous publications on Wallace, most importantly from *Existentialist Engagement in Wallace, Eggers, and Foer.*

[2] As becomes clear from this overview, several philosophical themes and thinkers potentially relevant to Wallace's work have been left out (e.g., issues of religion and gender; and thinkers such as Albert Camus, Jacques Derrida, Richard Rorty, and Maurice Merleau-Ponty). This is due to the inevitable limitations of an essay like this (in which I have chosen to include elements that can be taught both separately and in coherence) and to the fact that some of these issues and perspectives are addressed elsewhere in this collection. The topic of Wallace's thesis (fatalism) is not included in this essay, because the technical type of philosophy of which it is an expression has little connection to Wallace's later writing; however, the implications of the topic of fatalism (free will, meaningful action, et cetera) are covered.

[3] Wittgenstein's early philosophy is based on his so-called picture theory of language, which sees, in Wallace's words, "the paradigmatic function of language as mirroring or 'picturing' the world" ("The Empty Plenum" [*Review*] 224)—a theory that Wittgenstein in his later philosophy critiques as offering a much too narrow understanding of the many different ways in which language might be seen to function meaningfully.

[4] Sections 243–315 of Wittgenstein's *Philosophical Investigations* (see also Hacker 19). To help students interpret Wittgenstein's description of the impossibility of private language, the instructor can provide them with Wallace's own explanation thereof, as offered in Wallace's essay "Authority and American Usage" (*"Consider"* 87–88n32).

[5] Another key section from *Philosophical Investigations* on private language is section 258. The "many exotic new facts" section in *Infinite Jest* (200–10) connects addiction to solipsism and skepticism. As to secondary texts, Baker and Hacker's *Understanding and Meaning* (163–205) and Hacker's *Meaning and Mind* (15–30, 206–08, 224–53) offer highly illuminating essays on Wittgenstein's refutation of skepticism and solipsism; also see Jon Baskin on Wallace's fiction as Wittgensteinian therapeutic project and Patrick Horn on Wallace and solipsism (Horn claims Wallace partly misunderstood Wittgenstein's refutation of solipsism, while his fiction still successfully illustrates this refutation), including the suggestion that the ending of "Good Old Neon" ("Not another word" [181]) constitutes a "moral rebuke" (255).

[6] Sartre's fifty-page essay offers a relatively clear and succinct presentation of the ideas that are most relevant to Wallace's work (and that are elaborated in Sartre's *Being and Nothingness*).

[7] Interestingly, on the face of it, students might take the phrase to refer to overcoming the ego. Although this is not precisely what Sartre has in mind (he wants to indicate the location where the self is constituted—beyond consciousness—not to reject this constitution outright), there is an element of selflessness to Sartre's conception of the self: he conceives of it as a public (not private) entity that is subject to (in need of) constant change as a result of the constantly shifting relations between consciousness and the world (and thereby, philosophically, Sartre in fact transcends more traditional conceptions of the self or ego).

[8] Suggestions for further reading: the brief but difficult section "The Ontological Proof" (16–18) from the introduction to Sartre's *Being and Nothingness* and the chapter titled "Bad Faith" (70–95) could serve to deepen discussion based on *The Transcendence of the Ego* and to further connect "bad faith" and addiction. Wallace's short story "Good Old Neon" offers a philosophically very interesting portrayal of paralyzing, objectifying self-consciousness, and "The Devil Is a Busy Man" offers an example of self-reflective poisoning of experience. Recommended secondary texts include Richmond's introduction to *The Transcendence of the Ego*, the sections from Catalano's *A Commentary on Jean-Paul Sartre's* Being and Nothingness (39–41, 78–91) on the above-mentioned selections from Sartre's text, Zadie Smith's essay on Wallace, and the essays by both Boswell ("Constant Monologue") and Burn ("Paradigm") on the portrayal of consciousness in Wallace's work.

[9] This quotation in *The Pale King* refers to an older translation of *Either/Or*, by Walter Lowrie; for a more recent translation, see the Hong and Hong edition used throughout this section (285).

[10] Students can further explore the role of saintly characters in Wallace by reading James's lectures 14 and 15 ("The Value of Saintliness") and the description of prayer in lecture 19, "Other Characteristics" (415–28). Another AA / Ennet House section from *Infinite Jest* (for example, 343–74) could further illustrate the affinity between Wallace's description of his addict characters and James's "sick souls." The "Diapsalmata" from Kierkegaard's *Either/Or, Part I* (17–43) could be read to further explore the aesthete's dreadful awareness that the flight from boredom is unsuccessful. "Boredom as bliss" in *The Pale King* can be studied in the long Chris Fogle chapter (154–252). Recommended secondary texts include insightful essays by David Evans and by Thomas Tracey on the influence of James (and pragmatism) in Wallace's work as well as my own articles on the affinities between Wallace and Kierkegaard with regard to irony and boredom ("Beyond"; "Boredom"). My book *Existentialist Engagement in Wallace, Eggers, and Foer* also deals with these themes, including language; consciousness; and the relevance of Wittgenstein, Kierkegaard, and Sartre.

Desire, Self, and Other:
Wallace and Gender

Hamilton Carroll

The study of David Foster Wallace's fiction and nonfiction offers the advanced literature student the opportunity to think about not only questions of gender, sexuality, and identity that are at the forefront of recent social and cultural debates but also the often-overlooked relation between sociocultural gender dynamics, questions of desire, and the formal and thematic concerns of contemporary literature—a relation that is clearly visible across Wallace's oeuvre. Wallace frequently interrogates culturally constructed gender roles (which he tends to route through the topic of desire rather than in relation to sociological structures or the power dynamics of gender). At the same time, he often falls back on conservative views of gender—particularly as they relate to the sociocultural transformations that subtend the so-called crisis of masculinity that was a dominant cultural response to the sociopolitical gains of both second-wave feminism and the civil rights movement.

Studying and teaching Wallace through the lens of gender is a challenging task, therefore, but one that presents numerous opportunities for students to deepen their understanding of this influential author. While students will find that Wallace's engagement with questions of gender and sexuality is serious and sustained, they will also see that it is ambivalent and sometimes contradictory. While they will find frequent examples of strong female characters in his work, and will notice that he occasionally addresses questions of sexuality and desire through homosexual protagonists, they will see that he is just as likely to portray those characters in relation to the mores of heterosexual male characters or to offer female characters as unobtainable, near-fantasy objects of male desire. As such, Wallace's writing tends to recenter a conservative masculinist perspective that he, like many of his principal characters (both male and female), seems unable to escape from.

This essay highlights areas of Wallace's writing that are of particular concern to the study of gender and provides a range of ways in which students can be encouraged to think about them in relation to the themes through which Wallace is most typically understood: the reader-author relationship, narrative self-reflexivity, empathy, and the end of irony. At the same time, the essay points to locations where Wallace's famously empathetic mode of writing assumes or produces a male reading subject and succumbs to existing hierarchies of gender and suggests ways that students can be encouraged to consider the relation between this implied male reader and these other central themes.

A thorough examination of gender in Wallace will allow students to recognize how his work often adapts the language and positions of second-wave feminism while operating from the very positions of heteronormativity and male oppression it might otherwise seek to overcome. Like many of his peers, Wallace often appears to be motivated by a desire to move beyond the male-centered modes of authorship and subject matter that preoccupied his postmodern predecessors yet is unable to free himself completely from their influences as he recenters the male subject in sometimes problematic ways. This essay will suggest methods that will enable the advanced literature student to develop an understanding of how Wallace occupies this interesting position in relation to representations of gender and sexuality in contemporary literature.

Self and Other

Perhaps the most significant aspect of Wallace's attention to gender in his fiction is the repeated enlistment of the female other as an impossible ideal for the male subject. The most important figure of male desire in all of Wallace's fiction, *Infinite Jest*'s Joelle van Dyne, offers a complex and often ambivalent characterization of the female other. Sustained analysis of her character allows students to work through key themes that recur across Wallace's oeuvre, including the connection between beauty and ugliness; masculine desire; visual culture and celebrity; and the self-abnegating male subject.

Students' initial questions about Joelle usually concern the novel's ambivalent representation of her physical appearance; Joelle is described as a woman either so beautiful or so ugly (the novel offers both possibilities) that she feels the need to remain veiled at all times. She is both a member of U.H.I.D. (the Union of the Hideously and Improbably Deformed) and what Orin Incandenza, her former lover, calls the P.G.O.A.T., or the Prettiest Girl of All Time (249). Whether Joelle is truly beautiful or ugly is never fully disclosed in the novel, and she is variously described as either impossibly beautiful or hideously deformed following an acid attack (225). What is perhaps most important about the question of Joelle's appearance is not the ambiguity itself but the close connection it creates between bodily perfection and imperfection, and between the desiring subject and the desired object. Students should be encouraged to keep that ambiguity in play and should be dissuaded from trying to fix Joelle in one visual category or the other.

Students can be asked to locate passages in the text where Joelle's physical appearance is described and to ascertain who is doing the describing (the narrator, one of the other characters, Joelle herself, etc.). The first chapter in which she is represented to the reader at length, "7 November—Year of the Depend Adult Undergarment" (219–40), is a rich source of such descriptions. For example, Joelle is described in quick succession as "excruciatingly alive and encaged" (222), "like some grotesque clown" (223), "look[ing] like death" (229), and "prettier" than the "giant flawless 2D beauties iridescent on the screen" (237). Once such examples have been located, and their provenance secured, students can be asked to discuss the effect of these representations on both reader and characters. Students can discuss the implied reader Wallace constructs and whether that reader is gendered.

The discussion of the relation between narcissism and desire in Leo Bersani and Adam Phillips's short book *Intimacies* (esp. 57–118) can be used to think about the complex relation between desire and the self that is central to a full understanding of the figure of the other in Wallace's fiction. For example, students can consider how Bersani and Phillips's concept of "narcissistic pleasure that sustains human intimacy" (72) can frame a theory of the relationship between the self and the other in Wallace. Students can examine how desire for the other is often a means of defining the self for Wallace's male characters, and how Joelle exists in a state of social isolation.

If Joelle van Dyne is represented as an unparalleled object of desire, she is also, significantly, a minor celebrity. The pernicious effect of visual culture is a central theme in *Infinite Jest*, and it is often cast in highly gendered terms. Students will need to think through the relation developed in the novel between desire, gender, and contemporary forms of American celebrity culture. For example, Joelle, who has attracted fans as the host of a radio show under the pseudonym Madame Psychosis, also embodies the power of visual culture with her appearance in James Incandenza's irresistible and deadly film referred to as the Entertainment. She wonders whether she was responsible for the filmmaker's suicide: "Did she kill him, somehow, just inclined veilless over that lens?" (231). Understanding the long-standing links between gender and visual culture is an important task for the student of gender in Wallace's writing. Laura Mulvey's seminal essay "Visual Pleasure and Narrative Cinema" can usefully ground this discussion. Molly Haskell's equally important study of women in cinema, *From Reverence to Rape: The Treatment of Women in the Movies*, particularly the final chapter of the second edition, can help students discuss the dual representational load that women typically are required to bear. As Haskell usefully points out, female characters are often idealized or abjected, and frequently both at the same time: mother and lover, beautiful and ugly, angel and whore. Thinking through this observation in relation to Joelle van Dyne will allow students to develop an understanding of the relation between gender and characterization.

A discussion of this dual burden also provides a good opportunity for students to begin to think about the important topic of maternal relationships in Wallace's writing. The Entertainment's deadly power is frequently cast in terms of the irresistible appeal of narcissistic mother-love, and Joelle occupies a doubled dichotomy of beauty/ugliness and mother/lover. Haskell's discussion of the double bind of female agency is a productive starting point for a discussion not only of the capacity of the Entertainment to cause catatonia and death in its viewers but also of the connection between desire and maternal relationships that it represents in *Infinite Jest*. In Wallace's writing the female object of desire is often a location—or trajectory—that allows the relationship of the sexually mature adult male to his mother-centric infant self to be worked through. Maternal and sexual desire are frequently commingled in Wallace's fiction; the male character is unable to escape the bonds of one in order to fully enter the pleasures of the other. Referring to the foundational power of the figure of the mother in human romantic and sexual relationships as it is developed in psychoanalysis, in *Intimacies*, Phillips eloquently states, "we live our lives forward but we desire backwards" (105). Taking this observation as a starting point, students can be asked to think about the complex temporal structuring of *Infinite Jest* and the relation between desire and time that the novel develops. Narrative time is one of the key ways in which characters are placed in relation to the world of the novel and to the reader; it is significant that *Infinite Jest* opens with an account of an episode that takes place near the end of its chronological timeline. Desire operates in a dual relation to this opening: the reader desires to understand what led the character of Hal Incandenza to this point, but the episode also offers a point in time through which prior events—that are related later—can be understood. It is an episode that has yet to happen in the story but that is located in the past of the plot. As such, it is an example of the ways in which plotting organizes narrative's desire for closure.

The relationship between the unobtainable female other and the desiring male subject also receives sustained treatment in *The Pale King*, most notably in a lengthy chapter toward the end of the novel (444–509). The chapter primarily consists of an extended conversation in a bar between Shane Drinion, one of the novel's numerous male characters, and Meredith Rand, a "wrist-bitingly attractive" coworker (447). Meredith Rand serves as a useful counterpoint to Joelle van Dyne: as central female characters, written fifteen years apart, in novels otherwise populated almost exclusively by men, these characters allow students to consider how Wallace's understanding of female agency and male desire shifts across the course of the author's career. Much of the information readers are given about Meredith Rand concerns her physical beauty, and students should note the language used in this passage. Do these narrative descriptions betray a gendered perspective, for example? The chapter begins with an account of intergender social interactions among a group of work colleagues and states that the "energy and dynamics of the Pod C table change when Meredith Rand is present for Happy Hour" (446–47). Having observed that such changes are commonplace and "familiar enough to everyone to not spend time enumerating," the narrator concludes, "suffice it that Meredith Rand makes the Pod's males self-conscious" (447). This observation is followed by a description of the negative effect of the men's reactions to Meredith on the other women present.

The remainder of the chapter consists of a sustained conversation between Meredith and Shane, the only man in the group who is seemingly unaffected by her beauty. This conversation is significant because it is described largely from Meredith's point of view, sometimes in retrospect, and contains elements of direct speech. Students can be asked to compare the various ways in which information is provided about the conversation and to compare Meredith's later thoughts about it to the examples of direct speech. Because Meredith both participates in this conversation and is shown reflecting on it, this comparison will allow students to further develop their understanding of the complex relation in Wallace's writing between subjectivity and narrative. Drinion's lack of desire is apparent to Meredith and allows her to feel comfortable talking to him about topics that she wouldn't raise with more predatory or sexually invested coworkers. As such, she provides an example of Wallace attempting to think through male desire from the perspective of the unobtainable other. However, because the example of Meredith Rand relies on traditional sociocultural links between desire and gender, it serves more to recenter a traditional masculinist perspective than to offer an alternative to it. As an object of male desire, Meredith Rand is denied agency, even as she is given a voice. The potentially problematic gendered relations that are underscored by the fact that Meredith is offered to the reader as an object of sexual desire, in other words, aren't changed by her ability to converse freely with Shane. Moreover, given the frequency with which adult male sexual desire is routed through the figure of the mother in Wallace's fiction, students can gain a great deal from a discussion of the fact that Drinion grew up in an orphanage.

If the male protagonists of Wallace's fiction are often caught in an infantile relationship with the mother figure, they are also incapacitated by patriarchal overdetermination, as demonstrated by intergenerational masculine relationships in Wallace's writing. One particularly illuminating chapter that is vital for any discussion of gender in the novel appears early in *Infinite Jest* ("Winter B.S. 1960—Tucson, AZ," 157–69), which consists entirely of a speech given by James Incandenza's father. While the chapter's lament about the shift from one generation's experience to that of the next is not uncommon, there is an interesting claim being made about the presence of parents in the lives of their children. The parents of James's generation incapacitate their children not by absence or disinterest but by their opposite. Like the suffocating mother-love of the Entertainment, the taken-for-granted aspect of the child's relationship to the parent is understood to disable children in other ways.

This intergenerational dysfunction is a key aspect of the so-called crisis of masculinity that subtends many discussions of contemporary masculinity; the crisis names a perceived shift in forms of masculine activity that accompany the historical transition from blue-collar manual labor and manufacturing to the postwar world of white-collar labor and the more recent service economy. Students can be asked to note some of the many examples of interfamilial communication that take place in the novel (between fathers and sons, mothers and sons, fathers and daughters, and siblings). These examples can then be used to discuss the various forms of male disenfranchisement contained within the novel and to develop an understanding of their importance to the novel's central themes.

Perhaps the most useful introduction to the topic of American masculinities is Michael Kimmel's study *Manhood in America*. While the book's early chapters provide a helpful historical overview of masculine culture in the United States, its final section, "The Contemporary 'Crisis' of Masculinity," is particularly relevant to Wallace's representations of contemporary male anxieties of selfhood. The afterword to R. W. Connell's equally important study *Masculinities* also can help ground this discussion by introducing students to the sociological study of gender. The assignment of these key texts in the study of contemporary masculinities will help students analyze these pages and will provide context for later discussions.

Male Abjection

Like the female other, the male subject is also portrayed in relation to its own abjection. Male abjection in Wallace's writing is often represented through the inability of characters to control both body and mind. Masturbation functions, in Wallace's fiction and nonfiction alike, as a trope through which the male subject struggles with desire, gratification, and compulsion—with the relation between the inner life of the subject and its external manifestations. As is so often the case with Wallace, in his representations of masturbation an everyday activity is rendered abnormal through its representation as excess. Masturbation is understood in Wallace's oeuvre to be commonplace but nevertheless a topic of shame or psychic insecurity.

This double significance is perhaps most clearly visible in the essay "Big Red Son," the introductory paragraphs of which contain a discussion of the phenomenon of autocastration as a means of controlling unmanageable sexual desire. The introduction concludes with the suggestion that the essay's authors (it was published under double pseudonyms) have found an alternative way for men to curb their sexual desires: attendance at the Annual AVN Awards, produced by *Adult Video News*. One might begin discussion of the essay by asking why the author chose to open the article, the subject proper of which is the AVN awards show, with a story of men driven to self-harm by sexual desire. Students should be encouraged to think about how this discussion of male self-harm and pornography is routed through the subject of desire and the impossibility of its achievement (a recurring topic in Wallace's writing).

Such a discussion might bring students back to the topic of the unobtainable object of desire previously discussed through the character of Joelle van Dyne but can also move students towards an understanding of the male-centric nature of masturbation in Wallace's writing (which is almost exclusively understood to be a male activity). Students can be asked to locate these and other examples of the trope of masturbation and ask what it might mean that Wallace's female characters are so rarely represented as desiring subjects.

The article goes on to discuss not only the AVN Awards but also the relation between masturbation (the necessary corollary of the billion-dollar pornography industry), addiction, and pornography—a relation that likewise is understood in the essay to be an exclusively male problem. For example, Wallace observes that "certain antiporn arguments in the 1990s are now centered on adult entertainment's alleged effects on the men who consume it" rather than on the plight of female performers (18). These effects are cast in relation to the "grievous psychic harm" caused by addiction (19). That the male desiring—consuming—

subject is the primary focal point of the essay's underlying concerns suggests just how firmly fixed on the male psyche Wallace's attention is.

Students can be asked to compare Wallace's representation of the American pornography industry and its deleterious effect on its male consumers with the argument developed by Susan Faludi in "Waiting for Wood: A Death on the New Frontier," first published in the *New Yorker* as "The Money Shot" in 1995. Three years before Wallace, Faludi attended the awards show and the International Consumer Electronics Show (CES) in Las Vegas, interviewed producers and actors, and charted the shift from celluloid to video (and then DVD) that the industry underwent in the 1980s and 1990s. One primary difference between the two essays is that Faludi does not consider the consumers of pornography at all; her attention is focused entirely on the experience of male performers (and of Cal Jammer, an actor who had recently committed suicide, in particular). While Wallace only mentions Jammer's suicide in passing (and alongside a number of female suicides), for Faludi, his plight is typical of the modern American man, cut off from a world of manual labor and direct masculine activity. The comparison of Wallace and Faludi will allow students to return to the conversation about masculinity in relation to patriarchal affiliations in *Infinite Jest*. Typically perceived to hold the power in monetized sexual encounters such as the consumption of pornography, the male subject is shown here to be brought down by them, rendered powerless in the face of putative female empowerment (in the image of the successful porn star) on the one hand and by their own intolerable desires on the other. Students wishing to consider in more detail the subject of pornography and gender can be pointed to Linda Williams's study *Hard Core: Power, Pleasure, and the "Frenzy of the Visible,"* particularly chapter 5, "Generic Pleasures," which discusses, among other things, pornography in the age of video (120–52).

Narrating Subjects

Though frequently caught between perceptions of overwhelming female power and stultifying masculine inadequacy, Wallace's male characters also often hold a great deal of power as narrators. The male narrator's dangerous appropriation of the female to serve his own narcissistic needs is a common subject in Wallace's fiction and a major theme of his exploration of gender roles. This theme can be discussed through the analysis of "B.I. #20" in the short story collection *Brief Interviews with Hideous Men*, which students can be asked to read alongside one or two key critical readings.

In "B.I. #20" the speaker's co-opting of the suffering female other for his own empathic escape from solipsism provides one of the best examples of form meeting theme in Wallace's fiction. The speaking male subject tells the female interviewer (whose speech we never read) how he came to fall in love with a woman whom he had originally considered to be merely "a body that [his] body found sexually attractive and wanted to have sexual intercourse with and it was not really any more noble or complicated than that" (249). Following their first sexual encounter, the woman relates to the man the story of an "unbelievably horrifying incident in which she was brutally accosted and held captive and very nearly killed" (245). The speaker uses his account of his empathic response to the woman's story as an opportunity to construct a version of the self, both for himself and for the female interviewer. Students will need to be guided through the various layers of the narrative and to be encouraged to think about the narrator's positioning of himself in relation to the story that he is telling. How, students can be asked, does the storyteller construct a version of himself from his story about another person's experiences?

A helpful theoretical grounding for a discussion of this relationship between self and other can be found in Lauren Berlant and Lee Edelman's book *Sex; or, The Unbearable*, particularly their discussion of negativity, which they call a "scene of relationality" that "denotes . . . the relentless force that unsettles the fantasy of sovereignty" (viii). The connection between sex, desire, and sovereignty developed by Berlant and Edelman provides useful ways to think about these topics in Wallace's writing. In addition to the helpful preface, students can be asked to read the first chapter, "Sex without Optimism" (1–34), which establishes a theoretical framework for discussing Wallace's representations of the unobtainable other. In particular, the discussion of "fantasies of repairing what's broken" (20) that grounds the chapter's discussion of cuteness provides a provocative and helpful way of thinking about the desires that many of Wallace's male characters project onto the figure of the other. In this particular instance, it can be used to help students understand the links made in this short story between the narrative of male agency and female empowerment or disempowerment. What, students can be asked, does the male narrator's lengthy and detailed discussion of not only the woman's abduction and rape but also his reaction to it say about power, gender, and the field of sexual relationships?

Students will also find useful the discussion of narcissistic pleasure in *Intimacies* that was used to ground the discussion of Joelle van Dyne and the unobtainable female other, particularly Bersani's discussion in the chapter "The Power of Evil and the Power of Love" of the relation between the actions of predatory killers such as Jeffrey Dahmer and so-called normal human sexual or romantic interaction (57–88). Students can be asked to think about how Bersani's discussion provides a model for understanding the clear parallels that are drawn in "B.I. #20" between the male narrator's predatory seduction of the woman and the actions of her kidnapper and rapist.

The seminal work of Judith Butler on gender can also help students navigate this tricky terrain. Butler's *Undoing Gender* contains some useful essays that students can be asked to read alongside Wallace's short story. In addition to the introduction, which provides an overview of Butler's concerns and establishes the concept of gender as a "kind of doing" (1) and not a fixed or stable category, the first and second chapters in particular can be used to facilitate a discussion of gender as a social and performative act grounded in, and productive of, power. Butler's insistence that "power emerges in language" (13) and that gender "is a form of social power" (48) can facilitate a useful discussion about the relation between masculine identity, as it is represented in the story, and narrative authority. For example, students can be asked to locate examples of gendered language in the story and to think about the power relationships that they produce between the speaker, the listener, and the subject of the story. How, for example, does being denied a speaking voice disempower the female interviewer; can she properly be considered to be a character in the story? How does the interviewee's choice of language empower him? What is the significance of the handful of occasions when the interviewer relates the opinions that his male friends hold of the woman he is describing? Should the woman be understood to be a character, or is she merely an object of discussion for the male interviewee?

The discussion of loneliness in "What Survives," the second chapter of *Sex; or, The Unbearable,* serves as a useful theoretical approach to the frequent incapacity of Wallace's characters to form lasting romantic relationships and their reliance on the fantasy of unobtainability to shore up their sense of fully incorporated selfhood. Loneliness, in Berlant's helpful formulation, is "a kind of relation to a world whose only predictable is in the persistence of inaccessible love" (37). This formulation—which might have come straight from Wallace himself—enables the student to think in productive ways about the relationship between the self and the other when communication is seemingly denied by the impossibility of forming interpersonal relationships that are able to overcome the veils, masks, or walls put up by the desiring subject.

"B.I. #20" is a highly complex story in which three narrative temporalities are at work at the same time: the story of the woman's rape and near murder, the story of the woman telling the man her story following their first sexual encounter, and the story of the man telling the interviewer the story of his response to the woman's story. Finally, the scene of the interview is also presented as an attempted seduction of the female interviewer by the male subject (he repeatedly offers to buy her another drink, for example). The interview continually moves between these different narrative spaces and foregrounds their construction. As such, Wallace's story develops through multiple layers of irony and self-conscious narrative construction that mimic the layers of construction of self and other required in order for the male narrator to re-create the other in his image (which is a primary interest of the story itself).

In the first chapter of *Undoing Gender,* entitled "Beside Oneself: On the Limits of Sexual Autonomy," Butler says that grief "often interrupts the self-conscious account of ourselves we might try to provide in ways that challenge the very notion of ourselves as autonomous and in control." She goes on to claim that "[t]he very 'I' [of the speaking self] is called into question by its relation to the one to whom [it] address[es itself]" (19). The relation that Butler elucidates here between strong emotions, the self-conscious speaking subject, the interlocutor, and the act of storytelling can be used to consider the power dynamics at play in Wallace's short story. For example, students can be asked what it means that the female subject of the story is denied direct representation and that her story is given only indirectly as a subordinate component of the narrator's. Students also will need to consider the position of the reader in these power relations. A discussion of Wallace's use in this story of the interview format and of the second person can help to facilitate this discussion. For example, students can be asked to consider the fact that the (female) interviewer's questions have been left out of the story and to consider what effect this omission has on its meaning. This is also an opportunity to discuss the implied addressee of the second-person narrative, asking whether the "you" of the second person has the effect of hailing the reader, whether Wallace's implied reader is usually male, and, if so, what it might mean that this "you" is a woman.

Questions of Desire

The examples discussed so far demonstrate the almost exclusively heteronormative context in which Wallace explores the issues of identity formation and gender. By comparison, in the short story "Little Expressionless Animals" (which opens Wallace's first collection, *Girl with Curious Hair*), the author represents a lesbian relationship between two of the story's central characters, Julie and Faye. The story is valuable to the student of gender not only because of its representations of same-sex desire but also because it develops topics that occur throughout Wallace's fiction: the construction of the self through the other, the public self and private desire, celebrity culture, and maternal and paternal relationships and their effects on adult sexuality.

Julie and Faye's relationship is one in which the boundaries of sexual identity are understood to be fluid and negotiable: "being involved with a woman doesn't automatically make you a lesbian" and "lesbianism is simply one kind of response to Otherness," Julie tells Faye (32). Such statements locate the couple's frequent conversations about sexuality in clearly recognizable Wallace terrain. One productive classroom exercise is to task students with interrogating the various reasons that Faye and Julie imagine giving if asked to explain their lesbianism (33–37, 40–42). Students should be encouraged to recognize that many of these explanations locate the origin point of lesbianism either in the failure of a heterosexual relationship or in a retreat from the strictures of male duplicity. Through a discussion of these examples, students can consider precisely what forms of "Otherness" lesbianism is understood to be a response to. Cast in slightly different terms, students can be asked to consider why—and with what effect—a story about two women involved in a romantic-sexual relationship is so preoccupied with the topic of male sexual desire. Can lesbianism only be understood as a response to or a retreat from men?

In the story Wallace also presents love as a form of narcissistic interpersonal exchange that will be familiar to students from texts already studied. For example,

Julie tells Faye that "the whole point of love is to try to get your fingers through the holes in the lover's mask" (32). As a successful contestant on a television quiz show, Julie is a celebrity and only leaves the house in disguise, often dressed as a man. Students might be asked here to think about the relation between the male mask and Julie's various disguises and Joelle van Dyne's veil in *Infinite Jest*. Where does the self reside in these examples, in the public-facing mask or in the private consciousness hidden behind it? What is the relation between male desire and disguise? What does it mean that Julie is often dressed as, or mistaken for, a man when she is in disguise?

The final story Julie offers as an explanation for lesbianism appears to be her own and should be considered in some depth (especially because it repeats in a different context the information given in the story's opening paragraph). Julie offers Faye the story of her mother's abandonment of her and her younger brother at the behest of a controlling lover. Students can be asked to think about the relation between form and thematic content that is produced by this temporal structuring. How does the direct link that is made between the opening paragraph and Julie's closing narrative affect the meaning of the story?

Julie's incapacitating fear of all animals stems from her abandonment. Left in a field as a child, with a cow gazing blankly on her plight, she now "cannot stand animals, because animals' faces have no expression"; similarly, "[a] man's face has nothing on it" and "there are no holes for your fingers in the masks of men" (41). Students can be asked to think about the link that is being drawn here between men and animals and to judge how far—if at all—Wallace moves beyond the stereotype of men as predatory animals in his assessment of male behavior. How, for example, does the typical dichotomy that places animals on the side of nature and instinct and humans on the side of civilization and rationality operate here? Is it being complicated or is Wallace relying on its explanatory power?

A consideration of Wallace's writing that foregrounds questions of gender does more than just allow the advanced literature student to understand how significant the topic is to the author; it provides an explanatory mechanism through which many of his most important themes can be understood with more nuance and clarity. Like all of his primary subjects, questions of gender and desire were ones that Wallace took seriously—and with which he engaged with characteristic rigor and humor. At the same time, his principal literary influences and interlocutors were almost exclusively other male authors, and that fact is betrayed in his writing. Wallace's empathetic mode, his desire to place the reader in a position of power and responsibility alongside the author and the text, and his development of antirealist modes of realism are all dependent on the production of gendered subjects—more often than not male—as characters and as implied readers. To consider gender as deeply as Wallace did not only exposes some of his theoretical and representational limitations but also illuminates the care and attention he devoted to this important subject. It is this complexity that makes the subject of gender vital for any full understanding of Wallace's work.

Can Empathy Be Taught?
Wallace's Literary Ethics

Matthew Mullins

Empathy is more than a theme in David Foster Wallace's writing, which sets out to unseat his readers from their own psyches and to help them access the experiences and thoughts of others. Wallace explains the problem and promise of this enterprise in a well-known interview with Larry McCaffery: "We all suffer alone in the real world; true empathy's impossible. But if a piece of fiction can allow us imaginatively to identify with characters' pain, we might then also more easily conceive of others identifying with our own" (22). There may seem to be a contradiction in this theory. First Wallace says that true empathy is impossible in the real world, but then he suggests that identifying with characters in fiction might make it easier. The variety of definitions of *empathy*, as an ability, a quality, a power, and a capacity, can resolve any perceived contradiction. While some might consider empathy a zero-sum quality, others, like Wallace, think of it as an ability or capacity, something that can be enhanced. "True empathy," or full capacity, may very well be impossible, but this does not mean that empathy is entirely impossible.

Whether I am teaching Wallace to first-year students in an introductory literature course or to advanced students in a seminar on contemporary novels, whether I am teaching his shorter or longer fiction, I have found his ethics of empathy unavoidable. These experiences have raised the challenge of how to address empathy in my pedagogy. Like most teachers of literature, I was trained (on the job) to teach context, content, and form. These conventions of the literature classroom are all more or less easy to teach and test. I can tell in short order if my students know when a text was published or if they understand the difference between first-person and third-person narration and how that difference affects a given story. It is more difficult to assess whether or not a student has become more empathetic, yet every teacher can probably name students for whom literature has been an important component of their expanding worlds. In fact, there is some evidence of a correlation between literature and empathy. A recent study demonstrates that reading literary fiction can improve our "ability to detect and understand others' emotions" (Kidd and Castano 277). If we are going to capitalize on Wallace's investment in fiction as a means of enhancing readers' capacities for empathy, then we must not only examine empathy in his writing but also foster empathy in the classroom.

Fortunately for teachers of literature, Wallace's ethics of empathy are entangled with his literary historical context as well as with the content and form of his fiction. This essay is devoted to strategies for framing empathy in a literary historical approach to Wallace and a few brief implications for how these strategies might alter the way we situate Wallace on the syllabus. In their love for and frustration with Wallace, my students have taught me that I can teach until I am blue in the face but I cannot learn for them. Wallace's literary ethics have turned my pedagogical focus toward creating a space where students can build the kinds of learning environments in which they are most likely to identify with others and create new knowledge for themselves. And so this essay is not only about teaching Wallace but also about how teaching Wallace affects our teaching.

My approach to teaching Wallace has been integrally shaped by how his fiction makes it possible for readers to confront the inner workings of other minds. Building on the postmodern legacy of metafiction, he asks us to think like writers rather than readers, to know his characters so well that we can fill the gaps in their stories. Wallace's work thus provides a postmodern example of fiction that operates according to what Lisa Zunshine and others call "theory of mind," demanding of us the kind of empathy we need in our daily lives as we interact with friends and strangers whose thoughts and motives are not always apparent (6). It's one thing to explain this to students, but it's another to structure your class so that they must take a similarly active role in imagining the experiences of others. It's another thing still for teachers to take such an approach to thinking about students, to be thoughtful and reflective about what it takes for them to understand the material as we do. Ultimately, Wallace's fiction teaches us that we should act toward others as if there is more to them than we can know, and it stretches our capacity to imagine just how much more.

Postmodernism, Metafiction, and Empathy

In 2013, David Comer Kidd and Emanuele Castano published a study in *Science* that seems to validate Wallace's theory of fiction. They offer evidence that reading literary fiction promotes and refines "interpersonal sensitivity throughout our lives." They attribute this ability to the way literary fiction asks readers to delve deeply into the minds of its characters and approach them actively rather than in the passive manner more typical of popular fiction and nonfiction. Using Roland Barthes's terminology, Kidd and Castano assert that "writerly" literary fiction promotes empathy through active participation in the text (*S/Z* 4–5). Citing Jerome Bruner, Kidd and Castano argue that the writerly disposition of literary fiction "engages readers in a discourse that forces them to fill in gaps and search 'for meanings among a spectrum of possible meanings'" (377). This distinction between writerly and readerly approaches resonates with the form of metafiction developed by writers of the generation before Wallace, including John Barth, Robert Coover, Donald Barthelme, and others to whom Wallace is both heir and reactionary. What may seem like a standard point of literary historical context, then, can be an entrance to the world of Wallace's ethics of empathy through the writerly ethos of postmodern metafiction. Metafiction's model of discourse provides Wallace with a ready-made form for the fundamentally empathetic task of asking readers to engage his fictional worlds from a perspective other than their own. We might say that Wallace takes the formal demands of metafiction to their logical moral conclusions by using them as practice for filling in the gaps we all encounter in imagining the experiences of others.

I introduce metafiction in class with the opening story of John Barth's collection *Lost in the Funhouse*, "Frame-Tale," whose Möbius-strip structure makes the two-page story infinitely long. Front-and-back copies of "Frame-Tale" are ideal as they enable students to follow Barth's instructions and create their own Möbius strip. I either project this quotation from the introduction to Linda Hutcheon's *Narcissistic Narrative: The Metafictional Paradox* on a screen or include it on the "Frame-Tale" handout to work through with the class (advanced students might read Hutcheon's entire introduction): "'Metafiction,' as it has now been named, is fiction about fiction—that is, fiction that includes within itself a commentary on its own narrative and/or linguistic identity" (1). I lead a discussion of Barth's self-conscious story as an invitation for readers to imagine how narrative works by taking on the role of the author. In navigating from Barth to Wallace, the strategies discussed below for teaching "Lyndon" work well with nearly all of Wallace's fiction. For beginning students I recommend the relatively shorter and most overt metafiction, especially stories such as "Here and There," "Forever Overhead," "The Depressed Person," "Octet," and "Good Old Neon." More advanced students will be able to map these strategies onto entire collections, such as *Brief Interviews with Hideous Men*, or to jump directly into the novels.

"Lyndon"

If Barth brings the fictional world to the reader, then "Lyndon" brings a figure from the reader's world into the fictional world. "Lyndon" reimagines the life and career of Lyndon Baines Johnson through the first-person narration of a closeted aide named David Boyd and includes many metafictional features that collapse the distance between writer and reader and blur the lines between fact and fiction: fabricated newspaper headlines, quotations from staff members, associates, and other figures, an impassioned speech given by LBJ to a fourth-grade class, and, perhaps most outrageous, quotations from campaign speeches given from helicopters. Some beginning students may struggle to read the story as fiction, and this struggle is key. Here I turn to Hutcheon's *A Poetics of Postmodernism*. With the general concept of metafiction outlined, students typically welcome Hutcheon's theory of "historiographic metafiction" as a category for making sense of "Lyndon." Hutcheon defines historiographic metafiction as narratives "which are both intensely self-reflexive and yet paradoxically also lay claim to historical events and personages" (5). Readers of "Lyndon" are as active as readers of "Frame-Tale" as they struggle to distinguish between fact and fiction.

With Barth, Hutcheon, and Wallace under their belts, students can begin to make connections between Barth's and Wallace's metafiction. As we dig more deeply into "Lyndon," I hope students will recognize for themselves that the "narcissistic narrative" form developed by Wallace's precursors deeply influenced his own ethics of empathy. I stress that Hutcheon does not mean "narcissistic" in a pejorative sense but rather as a description of these texts' self-reflexivity. While many scholars, and even Wallace himself, may see the metafictional masters as more concerned with style than with emotion or empathy, I would point out that Wallace's own empathetic style is built on this metafictional foundation, and that writers like Barth insist that if their so-called experimental work is not also "*moving*, then the experiment is unsuccessful" (*Friday Book* 79).

As they become active participants in David Boyd's world, students come to see that metafiction's writerly mode is also what makes it such an effective form for empathy. To illustrate this point, I introduce Wallace's interview with McCaffery. Specifically, I ask students to engage Wallace's claim that

> a big part of serious fiction's purpose is to give the reader, who like all of us is sort of marooned in her own skull, to give her imaginative access to other selves. Since an ineluctable part of being a human self is suffering, part of what we humans come to art for is an experience of suffering, necessarily a vicarious experience, more like a sort of *generalization* of suffering. (22)

Wallace goes on to say that one of the values of metafiction in particular is that it reveals "fiction as a mediated experience" (40). In the course of reading, one becomes aware of the text as something written, and something whose construction one must complete. That is, the reader assumes a writerly orientation toward the text. Wallace utilizes this meta-awareness by asking us to take the empathetic steps of fleshing characters out, imagining their rationales, and wrestling with the gap between fact and fiction. It is this kind of imaginative work that requires, and for Wallace may even develop, empathy.

Students will certainly feel the metafictional pull of "Lyndon," as most of the characters' backstories are scattered and difficult to piece together into coherent narratives. David Boyd is a gay man living in the 1950s and 1960s. He is kicked out of Yale Business School, he marries a woman he does not love and lives under constant pressure from her family, and by the end of the story his husband, René Duverger, is slowly dying of AIDS. Duverger suffers, feeling that David shares his life with LBJ and not with him. LBJ shoulders the weight of a nation, his body breaking down under the burden. Lady Bird Johnson lives as if her husband is dead already. But, to imagine the pain of others, students need to identify with David's, Duverger's, LBJ's, or Lady Bird's suffering, and they need to assume a writerly perspective in order to do so. "Lyndon" primarily requires us to assume that perspective by forcing us to parse fact and fiction and by presenting us with significant gaps in characters' lives.

Asking students to choose a character like David Boyd, with his scattered backstory, and recompose his life in a single, historically linear paragraph, encourages them to take on another person's perspective. Or students might fill in the missing pieces in the life of another character, perhaps Duverger. Wallace makes astounding connections between characters in the story without ever revealing how those connections are originally forged. Asking students to fill in these gaps encourages them to assume the kind of writerly stance necessary for imagining the world from some else's point of view.

The first time I taught "Lyndon," I had not yet begun making the explicit connection between metafictional form and empathy, and I was struck by students' lack of interest in the story as historiographic metafiction. Once they recognized how Wallace was blurring the lines between fact and fiction, the class as a whole got it: narrative shapes our understanding of history, and media do more than merely transmit information and images. But they were much more interested in how a loudmouthed Texan, the all-powerful leader of the free world, could grow so close to a young man whose interracial homosexual relationship was being destroyed by AIDS as his husband lay dying. The relationships between David and LBJ, LBJ and Duverger, and Lady Bird and David seemed to stretch students' suspension of disbelief even more than the image of the thirty-sixth president of the United States pleading with a group of fourth graders.

The moment that most bewildered them was the final scene, in which LBJ has been confined to his bed and David is summoned to the Johnson residence only to find his recently disappeared husband there with his previously indomitable boss. In our last view, LBJ lies in bed surrounded by papers with Duverger by his side, the black man's hand on the white man's face. The president is gravely ill. Duverger seems nearly dead. Nothing can prepare David (or us) for this moment. How have LBJ and Duverger even met? Are they lovers? What precipitated such intimacy? These questions are not answered in any satisfactory way. Lady Bird and David talk past one another about their "two husbands," frequently misunderstanding just which husband the other is talking about (116). Just as we are asked to navigate the fact/fiction divide, these ambiguities require readers to participate in the construction of the story, to create backstories and imagine how such relations could be forged.

This writerly approach to reading can help us teach empathy by creating opportunities for students to imagine their own minds and actions as somehow related to those of others. Wallace provides models in the merging psyches of his characters. LBJ becomes so thoroughly identified with David that Lady Bird explains, "You stand in relations, my husband says. You contain one another. He says he owns the floor you stand on. He says you are the sky whose presence and meaning have become everyday" (116). Duverger and LBJ seem to have merged as well; the story ends with David reading LBJ's facial expressions by the movements of Duverger's hand. Once students have registered empathy between characters, empathy between characters and readers may still require a significant jump. This is when metafiction comes back into the discussion. Toon Staes maintains that Wallace's "immersive narrative world is only effective if the reader, listener, or viewer actively co-creates it" (415). (Advanced students should follow Staes with Suzanne Keen's *Empathy and the Novel*.) Wallace employs meta-fictional means toward empathetic ends by crafting narratives that ask us to rationalize the innermost workings of characters' minds just as we rationalize our own.

Implications for Teaching Wallace

"Lyndon" also offers the opportunity to take this barrier-shattering approach to other conventional boundaries. While the existing scholarship on Wallace occasionally addresses gender and sexuality, for instance, it has only recently raised questions about race, and yet this most visible, hotly contested, and historically conscious identity marker often creates the very kinds of islands on which we are likely to be marooned. "Lyndon" presents us with empathetic constructions of race in addition to the more obvious treatment of same-sex marriage. We might consider, for instance, Duverger's hand over LBJ's face as an invitation to explore the black-white binary in American fiction and what Toni Morrison calls the "Africanist presence" (5). Other Wallace stories are equally promising. One particularly good example is "Another Pioneer," a metafictional romp that interrogates the construction of whiteness. Such connections between the blurred reader/writer boundaries of metafiction and those of race demonstrate how emphasizing empathy can expand the possibilities for situating Wallace on the syllabus.

This expanded view of Wallace also has significant implications for how we teach him in his literary-historical context. First, we might ask, If metafiction gave Wallace the tools to develop his literary empathy, then isn't it possible that the metafictional writers who preceded him were just as invested in empathy as they were in experimentation? The temptation to reduce writers like Barth to formal game players is strong, especially in the classroom, where simplistic juxtapositions can give students clear categories for making sense of what they read. The fact that Wallace himself viewed the early metafictional writers in this way only heightens the temptation. On this point, I might explain or assign a story from the Ambrose cycle in *Lost in the Funhouse* and ask students to consider Ambrose's desire and struggle to relate to others. I also share some of Barth's introductory remarks from early public readings of stories from *Funhouse*. Barth maintains, "Heartless skill has its appeal; so does heartfelt ineptitude; but what we want is passionate virtuosity. If these pieces aren't also *moving*, then the experiment is unsuccessful, and their author is lost in the funhouse indeed" (*Friday Book* 79). Second, Wallace's empathy can help us rethink what scholars have variously identified as two distinct phases, stages, or generations of postmodernism, the first traditionally treated as the territory of white, male writers, the second as the territory of women and writers of color. Amy Elias provides a concise overview of this division in her introduction to *Sublime Desire*, and Wendy Steiner interrogates its problems in "Rethinking Postmodernism."

If time permits, students might read Wallace's novella "Westward the Course of Empire Takes Its Way," a rewrite of Barth's Ambrose cycle, as a means of considering similarities not just in form and content but in empathetic imperative as well. For instance, Barth scatters unfinished sentences throughout his title story. Are these merely playful, or might they be invitations to rationalize the thoughts and actions of his characters? Students might also compare the metafictional strategies of Barth and Wallace with those in Toni Morrison's "Recitatif" and Alice Walker's "Everyday Use." For instance, reading "Lyndon" can better prepare students to notice how and consider why Morrison withholds the racial identities of her two main characters in "Recitatif." Or we could reverse the order and build on Morrison's interrogation of her reader's assumptions to examine how that story shapes our reading of "Lyndon"'s closing scene between Duverger and LBJ. My goal here is to leverage Wallace's metafictional empathy and his commitment to engendering empathy across recognizable cultural boundaries to create some meta-awareness about how categories such as metafiction or postmodernism may cause us to read texts in certain ways to the exclusion of others.

If the objective of the teacher is to help students learn, then it seems our true responsibility is to create an environment in which learning is possible. Teaching is thus a fundamentally empathetic enterprise as we do our best to imagine what conditions might best facilitate student learning. Asking students to take responsibility for their own learning prompts them to collaborate in this process and makes them accountable to the teacher, to themselves, and to their classmates. Teaching Wallace's fiction can turn the classroom into a space in which we practice the very things we must do outside the classroom in order to empathize with others. This space is, finally, a collective space, one in which we may not be able to fully comprehend the experiences of others but in which we live in close enough proximity to try.

NOTES ON CONTRIBUTORS

Marshall Boswell is professor of English at Rhodes College. He is the author of three works of literary scholarship, *John Updike's Rabbit Tetralogy: Mastered Irony in Motion* (2001), *Understanding David Foster Wallace* (2004), and *The Wallace Effect: David Foster Wallace and the Contemporary Literary Imagination* (2019). He is also the author of two works of fiction, *Trouble with Girls* (2003) and *Alternative Atlanta* (2005). With Stephen J. Burn, he is coeditor of *A Companion to David Foster Wallace Studies* (2013), and he is the editor of *David Foster Wallace and "The Long Thing": New Essays on the Novels* (2014).

Mark Bresnan is instructor of English at Colorado State University. His research focuses on twenty-first-century American literature, and he has published essays on David Foster Wallace, Philip Roth, Jonathan Franzen, and Ben Fountain. He has a doctorate in English from the University of Iowa and has previously taught at New York University, Marymount Manhattan College, and Stevenson University.

Stephen J. Burn, reader at the University of Glasgow, is the author or editor of five books, most recently *American Literature in Transition, 1990–2000* (2017). He is the series editor for Bloomsbury's David Foster Wallace Studies and is editing David Foster Wallace's letters in collaboration with the Wallace estate.

Hamilton Carroll is associate professor of English at the University of Leeds. He is the author of *Affirmative Reaction: New Formations of White Masculinity* (2011). He has published widely on topics in contemporary American literature and culture in various edited collections and in journals such as *Comparative American Studies*, *Genre*, the *Journal of American Studies*, *Modern Fiction Studies*, *Studies in American Fiction*, and *Television and New Media*.

Ralph Clare is associate professor of English at Boise State University, specializing in twentieth- and twenty-first-century American literature. He is the author of *Fictions Inc.: The Corporation in Postmodern Fiction, Film, and Popular Culture* (2014) and the editor of *The Cambridge Companion to David Foster Wallace*. His latest book project, "Metaffective Fiction: Structures of Feeling in Contemporary American Literature," explores the role of emotion and affect in post-postmodern fiction.

Philip Coleman is associate professor in the School of English, Trinity College Dublin. He is the author of *John Berryman's Public Vision: Re-locating "the Scene of Disorder"* (2014) and he has edited *David Foster Wallace: Critical Insights* (2015). With Steve Gronert Ellerhoff, he has edited *George Saunders: Critical Essays* (2017), the first collection of essays on George Saunders.

Allard den Dulk is lecturer in philosophy, literature, and film at Amsterdam University College and research fellow at the Faculty of Humanities of the Vrije Universiteit Amsterdam. He is the author of *Existentialist Engagement in Wallace, Eggers and Foer: A Philosophical Analysis of Contemporary American Literature* (2015). Currently, he is working on a book tentatively titled "Wallace's Existentialist Intertexts: Comparative Readings with the Fiction of Kafka, Dostoevsky, Camus and Sartre."

Kathleen Fitzpatrick is director of digital humanities and professor of English at Michigan State University. She is the author of *Generous Thinking: A Radical Approach to Saving the University* (2019), *Planned Obsolescence: Publishing, Technology, and the Future of the Academy* (2011), and *The Anxiety of Obsolescence: The American Novel in the Age of Television* (2006).

Mary K. Holland is professor of English at the University at New Paltz, State University of New York. She is the author of *Succeeding Postmodernism: Language and Humanism in Contemporary American Literature* (2013) and has published essays on David Foster Wallace, Steve Tomasula, John Barth, A. M. Homes, and others. Currently she is working on a book tentatively titled "Contemporary Realisms: Literary Form and Function in the Twenty-First Century."

Matthew Luter is on the English faculty at St. Andrew's Episcopal School in Jackson, Mississippi. He is the author of *Understanding Jonathan Lethem* (2015). His articles, on authors including Don DeLillo, Ellen Douglas, Willie Morris, and Bret Easton Ellis, have appeared in journals including *Critique*, *The Southern Literary Journal*, *Genre*, and *Orbit: A Journal of American Literature*. He is a founding board member of the International David Foster Wallace Society.

Robert L. McLaughlin is professor of English at Illinois State University. He has published many articles on postmodern fiction, in particular on the work of Thomas Pynchon and David Foster Wallace. He is the author of *Stephen Sondheim and the Reinvention of the American Musical* (2016); coauthor, with Sally E. Parry, of *We'll Always Have the Movies: American Cinema during World War II* (2006); and editor of *Innovations: An Anthology of Modern and Contemporary Fiction* (1998).

Mike Miley teaches literature at Metairie Park Country Day School and film studies at Loyola University New Orleans. His work has appeared in *TheAtlantic.com*, *Bright Lights Film Journal*, *Critique*, *Music and the Moving Image*, *The Smart Set*, and elsewhere. He is also the author of the forthcoming book *Truth and Consequences: Game Shows in Fiction and Film*.

Matthew Mullins is assistant professor of English and the history of ideas at Southeastern Baptist Theological Seminary in Wake Forest, North Carolina, and the author of *Postmodernism in Pieces* (2016). His articles and reviews have appeared in *Callaloo*, *Arizona Quarterly*, *SubStance*, *Los Angeles Review of Books*, *The Comparatist*, and other venues. His research and teaching focus on contemporary fiction, critical race theory, and literary history.

Patrick O'Donnell is professor emeritus of English at Michigan State University. He is the author or editor of twelve books, including *The American Novel Now: Contemporary American Fiction Since 1980* (2010), *Latent Destinies: Cultural Paranoia and Contemporary U.S. Narrative* (2000), and, coedited with David W. Madden and Justus Nieland, *The Encyclopedia of Twentieth-Century American Fiction* (2011). He is a former editor of *MFS: Modern Fiction Studies*.

Jeffrey Severs is associate professor of English at the University of British Columbia. He is coeditor of *Pynchon's* Against the Day: *A Corrupted Pilgrim's Guide* (2011) and author of *David Foster Wallace's Balancing Books: Fictions of Value* (2017). His articles have been published in *Critique*, *Modern Fiction Studies*, *Twentieth-Century Litera-*

ture, MELUS, and *The Cambridge Companion to David Foster Wallace* (ed. Ralph Clare).

Lucas Thompson is lecturer at the United States Studies Centre at the University of Sydney. His first book, *Global Wallace: David Foster Wallace and World Literature,* was published in 2016. His articles have been published or are forthcoming in *New Literary History, Comparative Literature Studies, Texas Studies in Literature and Language,* and *Journal of American Studies,* among others.

Andrew Warren is the John L. Loeb Associate Professor of the Humanities in Harvard's Department of English, where he also codirects the Mahindra Humanities Center's Seminar in Dialectical Thinking. His first book, *The Orient and the Young Romantics,* was published in 2014, and his new project is entitled "Romantic Entanglements: The Figure of an Era, 1759–1845." He has published articles on Shelley, Radcliffe, Coleridge, De Quincey, Joyce, and Wallace, among others.

SURVEY PARTICIPANTS

Crystal Alberts, *University of North Dakota*
Maximillian Alvarez, *University of Michigan*
Diego Baez, *City Colleges of Chicago*
Kyle Beachy, *Roosevelt University*
Brandon Benevento, *University of Connecticut*
Alice Bennett, *Liverpool Hope University*
Cornel Bonca, *California State University, Fullerton*
Marshall Boswell, *Rhodes College*
Teresa Boyer, *California State University, Northridge*
Mark Bresnan, *Marymount Manhattan College*
Gerry Canavan, *Marquette University*
Joseph Cheatle, *Miami University*
Ralph Clare, *Boise State University*
Philip Coleman, *Trinity College, Dublin*
Carrie Conners, *LaGuardia Community College, City University of New York*
Thomas Cook, *University at Albany, State University of New York*
Joseph Donica, *School of the Art Institute of Chicago*
Sarah L. Eade
Sarah Etlinger, *Rock Valley College*
Bradley J. Fest, *University of Pittsburgh*
Julie Fifelski, *Fordham University*
Lindsay Gail Gibson, *Columbia University*
Jonathan Goodwin, *University of Louisiana, Lafayette*
Akiva Gottlieb, *University of Michigan*
Kevin Griffith, *Capital University*
Jennifer Gutman, *University at New Paltz, State University of New York*
Donald M. Hassler, *Kent State University*
Julie L. Hawk, *Georgia Institute of Technology*
Heather Houser, *University of Texas, Austin*
Caren Irr, *Brandeis University*
JT Jackson
Marianne Janack, *Hamilton College*
Michael Jauchen, *Colby Sawyer College*
Daniela Franca Joffe, *University of Cape Town*
Keith Leslie Johnson, *Georgia Regents University*
Royden Kadyschuk, *Columbia University*
Adam Kelly, *University of York*
Beth Kramer, *Boston University*
Don Lawson, *Wiley College*
Matthew Luter, *St. Andrew's Episcopal School*
Ryan Marnane, *Salve Regina University*
Katharina McAllister
Robert L. McLaughlin, *Illinois State University*

Maren Michel, *Justus-Liebig-Universität, Giessen*
Mike Miley, *Metairie Park Country Day School*
Shannon Minifie, *Queen's University*
Matthew Mullins, *Southeastern Baptist Theological Seminary*
Woods Nash, *University of Texas, Austin*
Justin Neuman, *Yale University*
Hillary Nunn, *University of Akron*
Jacqueline O'Dell, *Tufts University*
Kathleen O'Gorman, *Illinois Wesleyan University*
David B. Olsen, *Saint Louis University*
Jeffrey Paris, *University of San Francisco*
Scott Parker, *University of Minnesota*
Soong Phoon, *University of Auckland*
Jennifer Rhee, *Virginia Commonwealth University*
Josh Roiland, *University of Notre Dame*
Noah Salamon, *Sierra Canyon School*
Theo Savvas, *University of Bristol*
Christopher Schaberg, *Loyola University New Orleans*
Matthew Schultz, *Vassar College*
Robert Seguin, *Hartwick College*
Jeffrey Severs, *University of British Columbia*
Michael Sheehan, *Stephen F. Austin State University*
Robert Short, *University of Florida*
Albert Silva, *University of California, Santa Barbara*
Joseph Tabbi, *University of Illinois, Chicago*
David Tow, *Terra Linda High School*
Suzanne Webb, *Washington State University, Tri-Cities*
Alison Wielgus, *University of Iowa*
Thomas Winningham, *University of Southern California*
Conley Wouters, *Brandeis University*

WORKS CITED

Abrams, M. H. *A Glossary of Literary Terms*. 6th ed., Wadsworth Publishing, 1993.

Adams, Henry. "The Dynamo and the Virgin." *The Norton Anthology of American Literature: Volume C, 1865–1914*, edited by Nina Baym, 8th ed., Norton, 2012, pp. 390–97.

Allen, Graham. *Intertextuality*. 2nd ed., Routledge, 2011.

Alsup, Benjamin. "Saint David Foster Wallace and *The Pale King*." *Esquire Web Archive*, www.esquire.com/entertainment/books/reviews/a9606/the-pale-king-review-0411-5402611/. Accessed 12 Aug. 2015.

Anderson, Sherwood. *Winesburg, Ohio*. Penguin, 1992.

Apter, Emily. *Against World Literature: On the Politics of Untranslatability*. Verso, 2013.

———. *The Translation Zone: A New Comparative Literature*. Princeton UP, 2006.

Ashbery, John. "The One Thing That Can Save America." *Self-Portrait in a Convex Mirror,* by Ashbery, Penguin, 1976, pp. 44–45.

———. "Paradoxes and Oxymorons." *Shadow Train,* by Ashbery, Penguin, 1981, p. 25.

Baker, G. P., and P. M. S. Hacker. *Wittgenstein: Understanding and Meaning: An Analytical Commentary on the* Philosophical Investigations*: Volume 1*. Blackwell, 1980.

Bangs, Lester. *Psychotic Reactions and Carburetor Dung*. Edited by Greil Marcus, Knopf, 1987.

Barry, Peter. *Beginning Theory*. Manchester UP, 1995.

Barth, John. *The Friday Book: Essays and Other Nonfiction*. Johns Hopkins UP, 1984.

———. "An Interview with John Barth." By Charlie Reilly. *Contemporary Literature*, vol. 22, no. 1, 1981, pp. 1–23.

———. "John Barth: An Interview." By John J. Enck. *Wisconsin Studies in Contemporary Literature*, vol. 6, no. 1, 1965, pp. 3–14.

———. "The Literature of Exhaustion." Barth, *The Friday Book*, pp. 62–76.

———. *Lost in the Funhouse: Fiction for Print, Tape, Live Voice*. Doubleday, 1967.

———. "Lost in the Funhouse." *Lost in the Funhouse: Fiction for Print, Tape, Live Voice,* by Barth, Anchor Books, 1988, pp. 72–97.

Barthes, Roland. "The Death of the Author." *Image, Music, Text*, translated by Stephen Heath, Hill and Wang, 1977, pp. 142–48.

———. *S/Z*. Translated by Richard Miller, Hill and Wang, 1974.

Baskin, Jon. "Untrendy Problems: *The Pale King*'s Philosophical Inspirations." Bolger and Korb, pp. 141–56.

Bassnett, Susan. *Comparative Literature: A Critical Introduction*. Blackwell, 1993.

Baudrillard, Jean. "The Precession of Simulacra." *Simulacra and Simulation*, translated by Sheila Faria Glaser, U of Michigan P, 2010, pp. 1–42.

———. *Simulations*. Translated by Phil Beitchman et al. MIT Press, 1983.

Baym, Nina. "Realism and Naturalism." *The Norton Anthology of American Literature: Volume C, 1865–1914*, edited by Baym, 7th ed., W. W. Norton, 2007, pp. 902–03.

Begley, Adam. "The Art of Fiction CXXXV: Don DeLillo." *Conversations with Don De-Lillo*, edited by Thomas DePietro, U of Mississippi P, 2005, pp. 86–108.

Berlant, Lauren, and Lee Edelman. *Sex; or, The Unbearable*. Duke UP, 2014.

Bersani, Leo, and Adam Phillips. *Intimacies*. U of Chicago P, 2008.

The Bible. Authorized King James Version, Oxford UP, 1998.

Boddy, Kasia. "A Fiction of Response: *Girl with Curious Hair* in Context." Boswell and Burn, pp. 23–42.

Bolger, Robert K., and Scott Korb, editors. *Gesturing Toward Reality: David Foster Wallace and Philosophy*. Bloomsbury, 2014.

Boswell, Marshall. "Call for Papers—*Studies in the Novel*." U of Pennsylvania, 23 Aug. 2011, call-for-papers.sas.upenn.edu/node/42482. Accessed 30 July 2015.

———. "'The Constant Monologue inside Your Head': *Oblivion* and the Nightmare of Consciousness." Boswell and Burn, pp. 151–70.

———, editor. *David Foster Wallace*. Special issue of *Studies in the Novel*, vol. 44, nos. 3–4, 2012.

———, editor. *David Foster Wallace and "The Long Thing."* Bloomsbury, 2014.

———. *Understanding David Foster Wallace*. U of South Carolina P, 2004.

Boswell, Marshall, and Stephen J. Burn, editors. *A Companion to David Foster Wallace Studies*. Palgrave Macmillan, 2013.

Bretall, Robert, editor. *A Kierkegaard Anthology*. Princeton UP, 1946.

Breu, Christopher. *Insistence of the Material: Literature in the Age of Biopolitics*. U of Minnesota P, 2014.

Brown, Dan. *The Da Vinci Code*. Anchor, 2009.

Bucher, Matt. E-mail message to Kathleen Fitzpatrick. 26 May 2015.

Bucher, Matt, et al. "How to Read *Infinite Jest*." http://infinitesummer.org/archives/215, 17 June 2010. Accessed 24 Oct. 2016.

Burn, Stephen J., editor. *Conversations with David Foster Wallace*. UP of Mississippi, 2012.

———. *David Foster Wallace's* Infinite Jest: *A Reader's Guide*. 2nd ed., Continuum, 2013.

———. "A Map of the Territory: American Fiction at the Millennium." *Jonathan Franzen at the End of Postmodernism*, by Burn, Continuum, 2008, pp. 1–27.

———. "'A Paradigm for the Life of Consciousness': *The Pale King*." Boswell, *David Foster Wallace* [Bloomsbury], pp. 149–68.

———. "Toward a General Theory of Vision in Wallace's Fiction." *English Studies*, vol. 95, no.1, 2014, pp. 85–93.

Butler, Judith. *Undoing Gender*. Routledge, 2004.

Cahn, Steven M., and Maureen Eckert, editors. *Freedom and the Self: Essays on the Philosophy of David Foster Wallace*. Columbia UP, 2015.

Camus, Albert. *The Myth of Sisyphus: An Essay on the Absurd*. Translated by Justin O'Brien, Penguin Books, 2000.

Caponegro, Mary. *All Fall Down*. Coffee House, 2009.

Carlisle, Greg. *Elegant Complexity: A Study of David Foster Wallace's* Infinite Jest. Kindle ed., Sideshow Media Group, 2007.

Carver, Raymond. "What We Talk about When We Talk about Love." *What We Talk about When We Talk about Love.* Vintage, 1989, pp. 137–54.

Casanova, Pascale. *The World Republic of Letters.* 1999. Translated by M. B. DeBevoise, Harvard UP, 2004.

Catalano, Joseph S. *A Commentary on Jean-Paul Sartre's* Being and Nothingness. U of Chicago P, 1985.

Cateforis, Theo, editor. *The Rock History Reader.* 2nd ed., Routledge, 2013.

Cheever, Leonard A. "Lacan, Argentine Politics, and Science Fiction in Manuel Puig's *Pubis Angelical.*" *South Central Review,* vol. 5, no.1, 1988, pp. 61–74.

Clare, Ralph. "The Politics of Boredom and the Boredom of Politics in *The Pale King.*" Boswell [Bloomsbury], pp. 187–207.

Cohen, Samuel. "The Whiteness of David Foster Wallace." *Postmodern Literature and Race,* edited by Len Platt and Sara Upstone, Cambridge UP, 2015, pp. 228–43.

Cohen, Samuel, and Lee Konstantinou, editors. *The Legacy of David Foster Wallace.* U of Iowa P, 2012. New American Canon.

Connell, R. W. *Masculinities.* 2nd ed., U of California P, 2005.

Costello, Mark. Preface. *Signifying Rappers: Rap and Race in the Urban Present,* by Costello and David Foster Wallace, Back Bay, 2013, pp. v–xx.

Crane, Stephen. "The Open Boat." *The Norton Anthology of American Literature: Volume C, 1865–1914,* edited by Nina Baym, 8th ed., Norton, 2012, pp. 990–1006.

Crèvecoeur, J. Hector St. John de. "Letter III: What Is an American." *Letters from an American Farmer,* edited by Warren Barton Blake, E. P. Dutton and Co., 1912, pp. 39–68.

Damrosch, David. *How to Read World Literature.* Wiley-Blackwell, 2009.

——. *What Is World Literature?* Princeton UP, 2003.

Debord, Guy. *The Society of the Spectacle.* 1967. Translated by Donald Nicholson Smith, Zone, 1994.

"The Decemberists—Calamity Song." *YouTube,* 16 Aug. 2011, youtube.com/watch?v=xJpfK7l404I. Accessed 25 Oct. 2016.

Deleuze, Gilles, and Felix Guattari. *Kafka: Toward a Minor Literature.* 1975. Translated by Terry Cochran, U of Minnesota P, 1986.

DeLillo, Don. *End Zone.* 1972. Penguin, 1986.

——. *Falling Man.* Scribner, 2007.

——. *Underworld.* Scribner, 1997.

——. *White Noise.* Scribner, 1985.

De Man, Paul. "Semiology and Rhetoric." Leitch, pp. 1365–78.

DeMarco, Amanda. "The Mistake on Page 1,032: On Translating Infinite Jest into German." Publishing Perspectives, 4 Mar. 2010, publishingperspectives.com/2010/03/the-mistake-on-page-1032-on-translating-infinite-jest-into-german.

Derrida, Jacques. "From *Of Grammatology*." Leitch, pp. 1688–97.

———. *Given Time: I. Counterfeit Money*. Translated by Peggy Kamuf, U of Chicago P, 1992.

———. "Structure, Sign, and Play in the Discourse of the Human Sciences." *Writing and Difference*, by Derrida, 1967. Translated by Alan Bass, U of Chicago P, 1978, pp. 278–93.

DFW Wiki. 2009. machines.kfitz.info/dfwwiki. Accessed 24 Oct. 2016.

Díaz, Junot. *The Brief Wondrous Life of Oscar Wao*. Riverhead, 2007.

Dreiser, Theodore. "The Second Choice." *The Heath Anthology of American Literature, 1910–1945*, edited by Paul Lauter, vol. D, 6th ed., Cengage Learning, 2010, pp. 1363–75.

Dulk, Allard den. "Beyond Endless 'Aesthetic' Irony: A Comparison of the Irony Critique of Søren Kierkegaard and David Foster Wallace's *Infinite Jest*." Boswell, *David Foster Wallace* [44.3], pp. 325–45.

———. "Boredom, Irony, and Anxiety: Wallace and the Kierkegaardian View of the Self." Boswell, *David Foster Wallace* [Bloomsbury], pp. 43–60.

———. *Existentialist Engagement in Wallace, Eggers, and Foer: A Philosophical Analysis of Contemporary American Literature*. Bloomsbury, 2015.

Elias, Amy J. *Sublime Desire: History and Post-1960s Fiction*. Johns Hopkins UP, 2001.

Eliot, T. S. "*Ulysses*, Order, and Myth." *The Selected Prose of T. S. Eliot*, edited by Frank Kermode, Harcourt Brace Jovanovich, 1975, pp. 175–78.

Emerson, Ralph Waldo. "Self-Reliance." *The Norton Anthology of American Literature: Volume B, 1820–1865*, edited by Nina Baym, 7th ed., W. W. Norton, 2007, pp. 1163–80.

Espen, Hal. "Kael Talks." *The New Yorker*, 21 Mar. 1994, pp. 134–43.

Evans, David. "'The Chains of Not Choosing': Free Will and Faith in William James and David Foster Wallace." Boswell and Burn, pp. 171–89.

Faludi, Susan. *Stiffed: The Betrayal of the American Man*. Perennial, 1999.

Farber, Manny. "White Elephant Art vs. Termite Art." *Farber on Film: The Complete Film Writings of Manny Farber*, edited by Robert Polito, Library of America, 2009, pp. 533–42.

Ferris, Joshua. *Then We Came to the End*. Penguin, 2007.

Fitzpatrick, Kathleen. "Infinite Summer: Reading in the Social Network." *The Legacy of David Foster Wallace: Critical and Creative Assessments*, edited by Lee Konstantinou and Samuel Cohen, U of Iowa P, 2012, pp. 182–207.

———. "The Literary Machine: Blogging the Literature Course." *Teaching Language and Literature Online*, edited by Ian Lancashire, Modern Language Association, 2009, pp. 205–16.

Flower, Linda, et al., editors. *Making Thinking Visible: Writing, Collaborative Planning, and Classroom Inquiry*. NCTE, 1994.

Foer, Jonathan Safran. *Everything Is Illuminated*. Harper Perennial, 2003.

"Framework for Success in Postsecondary Writing." Council of Writing Program Administrators / National Council of Teachers of English / National Writing Project, 2011.

Franzen, Jonathan. *The Corrections*. Farrar, Straus and Giroux, 2001.

———. "Farther Away." *Farther Away*, by Franzen, Farrar, Straus and Giroux, 2012, pp. 15–52.

———. *Freedom*. Farrar, Straus and Giroux, 2010.

———. *How to Be Alone*. Farrar, Straus and Giroux, 2003.

———. "Mr. Difficult." Franzen, *How to Be Alone*, pp. 238–69.

———. "Why Bother?" Franzen, *How to Be Alone*, pp. 55–97.

Gaddis, William. *J R*. Knopf, 1975.

Gardner, John. *On Moral Fiction*. Basic Books, 1977.

Gass, William H. "Philosophy and the Form of Fiction." *Fiction and the Figures of Life*, by Gass, Nonpareil, 1979, pp. 3–26.

Genette, Gérard. *Paratexts: Thresholds of Interpretation*. Cambridge UP, 1997.

Geyh, Paula, et al., editors. *Postmodern American Fiction*. W. W. Norton, 1998.

Gilder, George F. *Life after Television*. Whittle Direct Books, 1990. Annotated copy housed as part of the David Foster Wallace library, Harry Ransom Center, University of Texas, Austin.

Giles, Paul. *Antipodean America: Australasia and the Constitution of U.S. Literature*. Oxford UP, 2013.

———. "Sentimental Posthumanism: David Foster Wallace." *Twentieth-Century Literature*, vol. 52, nos. 3–4, 2011, pp. 291–308.

Gilmour, David. *The Film Club*. Twelve, 2008.

Glasgow David Foster Wallace Research Group. *Bibliography of Secondary Criticism*. University of Glasgow, davidfosterwallaceresearch.wordpress.com.

Greco, Arnaldo. "Breve intervista con un uomo meraviglioso." *La Repubblica*, 18 Dec. 2010, p. 98.

Green, Jeremy. *Late Postmodernism: American Fiction at the Millennium*. Palgrave Macmillan, 2005.

Hacker, P. M. S. *Wittgenstein: Meaning and Mind: An Analytical Commentary on the Philosophical Investigations: Volume 3*. Blackwell, 1990.

Halford, Macy. "Our Live Chat with Lydia Davis." *The New Yorker*, 10 Dec. 2009. www.newyorker.com/books/book-club/our-live-chat-with-lydia-davis.

Harkin, Christine. "Silences and Hypertext: Blogging the Death of David Foster Wallace." Footnotes: New Directions in David Foster Wallace Studies, City University of New York, 20 Nov. 2009. Unpublished conference paper.

Harris, Charles B., editor. *Proofread or Die! Writings by Former Students and Colleagues of David Foster Wallace*. Lit Fest, 2016.

Haskell, Molly. *From Reverence to Rape: The Treatment of Women in the Movies*. 2nd ed., U of Chicago P, 1987.

Hassan, Ihab. *The Postmodern Turn: Essays in Postmodern Theory*. Ohio State UP, 1987.

Hawthorne, Nathaniel. "Young Goodman Brown." *The Norton Anthology of American Literature: Volume B, 1820–1865*, edited by Nina Baym, 7th ed., W. W. Norton, 2007, pp. 1289–98.

Hayes-Brady, Clare. *The Unspeakable Failures of David Foster Wallace: Language, Identity, and Resistance*. Bloomsbury, 2016.

Hayles, N. Katherine. "The Illusion of Autonomy and the Fact of Recursivity: Virtual Ecologies, Entertainment, and *Infinite Jest*." *New Literary History*, vol. 30, no.3, 1999, pp. 675–97.

Herbert, Zbigniew. *Mr. Cogito*. Translated by Bogdana Carpenter and John Carpenter, Oxford UP, 1993.

Hering, David, editor. *Consider David Foster Wallace: Critical Essays*. Sideshow Media Group, 2010.

———. *David Foster Wallace: Fiction and Form*. Bloomsbury, 2016.

Herman, Luc, and Toon Staes. *Unfinished: Critical Approaches to David Foster Wallace's* The Pale King. Special issue of *English Studies*, vol. 95, no. 1, 2014.

Hoberek, Andrew. "The Novel after David Foster Wallace." Boswell and Burn, pp. 211–28.

Holland, Mary K. *Succeeding Postmodernism: Language and Humanism in Contemporary American Literature*. Bloomsbury, 2013.

Horn, Patrick. "Does Language Fail Us? Wallace's Struggle with Solipsism." Bolger and Korb, pp. 245–70.

Hutcheon, Linda. *Narcissistic Narrative: The Metafictional Paradox*. Methuen, 1984.

———. *A Poetics of Postmodernism: History, Theory, Fiction*. Routledge, 1988.

Hyde, Lewis. *The Gift: Creativity and the Artist in the Modern World*. 25th Anniversary Edition, Vintage, 2007.

Jackson, Edward, and Joel Nicholson-Roberts. "White Guys: Questioning *Infinite Jest*'s New Sincerity." *Orbit*, vol. 5, no. 2, 2017, www.pynchon.net/articles/10.16995/orbit.182/. Accessed 25 Aug. 2017.

Jacobs, Timothy. "American Touchstone: The Idea of Order in Gerard Manley Hopkins and David Foster Wallace." *Comparative Literature Studies* 38, no. 3, 2001, pp. 215–31.

James, Henry. *The Art of the Novel: Critical Prefaces*. Edited by R. P. Blackmur, U of Chicago P, 2011.

———. "The Question of the Opportunities." *Henry James: The American Essays*, edited by Leon Edel, Vintage, 1956, pp. 197–204.

James, William. *The Varieties of Religious Experience. William James: Writings 1902–1910*, edited by Bruce Kuklick, Library of America, 1987, pp. 1–478.

Jameson, Fredric. *The Antinomies of Realism*. Verso, 2013.

———. "Postmodernism and Consumer Society." *The Cultural Turn: Selected Writings on the Postmodern, 1983–1998*, by Jameson, Verso, 2009, pp. 1–20.

———. *Postmodernism; or, The Cultural Logic of Late Capitalism*. Duke UP, 1991.

Joyce, James. *A Portrait of the Artist as a Young Man*. 1916. Penguin, 1992.

Kael, Pauline. *The Age of Movies: Selected Writings of Pauline Kael*. Edited by Sanford Schwartz, Library of America, 2011.

Kafka, Franz. *The Complete Stories*. Translated by Willa and Edwin Muir, Schocken, 1995.

Keen, Suzanne. *Empathy and the Novel*. Oxford UP, 2007.

Kelly, Adam. "David Foster Wallace and the New Sincerity in American Fiction." Hering, *Consider*, pp. 131–46.

Kidd, David Comer, and Emanuele Castano. "Reading Literary Fiction Improves Theory of Mind." *Science*, vol. 42, no. 6156, 2013, pp. 377–80.

Kierkegaard, Søren. *The Concept of Anxiety: A Simple Psychologically Orienting Deliberation on the Dogmatic Issue of Hereditary Sin*. Edited and translated by Howard V. Hong and Edna H. Hong, Princeton UP, 1981.

———. *The Concept of Irony, with Continual Reference to Socrates / Notes of Schelling's Berlin Lectures*. Edited and translated by Howard V. Hong and Edna H. Hong, Princeton UP, 1989.

———. *Concluding Unscientific Postscript to* Philosophical Fragments, *Volume 1*. Edited and translated by Howard V. Hong and Edna H. Hong, Princeton UP, 1992.

———. *Either/Or, Part I*. Translated by Howard V. Hong and Edna H. Hong, Princeton UP, 1987.

Kimmel, Michael. *Manhood in America: A Cultural History*. 3rd ed., Oxford UP, 2011.

Klosterman, Chuck. *Fargo Rock City*. Scribner, 2001.

Kolb, Jr., Harold. *The Illusion of Life: American Realism as a Literary Form*. UP of Virginia, 1969.

Konstantinou, Lee. "No Bull: David Foster Wallace and Postironic Belief." *The Legacy of David Foster Wallace: Critical and Creative Assessments*, edited by Konstantinou and Samuel Cohen, U of Iowa P, 2012, pp. 83–112.

Lacan, Jacques. *Écrits: A Selection*. Translated by Alan Sheridan, W. W. Norton, 1977.

Lahiri, Jhumpa. "Sexy." *The Norton Anthology of American Literature: Volume E, Literature Since 1945*, edited by Nina Baym, 7th ed., W. W. Norton, 2007, pp. 3249–65.

Lawall, Sarah, editor. *Reading World Literature: Theory, History, Practice*. U of Texas P, 2007.

LeClair, Thomas. *In the Loop: Don DeLillo and the Systems Novel*. U of Illinois P, 1987.

———. "The Prodigious Fiction of Richard Powers, William Vollmann, and David Foster Wallace." *Critique*, vol. 38, 1996, pp. 12–37.

Leitch, Vincent B., editor. *The Norton Anthology of Theory and Criticism*. W. W. Norton, 2010.

Lethem, Jonathan. *Chronic City*. Doubleday, 2009.

Levin, Jenifer. "Love Is a Federal Highway." *The New York Times*, 5 Nov. 1989, www .nytimes.com/1989/11/05/books/love-is-a-federal-highway.html.

Lewis, R. W. B. *The American Adam: Innocence, Tragedy, and Tradition in the Nineteenth Century*. U of Chicago P, 1955.

Lipsky, David. *Although of Course You End Up Becoming Yourself*. Broadway Books, 2010.

Long, Elizabeth. "Textual Interpretation as Collective Action." *Discourse*, vol. 14, no. 3, 1992, pp. 104–30.

Lucchetti, Roberto, and Roberto Natalini, editors. *David Foster Wallace e la Matematica*. Special issue of *Lettera Matematica Pristem*, vol. 95, 2015.

Manaitis, Nick. E-mail message to Kathleen Fitzpatrick. 21 June 2015.

Max, D. T. *Every Love Story Is a Ghost Story: A Life of David Foster Wallace*. Viking, 2012.

———. "The Unfinished." *The New Yorker*, 9 Mar. 2009, pp. 48–61.

May, Charles E. *The New Short Story Theories*. Ohio UP, 1994.

McCaffery, Larry, editor. *After Yesterday's Crash: The Avant-Pop Anthology*. Penguin, 1995.

———. "A Conversation with David Foster Wallace." *The Review of Contemporary Fiction*, vol. 13, no. 2, 1993, pp. 127–50.

McCarthy, Tom. *Satin Island*. Jonathan Cape, 2015.

McGinn, Marie. *Wittgenstein and the* Philosophical Investigations. Routledge, 1997.

McGurl, Mark. *The Program Era: Postwar Fiction and the Rise of Creative Writing*. Harvard UP, 2009.

McHale, Brian. "*The Pale King*; or, The White Visitation." Boswell and Burn, pp. 191–210.

———. *Postmodernist Fiction*. Routledge, 1987.

McLaughlin, Robert L, editor. *Innovations: An Anthology of Modern and Contemporary Fiction*. Dalkey Archive Press, 1998.

———. "Post-Postmodern Discontent: Contemporary Fiction and the Social World." *Symploke*, vol. 12, nos. 1–2, 2004, pp. 53–68.

McLuhan, Marshall. *Understanding Media: The Extensions of Man*. McGraw-Hill, 1964.

Mendelson, Edward. "Encyclopedic Narrative: From Dante to Pynchon." *Modern Language Notes*, vol. 91, no. 6, 1976, pp. 1267–75.

Miller, Adam. *The Gospel According to David Foster Wallace*. Bloomsbury, 2016.

Miller, Laura, et al. "Everything and More: *The Pale King* by David Foster Wallace." Panel discussion, PEN World Voices Festival, 26 Apr. 2011, pen.org/video/everything-and-more-pale-king-david-foster-wallace/. Accessed 24 Oct. 2016.

Moody, Rick. *The Diviners*. Little, Brown, 2005.

Moore, Steven. *J R: A Scene Outline*. The Gaddis Annotations, www.williamgaddis.org/jr/jrscenes.shtml. Accessed 24 Oct. 2016.

Moraru, Christian. *Cosmodernism: American Narrative, Late Globalization, and the New Cultural Imaginary*. U of Michigan P, 2011.

Morris, Pam. *Realism*. Routledge, 2003.

Morrison, Toni. *Playing in the Dark: Whiteness and the Literary Imagination*. Vintage, 1992.

Morrissey, Tara, and Lucas Thompson. "'The Rare White at the Window': A Reappraisal of Mark Costello and David Foster Wallace's *Signifying Rappers*." *Journal of American Studies*, vol. 49, no. 1, 2014, pp. 77–97.

Mulvey, Laura. "Visual Pleasure and Narrative Cinema." *Screen*, vol. 16, no. 3, 1975, pp. 6–18.

"Narcissism." DFW Wiki. 2009. machines.kfitz.info/dfwwiki/index.php?title=Narcissism. Accessed 24 Oct. 2016.

Nealon, Jeffrey T. *Post-Postmodernism, or, the Cultural Logic of Just-in-Time Capitalism*. Stanford UP, 2012.

Nørretranders, Tor. *The User Illusion: Cutting Consciousness Down to Size*. Translated by Jonathan Sydenham, Penguin, 1998.

Norris, Margot. *Suspicious Readings of Joyce's* Dubliners. U of Pennsylvania P, 2003.

Olsen, Lance. "A Flash Poetics of Illegibility." *The Force of What's Possible: Writers on Accessibility and the Avant-Garde*. Edited by Lily Hoang and Joshua Marie Wilkinson, Nightboat, 2015, pp. 246–50.

———. "Termite Art; or, Wallace's Wittgenstein." *The Review of Contemporary Fiction*, vol. 13, no. 2, 1993, pp. 199–215.

———. *Theories of Forgetting*. FC2, 2014.

Olsen, Lance, with Trevor Dodge, editors. *Architectures of Possibility: After Innovative Writing*. Guide Dog Books, 2012.

Park, Ed. *Personal Days*. Vintage, 2008.

Peck, Dale. "Well, Duh." Review of *Infinite Jest*, by David Foster Wallace. *London Review of Books*, 18 Jul. 1996, pp. 14–15.

Penrose, Ann, and Barbara Sitko, editors. *Hearing Ourselves Think: Cognitive Research in the College Writing Classroom*. Oxford UP, 1993.

Perec, Georges. *The Art and Craft of Approaching Your Head of Department to Submit a Request for a Raise*. 1968. Translated by David Bellos, Verso, 2011.

Potts, Sam. *Infinite Jest Diagram*. sampottsinc.com/ij/. Accessed 24 Oct. 2016.

Powers, Richard. *Gain*. Farrar, Straus and Giroux, 1998.

———. *Galatea 2.2*. Farrar, Straus and Giroux, 1995.

———. "Literary Devices." *Zoetrope: All-Story*, vol. 6, no. 4, 2002, pp. 8–15.

Puig, Manuel. *Betrayed by Rita Hayworth*. Translated by Suzanne Jill Levine, Bard, 1979.

———. *Eternal Curse on the Reader of These Pages*. U of Minnesota P, 1999.

———. *Heartbreak Tango*. 1969. Translated by Suzanne Jill Levine, Dalkey Archive Press, 2010.

Raban, Jonathan. "Divine Drudgery." Review of *The Pale King, The Broom of the System, Fate, Time and Language, Everything and More*, and *Infinite Jest*, by David Foster Wallace. *The New York Review of Books*, 12 May 2011. www.nybooks.com/articles/2011/05/12/divine-drudgery/. Accessed 1 Sept. 2011.

Ramal, Randy. "Beyond Philosophy: David Foster Wallace on Literature, Wittgenstein, and the Dangers of Theorizing." Bolger and Korb, pp. 177–98.

Reed, Ishmael. *Juice!* Dalkey Archive Press, 2011.

reidau. "Its Been Thoroughly Enjoyed." *David Foster Wallace*, 4 May 2009, machines.kfitz.info/166-2009/2009/05/04/its-been-thoroughly-enjoyed/. Accessed 24 Oct. 2016.

Remski, Mathew. *Silver*. Insomniac, 1998.

Rossiter, Clinton, editor. *The Federalist Papers*. Signet, 2003.

Russell, Karen. *St. Lucy's Home for Girls Raised by Wolves*. Knopf, 2006.

Ryan, Judith. *The Novel after Theory*. Columbia UP, 2014.

Ryerson, James. "Introduction: A Head That Throbbed Heartlike." Wallace, *Fate*, pp. 1–33.

Sartre, Jean-Paul. *Being and Nothingness: An Essay on Phenomenological Ontology.* Translated by Hazel E. Barnes, Routledge, 2010.

————. *The Transcendence of the Ego: A Sketch for a Phenomenological Description.* Translated by Andrew Brown, Routledge, 2004.

Saunders, George. "A Mini-Manifesto." *MFA vs. NYC*, edited by Chad Harbach, n+1 / Farrar, Straus and Giroux, 2014, pp. 31–4.

Scanlon, Suzanne. "Final Exam." Harris, pp. 115–26.

Scott, A. O. "The Panic of Influence." Review of *Brief Interviews with Hideous Men*, by David Foster Wallace. *The New York Review of Books*, 10 Feb. 2000, pp. 39–43.

Severs, Jeffrey. *David Foster Wallace's Balancing Books: Fictions of Value.* Columbia UP, 2017.

Seyhan, Azade. "'World Literatures Reimagined': Sara Suleri's *Meatless Days* and A.H. Tanipinar's *Five Cities*." *Modern Language Quarterly* 74, no. 2, 2013, pp. 197–215.

Smith, Zadie. "*Brief Interviews with Hideous Men*: The Difficult Gifts of David Foster Wallace." *Changing My Mind: Occasional Essays*, by Smith, Hamish Hamilton, 2009, pp. 257–300.

"Solipsism." DFW Wiki, 2009, machines.kfitz.info/dfwwiki/index.php?title=Solipsism. Accessed 24 Oct. 2016.

Sontag, Susan. "Against Interpretation." *"Against Interpretation" and Other Essays*, by Sontag, Picador, pp. 3–14.

Spivak, Gayatri Chakravorty. *An Aesthetic Education in the Era of Globalization.* Harvard UP, 2012.

————. *Death of a Discipline.* Columbia UP, 2003.

————. *In Other Worlds.* Routledge, 2006.

Staes, Toon. "Rewriting the Author: A Narrative Approach to Empathy in *Infinite Jest* and *The Pale King*." *Studies in the Novel*, vol. 44, no. 4, 2012, pp. 409–27.

Steiner, Wendy. "Rethinking Postmodernism." *The Cambridge History of American Literature, Volume 7: Prose Writing, 1940–1990*, edited by Sacvan Bercovitch, Cambridge UP, 1999, pp. 425–50.

Storrs, Francis. "The Dan Brown Code." *Boston Magazine*, September 2009, bostonmagazine.com/2009/08/the-dan-brown-code/3/. Accessed 30 July 2015.

Sundquist, Eric J. *American Realism: New Essays.* Johns Hopkins UP, 1982.

Sunstein, Cass R. *Infotopia: How Many Minds Produce Knowledge.* Oxford UP, 2006.

"Talk:DFW Wiki." DFW Wiki, 2009, machines.kfitz.info/dfwwiki/index.php?title=Talk:DFW_Wiki.

Tanner, Tony. *City of Words: American Fiction, 1950–1970.* Harper Collins, 1971.

"Term Project." *David Foster Wallace*, 2009, machines.kfitz.info/166-2009/term-project/. Accessed 24 Oct. 2016.

"Themes Page." DFW Wiki, 2009, machines.kfitz.info/dfwwiki/index.php?title=Themes_Page. Accessed 24 Oct. 2016.

Thompson, Lucas. *Global Wallace: David Foster Wallace and World Literature.* Bloomsbury, 2016.

Thoreau, Henry David. "Resistance to Civil Government." *The Norton Anthology of American Literature: Volume B, 1820–1865*, edited by Nina Baym, 7th ed., W. W. Norton, 2007, pp. 1857–72.

Tocqueville, Alexis de. *Democracy in America: Volume 2*. Vintage, 1990.

Tracey, Thomas. "The Formative Years: David Foster Wallace's Philosophical Influences and *The Broom of the System*." Bolger and Korb, pp. 157–75.

Walkowitz, Rebecca L. "Unimaginable Largeness: Kazuo Ishiguro, Translation and the New World Literature." *Novel*, vol. 40, no. 3, 2007, 216–39.

Wallace, David Foster. "Authority and American Usage." Wallace, *"Consider,"* pp. 66–127.

——. "B.I. #20." Wallace, *Brief Interviews*, pp. 245–71.

——. "Big Red Son." Wallace, *"Consider,"* pp. 3–50.

——. "Borges on the Couch." Wallace, *Both*, pp. 285–94.

——. *Both Flesh and Not: Essays*. Little, Brown, 2012.

——. *Brief Interviews with Hideous Men*. Little, Brown, 1999.

——. *Brief Interviews with Hideous Men*. Back Bay, 2000.

——. *The Broom of the System*. Penguin, 1987.

——. "Certainly the End of *Something* or Other, One Would Sort of Have to Think." Wallace, *"Consider,"* pp. 51–59.

——. "Consider the Lobster." Wallace, *"Consider,"* pp. 235–54.

——. *"Consider the Lobster" and Other Essays*. Little, Brown, 2005.

——. "David Foster Wallace Interview with Charlie Rose." *YouTube*, uploaded by Manufacturing Intellect, 24 July 2015, www.youtube.com/watch?v=9lytSdSM-Kk.

——. *David Foster Wallace: The Last Interview and Other Conversations*. Melville House, 2012.

——. *The David Foster Wallace Reader*. Little, Brown, 2014.

——. "David Lynch Keeps His Head." Wallace, *Supposedly*, pp. 146–212.

——. "The Depressed Person." Wallace, *Brief Interviews*, pp. 37–69.

——. "The Devil Is a Busy Man." *The Heath Anthology of American Literature: Contemporary Period: Volume E, 1945 to the Present*, edited by Paul Lauter, 6th ed., Cengage Learning, pp. 3528–30.

——. "E Unibus Pluram: Television and U.S. Fiction." *The Review of Contemporary Fiction*, vol. 13, no. 2, 1993, pp. 151–94.

——. "E Unibus Pluram: Television and U.S. Fiction." Wallace, *Supposedly*, pp. 21–82.

——. E-mail message to Adelaide Cioni. March 29, 2006. Container 1.3, Bonnie Nadell's David Foster Wallace Collection, Harry Ransom Center, University of Texas, Austin.

——. E-mail message to Martina Testa. June 20, 2001. Container 31.8, David Foster Wallace Papers, Harry Ransom Center, University of Texas, Austin.

——. "The Empty Plenum: David Markson's *Wittgenstein's Mistress*." Wallace, *Both*, pp. 73–116.

——. "The Empty Plenum: David Markson's *Wittgenstein's Mistress*." *The Review of Contemporary Fiction*, vol. 10, no. 2, 1990, pp. 217–39.

——. "English 102—Literary Analysis I: Prose Fiction." *Teaching Materials from the David Foster Wallace Archive*, Harry Ransom Center, www.hrc.utexas.edu/press/releases/2010/dfw/teaching/. Accessed 1 Oct. 2015.

——. *Everything and More: A Compact History of Infinity*. W. W. Norton, 2003.

―――. *Fate, Time, and Language: An Essay on Free Will.* Edited by Steven M. Cahn and Maureen Eckert, Columbia UP, 2011.

―――. "Fictional Futures and the Conspicuously Young." Wallace, *Both,* pp. 37–72.

―――. "'A Frightening Time in America': An Interview with David Foster Wallace." By Ostap Karmodi. *NYR Daily, New York Review of Books,* 13 June 2011.

―――. "Getting Away from Already Being Pretty Much Away from It All." Wallace, *Supposedly,* pp. 83–137.

―――. *Girl with Curious Hair.* W. W. Norton, 1989.

―――. "Good Old Neon." Wallace, *Oblivion,* pp. 141–81.

―――. "Greatly Exaggerated." Wallace, *Supposedly,* 138–45.

―――. "Gus Van Sant Interviews David Foster Wallace." *Electric Literature,* May 1998, electriccereal.com/gus-van-sant-interviews-david-foster-wallace. Accessed 24 Oct. 2016.

―――. "Incarnations of Burned Children." Wallace, *Oblivion,* pp. 114–16.

―――. *Infinite Jest.* Little, Brown, 1996.

―――. Interview with Miriam Böttger. Zweites Deutsche Fernsehen, 2003, youtube.com/ watch?v=N5IDAnB_rns>. Accessed 24 Oct. 2016.

―――. Interview with Laura Miller. *Salon,* 9 Mar., 1996, salon.com/1996/03/09/wallace_5/. Accessed 24 Oct. 2016.

―――. Interview with Michael Silverblatt. *Bookworm,* KCRW, 11 Apr., 1996, kcrw.com/etc/programs/bw/bw960411david_foster_wallace. Accessed 24 Oct. 2016.

―――. "Joseph Frank's Dostoevsky." Wallace, *"Consider,"* pp. 255–74.

―――. Letter to Don DeLillo. 11 June 1992. David Foster Wallace Papers. Harry Ransom Center, University of Texas, Austin.

―――. Letter to Don DeLillo. 15 July 1992. David Foster Wallace Papers. Harry Ransom Center, University of Texas, Austin.

―――. "Little Expressionless Animals." Wallace, *Girl,* pp. 3–42.

―――. "Lyndon." Wallace, *Girl,* pp. 75–118.

―――. *McCain's Promise: Aboard the Straight Talk Express with John McCain and a Whole Bunch of Actual Reporters, Thinking about Hope.* Back Bay, 2008.

―――. "Mister Squishy." Wallace, *Oblivion,* pp. 3–66.

―――. "Mr. Cogito." Wallace, *Both,* pp. 121–23.

―――. "My Appearance." Wallace, *Girl,* pp. 173–201.

―――. *Oblivion: Stories.* Little, Brown, 2005.

―――. "Octet." Wallace, *Brief Interviews,* pp. 131–60.

―――. *The Pale King.* Little, Brown, 2011.

―――. "The Planet Trillaphon as It Stands in Relation to the Bad Thing." *The David Foster Wallace Reader,* pp. 5–19.

―――. "Quo Vadis—Introduction." *The Review of Contemporary Fiction,* vol. 16, no. 1, 1996, pp. 7–8.

―――. "A Radically Condensed History of Postindustrial Life." Wallace, *Brief Interviews,* p. 0.

―――. "Some Remarks on Kafka's Funniness." Wallace, *"Consider,"* pp. 60–65.

———. "The Soul Is Not a Smithy." Wallace, *Oblivion*, pp. 67–113.

———. "The Suffering Channel." Wallace, *Oblivion*, pp. 238–329.

———. "A Supposedly Fun Thing I'll Never Do Again." Wallace, *Supposedly*, pp. 256–353.

———. *A Supposedly Fun Thing I'll Never Do Again: Essays and Arguments*. Little, Brown, 1997.

———. "Tense Present: Democracy, English and the Wars over Usage." *Harper's*, April 2001, pp. 39–58.

———. *This Is Water*. Little, Brown, 2009.

———. "Tragic Cuban Émigré and a Tale of 'The Door to Happiness.'" Review of *The Doorman* by Reinaldo Arenas. *The Philadelphia Inquirer*, 14 July 1991.

———. "Up, Simba." Wallace, *"Consider,"* pp. 156–234.

———. "The View from Mrs. Thompson's." Wallace, *"Consider,"* pp. 128–40.

———. "Westward the Course of Empire Takes Its Way." Wallace, *Girl*, pp. 231–373.

Wallace, David Foster, and Mark Costello. *Signifying Rappers: Rap and Race in the Urban Present*. Ecco, 1990.

Wallace, David Foster, and Bryan A. Garner. *Quack This Way: David Foster Wallace and Bryan A. Garner Talk Language and Writing*. RosePen, 2013.

Wallen, James Ramsey. "What Is an Unfinished Work?" *New Literary History*, vol. 46, 2015, pp. 125–42.

Wellek, René. *Concepts of Criticism*. Edited by Stephen B. Nichols, Jr., Yale UP, 1963.

Welty, Eudora. "Where Is the Voice Coming From?" *The Oxford Book of American Short Stories*, edited by Joyce Carol Oates, Oxford UP, 1992, pp. 481–87.

Whitehead, Colson. *John Henry Days*. Doubleday, 2001.

———. *Zone One*. Doubleday, 2011.

Williams, Linda. *Hard Core: Power, Pleasure, and the "Frenzy of the Visible."* Expanded ed., U of California P, 1999.

Williams, Raymond. *Keywords: A Vocabulary of Culture and Society*. Oxford UP, 1985.

Wilson, Carl. *Let's Talk about Love: A Journey to the End of Taste*. Continuum, 2007.

Wimsatt, W. K., Jr., and Monroe Beardsley. "The Intentional Fallacy." *The Verbal Icon: Studies in the Meaning of Poetry*, by Wimsatt, U of Kentucky P, 1954, pp. 3–18n.

Wittgenstein, Ludwig. *Philosophical Investigations: The German Text, with a Revised English Translation*. Translated by G. E. M. Anscombe, Blackwell, 2001.

———. *Tractatus Logico-Philosophicus*. Translated by C. K. Ogden, Routledge, 1981.

Wood, James. "Human, All Too Inhuman." *New Republic*, 24 July 2000, newrepublic.com/article/61361/human-all-too-inhuman. Accessed 24 Oct. 2016.

Zunshine, Lisa. *Why We Read Fiction: Theory of Mind and the Novel*. Ohio State UP, 2006.